Survival

GLOBAL POLITICS AND STRATEGY

Volume 59 Number 5 | October–November 20

'Countries enjoy no inherent prerogative to join any security organisation they wish. Security organisations are not an intrinsic feature of the Westphalian state system or even the post-Second World War, UN-supervised international order. They are constructs designed to serve particular purposes for specific countries during certain periods.'

Michael O'Hanlon, NATO's Limits: A New Security Architecture for Eastern Europe, p. 9.

'Autocrats have traditionally used survival tactics aimed at countering threats emanating from the elite … As more dictators fall to protests, however, leaders are increasingly targeting the citizenry.'

Erica Frantz and Andrea Kendall-Taylor, The Evolution of Autocracy: Why Authoritarianism Is Becoming More Formidable, p. 65.

'The Trump administration's beginning in birtherism … is important. To begin with, it announced that racism would dominate the campaign and, it seemed likely, the presidency. It also sharply established the 45th president in his historical role as Obama's antithesis.'

Dana H. Allin, Charlottesville, p. 204.

Survival
GLOBAL POLITICS AND STRATEGY
Volume 59 Number 5 | October–November 2017

Contents

Cover: Wojtek Radwanski/AFP/Getty Images

On the cover
US soldiers are pictured prior to the beginning of the official welcoming ceremony of NATO troops to Orzysz, Poland, on 13 April 2017.

On the web
Visit www.iiss.org/publications/survival for brief notices on new books on South Asia, the Middle East, Economy, and Cyber Security and Emerging Technologies.

***Survival* editors' blog**
For ideas and commentary from *Survival* editors and contributors, visit www.iiss.org/politicsandstrategy.

Weaponry and Strategy

Review Essays

Book Reviews

Closing Argument

Survival

GLOBAL POLITICS AND STRATEGY

The International Institute for Strategic Studies
2121 K Street, NW | Suite 801 | Washington DC 20037 | USA
Tel +1 202 659 1490 Fax +1 202 659 1499 E-mail survival@iiss.org Web www.iiss.org

Arundel House | 6 Temple Place | London | WC2R 2PG | UK
Tel +44 (0)20 7379 7676 Fax +44 (0)20 7836 3108 E-mail iiss@iiss.org

14th Floor, GBCorp Tower | Bahrain Financial Harbour | Manama | Kingdom of Bahrain
Tel +973 1718 1155 Fax +973 1710 0155 E-mail iiss-middleeast@iiss.org

9 Raffles Place | #51-01 Republic Plaza | Singapore 048619
Tel +65 6499 0055 Fax +65 6499 0059 E-mail iiss-asia@iiss.org

Survival Online www.tandfonline.com/survival and www.iiss.org/publications/survival

Aims and Scope *Survival* is one of the world's leading forums for analysis and debate of international and strategic affairs. Shaped by its editors to be both timely and forward thinking, the journal encourages writers to challenge conventional wisdom and bring fresh, often controversial, perspectives to bear on the strategic issues of the moment. With a diverse range of authors, *Survival* aims to be scholarly in depth while vivid, well written and policy-relevant in approach. Through commentary, analytical articles, case studies, forums, review essays, reviews and letters to the editor, the journal promotes lively, critical debate on issues of international politics and strategy.

Published for the IISS by
Routledge Journals, an imprint of Taylor & Francis, an Informa business.

About the IISS The IISS, a registered charity with offices in Washington, London, Manama and Singapore, is the world's leading authority on political–military conflict. It is the primary independent source of accurate, objective information on international strategic issues. Publications include *The Military Balance*, an annual reference work on each nation's defence capabilities; *Strategic Survey*, an annual review of world affairs; *Survival*, a bimonthly journal on international affairs; *Strategic Comments*, an online analysis of topical issues in international affairs; and the *Adelphi* series of books on issues of international security.

SUBMISSIONS

To submit an article, authors are advised to follow these guidelines:

- *Survival* articles are around 4,000–10,000 words long including endnotes. A word count should be included with a draft. Length is a consideration in the review process and shorter articles have an advantage.
- All text, including endnotes, should be double-spaced with wide margins.
- Any tables or artwork should be supplied in separate files, ideally not embedded in the document or linked to text around it.
- All *Survival* articles are expected to include endnote references. These should be complete and include first and last names of authors, titles of articles (even from newspapers), place of publication, publisher, exact publication dates, volume and issue number (if from a journal) and page numbers. Web sources should include complete URLs and DOIs if available.
- A summary of up to 150 words should be included with the article. The summary should state the main argument clearly and concisely, not simply say what the article is about.
- A short author's biography of one or two lines should also be included. This information will appear at the foot of the first page of the article.
- *Survival* has a strict policy of listing multiple authors in alphabetical order.

Submissions should be made by email, in Microsoft Word format, to the Managing Editor, Matthew Harries, survival@iiss.org. Alternatively, hard copies may be sent to *Survival*, IISS–US, 2121 K Street NW, Suite 801, Washington, DC 20037, USA. Please direct any queries to Matthew Harries.

The editorial review process can take up to three months. *Survival*'s acceptance rate for unsolicited manuscripts is less than 20%. *Survival* does not normally provide referees' comments in the event of rejection. Authors are permitted to submit simultaneously elsewhere so long as this is consistent with the policy of the other publication and the Editors of *Survival* are informed of the dual submission.

Readers are encouraged to comment on articles from the previous issue. Letters should be concise, no longer than 750 words and relate directly to the argument or points made in the original article.

ADVERTISING AND PERMISSIONS

For advertising rates and schedules

USA/Canada: The Advertising Manager, Taylor & Francis Inc., 530 Walnut Street, Suite 850, Philadelphia, PA 19106, USA Tel +1 (800) 354 1420 Fax +1 (215) 207 0050.

UK/Europe/Rest of World: The Advertising Manager, Routledge Journals, Taylor & Francis, 4 Park Square, Milton Park, Abingdon, Oxfordshire OX14 4RN, UK Tel +44 (0) 207 017 6000 Fax +44 (0) 207 017 6336.

SUBSCRIPTIONS

Survival is published bi-monthly in February, April, June, August, October and December by Routledge Journals, an imprint of Taylor & Francis, an Informa Business.

Annual Subscription 2017

Institution	$842	£481	€706
Individual	$231	£137	€187
Online only	$737	£421	€618

Taylor & Francis has a flexible approach to subscriptions, enabling us to match individual libraries' requirements. This journal is available via a traditional institutional subscription (either print with online access, or online only at a discount) or as part of our libraries, subject collections or archives. For more information on our sales packages please visit http://www.tandfonline.com/page/librarians.

All current institutional subscriptions include online access for any number of concurrent users across a local area network to the currently available backfile and articles posted online ahead of publication.

Subscriptions purchased at the personal rate are strictly for personal, non-commercial use only. The reselling of personal subscriptions is prohibited. Personal subscriptions must be purchased with a personal cheque or credit card. Proof of personal status may be requested.

Dollar rates apply to all subscribers outside Europe. Euro rates apply to all subscribers in Europe, except the UK and the Republic of Ireland where the pound sterling rate applies. If you are unsure which rate applies to you please contact Customer Services in the UK. All subscriptions are payable in advance and all rates include postage. Journals are sent by air to the USA, Canada, Mexico, India, Japan and Australasia. Subscriptions are entered on an annual basis, i.e. January to December. Payment may be made by sterling cheque, dollar cheque, euro cheque, international money order, National Giro or credit cards (Amex, Visa and Mastercard).

Survival (USPS 013095) is published bi-monthly (in Feb, Apr, Jun, Aug, Oct and Dec) by Routledge Journals, Taylor & Francis, 4 Park Square, Milton Park, Abingdon, OX14 4RN, United Kingdom.

The US annual subscription price is $842. Airfreight and mailing in the USA by agent named Air Business Ltd, c/o Worldnet Shipping Inc., 156-15, 146th Avenue, 2nd Floor, Jamaica, NY 11434, USA. Periodicals postage paid at Jamaica NY 11431.

US Postmaster: Send address changes to Survival, C/O Air Business Ltd / 156-15 146th Avenue, Jamaica, New York, NY11434.

Subscription records are maintained at Taylor & Francis Group, 4 Park Square, Milton Park, Abingdon, OX14 4RN, United Kingdom.

ORDERING INFORMATION

Please contact your local Customer Service Department to take out a subscription to the Journal: **USA, Canada:** Taylor & Francis, Inc., 530 Walnut Street, Suite 850, Philadelphia, PA 19106, USA. Tel: +1 800 354 1420; Fax: +1 215 207 0050. **UK/ Europe/Rest of World:** T&F Customer Services, Informa UK Ltd, Sheepen Place, Colchester, Essex, CO3 3LP, United Kingdom. Tel: +44 (0) 20 7017 5544; Fax: +44 (0) 20 7017 5198; Email: subscriptions@tandf.co.uk.

Back issues: Taylor & Francis retains a two-year back issue stock of journals. Older volumes are held by our official stockists: Periodicals Service Company, 351 Fairview Ave., Suite 300, Hudson, New York 12534, USA to whom all orders and enquiries should be addressed. *Tel* +1 518 537 4700 *Fax* +1 518 537 5899 *e-mail* psc@periodicals.com *web* http://www.periodicals.com/tandf.html.

The issue date is October–November 2017.

The print edition of this journal is printed on ANSI conforming acid free paper.

NATO's Limits: A New Security Architecture for Eastern Europe

Michael O'Hanlon

Western relations with Russia are in a dangerous state. In the United States, evidence of Russian meddling in the 2016 election has produced a rare bipartisan consensus of inflexibility towards Moscow. President Donald Trump's long-stated goal of improved relations is thwarted, not least by the ongoing investigation of possible collusion between his campaign and Russian intelligence agencies. Yet, the goal itself is worthy. After all, Trump's two immediate predecessors had similar hopes for a better rapport with Russian President Vladimir Putin. Both failed. Putin and many of those around him are hard-edged autocrats, and there will likely be no easy way to put US–Russian relations fully back on track as long as they are in power. But it should be possible to reduce the risks of rivalry and war by focusing on what may be, in Putin's mind, the fundamental cause of the problem: NATO expansion.

It is time for Western nations to work out, and seek to negotiate, a new security architecture for the neutral countries of Eastern Europe. The countries in question collectively make a broken-up arc from Europe's far north to its south, plus parts of the Caucasus in Western Asia, encompassing Finland and Sweden; Ukraine, Moldova and Belarus; Georgia, Armenia and Azerbaijan; Cyprus; and Serbia and other Balkan states.[1] Most, though not all, of these countries are ambivalent themselves about NATO, and where there is interest in joining, it is often due to a recent sense of threat from Russia that a new security order might be able to mitigate substantially.

Michael O'Hanlon is a Senior Fellow at the Brookings Institution.

Survival | vol. 59 no. 5 | October–November 2017 | pp. 7–24 DOI 10.1080/00396338.2017.1375215

Moreover, many existing NATO members have publics that are already uncertain about their countries' military commitments to the eastern extremes of the Alliance, casting doubt on the feasibility and wisdom of any further expansion. Despite its evident difficulties, the Trump administration should try to build bipartisan and transatlantic support for pursuit of a new vision. The discussion process should begin within NATO, and then expand to include consultations with the neutral countries themselves. Subsequent, formal negotiations would include all of the aforementioned states as well as Russia.

This process would bring an end to NATO enlargement, provided that Russia resolved its territorial disputes with its neighbours and verifiably withdrew forces from their territories. It would also ultimately lead to the lifting of Western sanctions on Russia. And to be clear, the process would demand significant concessions from Moscow, including verified withdrawal of its forces, regular and irregular, from Ukraine and Georgia, and an end to interference in neighbouring countries' internal affairs. Crucially, Moscow would also have to recognise the rights of neutral states to join any economic or political association.

There is, of course, no guarantee that this concept would be well received in Russia, and even if it were accepted, it would not necessarily return US–Russian relations to the relatively tranquil state that characterised the relationship in the 1990s. But it would likely be a vast improvement over the current situation, and make Europe a much safer place.

The purpose of this article is not to revisit in detail the origins of the crisis in NATO–Russian relations, nor the contribution that NATO expansion may have made to the situation. Suffice it to say that NATO's enlargement has been generally well intentioned; leaders have been sincere in their desire to use the process to spread democracy and stability to Europe, and have made many efforts to mitigate Russian fears along the way. Yet the Russian objection to enlargement was predictable, and predicted. NATO should not seek to negotiate a new security order out of any sense of guilt or redress, but it should recognise that, whatever the merits and motivations of the expansion process to date, it has run its useful course and in fact become counterproductive.

A new security architecture for Europe needs to be based on several foundational concepts. The first, as a matter of moral principle and strategic necessity, is that all countries, big or small, east or west, are fully sovereign and have the inherent right to choose their own form of government, political leadership, diplomatic relations and economic associations. This is as true for Ukraine and Georgia, and other countries of Central Europe, as it is for America's traditional core allies or any other nation. No country should be relegated to a Russian sphere of influence. Indeed, all countries must be accorded every right to think of themselves as Western, as Finland has done for decades. Their future neutrality should concern only formal membership in mutual-defence security organisations; in other ways, they must be able to align themselves as they choose.

Membership of security organisations is a different matter, however. Great powers, like smaller powers, have natural incentives to ensure their own security. They are not entitled to fealty or tribute from smaller neighbours, but they do have the right to worry about their self-defence. Thus, even if the concept of spheres of influence – if taken to mean a region in which the big can bully the smaller and weaker – is not defensible, the concept of secure and defensible borders is valid. Russia has the right to be secure, and to feel secure.

Membership of security organisations is a different matter

For this and other reasons, countries enjoy no inherent prerogative to join any security organisation they wish. Security organisations are not an intrinsic feature of the Westphalian state system or even the post-Second World War, UN-supervised international order. They are constructs designed to serve particular purposes for specific countries during certain periods. If well designed, they will improve security first and foremost for their own members, but also for the regional or global order writ large, without prejudice to the security interests of other states. The effort to organise international society is an ongoing one that involves many different layers of interaction and organisation among states, with no clear role for alliances as a central organising feature.[2] Alliances may help in some cases; they may be irrelevant or cause damage in others. In Europe today, the prospect of further NATO enlargement, however indeterminate and far off, is almost certainly causing net harm.

Constructing an East European security architecture

A new security architecture for the neutral countries of Eastern Europe would be founded on the concept of sustained neutrality for those countries not now in NATO – at least in regard to joining a formal alliance based on a mutual-defence pledge like NATO's Article V. Specifically, it would provide that these states would not join NATO in the future – unless and until Russia itself showed interest in joining, or otherwise formally indicated that it would have no objection to further Alliance expansion at some point in the (presumably quite distant) future.[3] Armenia and Belarus could retain their current political and security associations with Russia, notably under the Collective Security Treaty Organization, since it seems fair to say that this is not seen as threatening or otherwise disruptive by any other country.

Ideally, this architecture would be codified in treaty form. The treaty could be a simple one because the architecture would not create a new organisation, though it would formalise certain types of monitoring and verification practices. A treaty, however, may be unattainable in the current climate, not least because the current US Senate would not ratify it. There are precedents, however, for far-reaching agreements that did not take the form of a treaty. These include the Helsinki Accords of 1975, the Paris Charter of 1990 and the NATO–Russia Founding Act of 1997. The importance of the Helsinki Accords, in particular, should not be discounted; though widely criticised as hortatory and empty at the time, they ultimately provided profound impetus for the settlement ending the Cold War. Writing things down, and agreeing to them, often turns out to matter. Indeed, even treaties that are not ratified often have some sway in global affairs, such as SALT II and the Convention on the Law of the Sea.

Neutral states under the treaty would also agree not to be covered by the security provisions of the European Union Treaty, even if they did join the EU in its other dimensions. This idea of separating out 'security membership' in the EU from economic and political membership was already broached by the Dutch prime minister in 2016, albeit in a different context.[4]

The Crimea issue could be approached separately in various ways. Russia's transgression there could effectively be forgiven, as a show of good faith by the West, and in recognition of the unusual history and character of that Russian-majority region. More realistically, the matter could simply be set aside, with the United States and other Western nations choosing not to recognise the annexation (and limiting their willingness to participate in certain types of activities or meetings there), but otherwise not treating it as an impediment to improved relations. Alternatively, a modest sanctions regime could be retained to sustain the objection to Russia's annexation, not necessarily in the expectation that Moscow would someday reverse course, but more as a point of principle. This might, however, be an instance in which it is counterproductive to stand too forcefully on principle, especially if a new security order is beckoning, and there is general agreement that the Crimea experience would not be repeated elsewhere in Europe.

The Ukrainian civil war would be ended, and the Russian presence there verifiably withdrawn, under this plan. The 2015 Minsk II agreement would in effect be implemented, and the Donbass region would receive some autonomy within Ukraine, as hostilities were ended. The 'frozen conflicts' in Transdniestr (Moldova), as well as South Ossetia and Abkhazia (Georgia), would also have to be resolved as part of this negotiation; so too would the status of Kosovo. In principle, internationally supervised referendums on independence or accession could be conducted in Transdniestr or the autonomous parts of Georgia, provided that the mechanisms were transparent and the outcomes verifiable. There would also be an understanding that Russia would not interfere militarily, through overt or covert means, on the territories of sovereign states to stir up similar problems in the future.

Under the plan, NATO would not offer new Membership Action Plans (MAPs) to any neutral or non-aligned country. At present, Bosnia and Herzegovina, and the Former Yugoslav Republic of Macedonia, have MAPs. These would ideally be transformed into mechanisms to help usher these states into a new security architecture rather than NATO itself. Were Kosovo's independence to be fully established at some point, it too would be given the opportunity to be part of the new security architecture, remaining neutral rather than seeking to join NATO.

Preferably, Finland and Sweden would also remain outside of NATO, despite their Western sensibilities and associations. Historically and practically, they have long traditions of finessing their security relationships as neutral countries outside of any alliance. The fact that this long-standing aspect of their strategic cultures is being called into question at present, especially in Sweden, is a reflection of the acute tensions in contemporary Western relations with Russia. It is hard to believe that NATO membership reflects the genuinely preferred outcome among most Swedes or Finns. If forced to choose between East and West, they will likely choose the latter, but more likely, they would prefer to avoid the choice. As such, a new security architecture that offered the promise of a much improved and stable relationship between the Western world and Russia would likely reduce the newfound openness to the NATO option in these two proudly self-reliant countries.

> *NATO's promises to Ukraine and Georgia would have to be disavowed*

While the proposal could in theory go forward even if some or all existing MAPs with Balkan states were implemented – and, indeed, even if Sweden and Finland joined NATO as well – this should not be the preferred course of action. Any decision by Sweden or Finland to join the Western alliance would implicitly reflect a lack of confidence in the effectiveness of any new security architecture. As the strongest states – and those with arguably the strongest traditions of neutrality – among the group under consideration, Finland and Sweden would do much to set the tone for perceptions of the new paradigm. Moreover, it is doubtful that Moscow would trust the intentions of the West, or be favourably inclined to negotiate a new security architecture, if NATO expansion was simultaneously proceeding apace, even if only in a limited way.

Most importantly, as part of the new architecture, NATO's public promises to Ukraine and Georgia in 2008 that they would someday be invited into the Alliance would have to be disavowed. These overtures would be superseded by the new East European Security Architecture (EESA) that would reliably ensure the countries' sovereignty – and that might prove negotiable far more quickly than any prospective NATO membership, given current strategic conditions. It is important to underscore that if the new architecture works as intended, it will be *preferable* to NATO membership for the simple reason that it is a far more credible and attainable arrangement, on a much shorter time horizon.[5]

Of course, no one can guarantee that it will be possible to negotiate an EESA. Certain neutral states might reject the concept, in the hope that NATO would someday reconsider and offer them membership instead. Strictly speaking, their acquiescence would not be needed, since they would not be asked to take any active steps or to join any new organisation. On the other hand, it could prove difficult to negotiate this arrangement, designed as it is to enhance their security, over their adamant objections. Ideally, they would take the public step of inviting it, after a consultation period.

In fact, there is a good chance that the idea will ultimately prove appealing to the neutral states, once discussed, explained and refined. Countries such as Ukraine and Georgia surely know that, whatever their long-term prospects, there is virtually no chance of near-term NATO membership being offered to them, due to their simmering conflicts with Russia and the lack of consensus about further Alliance expansion among current NATO members. At the same time, Russia knows that NATO has an underlying tendency towards expansion, and bases current policies on that expectation. The current state of affairs is thus in many ways the worst of all worlds. A new architecture would not create the same perverse incentives or profound uncertainties.

The structure being proposed here may strike some in the West as distasteful, or worse. It would allow Vladimir Putin – who has suppressed Russian political and civil society, and provoked unnecessary conflicts near his own borders – to claim that he was the Russian leader who stopped NATO in its tracks, preventing any further expansion. But we need to keep our eye on the ball. NATO membership for Ukraine and other nearby countries is not a viable means of resolving the current crisis; not even the most hawkish voices within NATO are calling for near-term Alliance membership for Ukraine or any other Central European state. Moreover, NATO expansion was never conceived as a way to pressure or punish Russia (except in the eyes of certain Russians, of course). Allowing Putin to claim some degree of vindication is a far less injurious outcome than running an unnecessarily heightened risk of war, and perpetuating a period of poor relations between Russia and the West that impedes cooperative action against other problems of mutual concern in the Middle East and Asia.

Indeed, a negotiated settlement could substantially reduce the risk of direct NATO–Russia conflict – a risk that, while still small, has grown significantly over the last three years. Efforts to assign blame for the current state of affairs must not be allowed to stand in the way of addressing problems that could impose enormous costs and risks if left unresolved. For example, a 2015 report by the European Leadership Network details how the intensity and gravity of incidents involving Russian and Western military forces have increased, raising the risk of an accident or military escalation between the world's leading nuclear powers.[6] Such incidents have hardly relented since then. Military-to-military contacts have also been inadequate; they should expand even before a new security order can be constructed, as General Joseph Dunford, chair of the US Joint Chiefs of Staff, has wisely suggested.[7]

A deal could also substantially improve Ukraine's prospects for finding peace and refocusing on political reform and economic recovery. It would also lower the chances of escalation in the current war. Similar considerations would apply in the case of Georgia.

While negotiations to devise and formalise the new security architecture were ongoing, most aspects of current Western policy should not change. Notably, sanctions should be sustained. They should not be expanded, however, unless Russia escalates its military activities further.

Once the EESA was agreed and at least partially implemented, sanctions on Russia could be lifted.[8] They could be removed step by step, in synchronisation with the verified withdrawal of Russian forces from the Donbass region of Ukraine, and from Abkhazia and South Ossetia in Georgia.

Future security cooperation between neutral states and NATO

Numerous aspects of this new security architecture require further detail. One key set of issues concerns ongoing security collaboration, in various forms, between NATO and those neutral countries that might be part of a future EESA. These activities are legitimate and non-threatening, and are often important to the security of the participating states. Thus, it will be essential not to interrupt or end such collaboration even with an EESA in place.

Consider firstly the issue of security assistance. The United States and other Western states already provide limited amounts of security assistance to most of the neutral countries in question. Much of it is intended to help ensure civilian control of the armed forces and to develop means of collaborating with NATO, through the Partnership for Peace programme as well as other activities, on security tasks of mutual interest. For example, the Partnership for Peace effort, overseen by the Euro-Atlantic Partnership Council, includes the following countries: Armenia, Austria, Azerbaijan, Belarus, Bosnia and Herzegovina, Ireland, Kazakhstan, Kyrgyzstan, Malta, Moldova, Montenegro, Russia, Serbia, Sweden, Switzerland, Tajikistan, the Former Yugoslav Republic of Macedonia, Turkmenistan, Ukraine and Uzbekistan.[9] Of these, 15 receive some financial support through Warsaw Initiative Funds – all but Austria, Ireland, Russia, Sweden and Switzerland.[10]

The *Rapid Trident* exercise, which took place in summer 2016 and involved NATO and several Partnership for Peace nations, serves as an example of such collaboration. The exercise focused on command and field training, with an emphasis on peacekeeping and stability operations, though its lessons were potentially applicable to other activities as well. Some 2,000 personnel took part, from a total of 14 countries (Ukraine, the United States, Belgium, Bulgaria, Canada, Georgia, Great Britain, Moldova, Lithuania, Norway, Poland, Romania, Sweden and Turkey). The exercise emphasised key tasks such as countering improvised explosive devices, convoy operations and patrolling.[11]

Another important example concerns Georgia, which has been collaborating with NATO under the Partnership for Peace since the 1990s. The programme provided a framework under which Georgia could send more than 200 soldiers to the peacekeeping operation in Kosovo from 1999 to 2008. Georgia has also been a key contributor to the NATO-led International Security Assistance Force mission, and now the *Resolute Support* mission, in Afghanistan. It deployed nearly 1,000 soldiers at the peak of the mission in early 2011; at that time, it was the second-largest non-NATO troop contributor to the operation, after Australia. Georgia also sent more than

2,000 troops to the Iraq War. It has a mountain-training site, accredited as a Partnership Training and Education Center by the Alliance, which offers courses and training to NATO members and other partner countries.[12]

Alliance maritime exercises have involved non-NATO countries too. Some are tailored to particular purposes, such as cold-weather training involving several allied states plus Finland and Sweden. The *Cold Response* exercise of March 2016 was one such example. These kinds of activities should be allowed to continue even under a new security architecture – as should maritime exercises emphasising search and rescue, or environmental surveillance and monitoring, or interdiction of international criminal and terrorist operations.[13]

Other types of military preparations motivated by a poor relationship with Russia might be phased out over time. Training on tasks such as anti-submarine warfare, or coordination of contingency planning for possible conflicts with Russia involving the Baltic Sea, should not be continued indefinitely once the relationship with Russia is stabilised – and the frequent provocations that Russian forces have carried out in recent years have presumably come to an end, a process that can be monitored and verified.[14] During the negotiation and early implementation phase of the new security order, these activities might continue, but would presumably not increase in scale or frequency.

The United States makes very few arms sales to the nations that participate in the Partnership for Peace. In 2015, for example, only Sweden, Ukraine and Uzbekistan received any weapons shipments, for a combined value of only about $50 million.[15] Similar levels of defence trade – and perhaps even modestly higher levels, should the economies of the affected countries experience accelerated growth – ought to be acceptable in the future.

NATO's Mediterranean initiatives and dialogues, which include a number of Arab and North African states and focus on issues such as refugee flows and Middle Eastern security, are also important. The threats they address are sufficiently acute that even more effective collaboration would be highly desirable.[16] Thus, one would not wish to cap, in any quantitative sense, possible future joint security activities. But most such efforts should also involve Russia, in some way.

How does one loosely cap cooperation in a way that will not produce disputes over which types of collaboration are allowable and which are not? It would admittedly be difficult, and probably undesirable, to be overly precise about exactly what limits to place on security assistance, arms sales and exercises. But there is still value in the idea of agreeing that future activities would not generally exceed the scale of past and ongoing efforts in these domains. A useful analogy is the US–China agreement in 1982 that the United States would cap (and gradually reduce) its arms sales to Taiwan.[17] China has argued for years that the agreement in fact committed Washington to wind down these arms transfers more quickly than has been the case; the two countries argue over the interpretation of that accord to this day. But the arguments, while sometimes acrimonious, occur within the parameters defined by the 1982 agreement, thus limiting the degree to which this issue has poisoned the broader relationship.

Verification and compliance

Even if it were successfully negotiated and implemented, a new EESA for today's neutral states might not be the end of the story. The same 'trust but verify' approach that Ronald Reagan famously articulated when negotiating with Soviet leaders would be required.

It is entirely possible that Russia is not simply an aggrieved state, acting in response to a sense of embitterment and encirclement, but also now a revanchist or revisionist power.[18] In that event, Moscow would most likely not be willing to negotiate the kind of security framework proposed here. Even if it did, it might do so cynically, seeing any agreement as merely a temporary truce to be rejected later, or as a means of constraining the West and lulling it into a false sense of complacency, while allowing Russia to carry out surreptitious activities in the states in question. Moscow might also seek to create a climate of intimidation that would produce a ring of partially subservient states near Russia's borders, despite Moscow's promise to allow full diplomatic and economic freedoms.

Therefore, in addition to sustaining prudent defensive measures such as the European Reassurance Initiative, and improving defences against Russian cyber attacks and political manipulation, Washington and other

Western capitals would need to devise a rigorous system of verification and a framework for responding to possible acts of non-compliance or even aggression by Moscow. The ultimate recourse, if the security architecture failed, would be to reopen the possibility of further NATO expansion. But that would be a last and least desirable resort. More modest steps need to be conceptualised, in advance, as well.

The first challenge is monitoring and verification. The Organization for Security and Co-operation in Europe (OSCE) would need to have the capacity and the formal responsibility to monitor compliance with the agreement, to handle any future disputes about security challenges faced by any of the countries covered by the accord, and to investigate and adjudicate complaints. With 700 monitors in Ukraine, the OSCE has played a key role in observing the ongoing fighting and tracking the involvement of various parties. This kind of capability should be sustained under the new EESA.

Certain elements of verification could be expected to be relatively straightforward. Monitoring the locations and movements of large quantities of conventional weaponry, as was done for years under the Treaty on Conventional Armed Forces in Europe (CFE Treaty), is not difficult. That treaty involved hundreds of inspections a year at declared sites, with stipulations requiring notification if equipment was moved or repositioned. Aircraft flying missions through the Open Skies arrangement – which has typically applied to some 100 flights per year over various parts of Eurasian and North American territory – can also contribute usefully to the effort.[19] Indeed, in the course of 2014, US intelligence was capable of tracking the movements of Russian equipment so well that at times it provided exact counts of the number of heavy military vehicles that had crossed the border with Ukraine. Observers from the OSCE were also capable of carefully monitoring such movements. Journalistic accounts, including interviews with captured fighters, commercially available imagery and social media are among the tools that together are increasingly likely to reveal any clandestine foreign military presence as its scale grows.[20]

In addition to national technical means and OSCE inspectors, a few other capabilities and methods could be authorised within the EESA as well. For example, the current observation provisions in the OSCE's Vienna Document should be improved to allow 'snap inspections' when countries conduct snap exercises, as suggested by the Netherlands' special envoy for conventional arms control, Lucien Kleinjan.[21]

Of course, determining who owns given pieces of equipment can be complex, as demonstrated by the Donbass experience in eastern Ukraine since 2014. So-called Russian volunteers operated in that region, bringing weaponry with them and at times transferring it to Ukrainian separatists. Determining who was who required, among other things, sophisticated American signals intelligence – including sources and methods that the United States was not willing to share in all cases.[22] Moreover, Russia retained some degree of deniability for the actions of these so-called volunteers, at least in its own mind, and even if most others were not fooled for long. Russia's *maskirovka* (military-deception) policies can employ a range of tactics: for example, special forces deployed in small numbers and embedded within friendly local populations, and the hiding of military capabilities and supplies within humanitarian-supply convoys.[23] Fortunately, as the scale and frequency of such activities increase, their deniability tends to decline.

If Russia suspended its withdrawal or otherwise violated its commitments, consequences would ensue. Sanctions could and should be reimposed with the same kind of 'snapback' automaticity that was worked out through UN channels in regard to Iran's compliance with the Joint Comprehensive Plan of Action.

If a violation were sufficiently serious, however, and redress could not be achieved, the entire deal could be declared dead. In other words, if Russia again invaded part of Ukraine, for example, the United States and other NATO states, as well as the European Union more broadly, would retain the right to respond. Appropriate steps could include reimposing economic sanctions, providing lethal arms to Ukraine's military and even considering NATO membership for Ukraine. This latter step is not necessarily an outcome that I would advocate, depending on circumstances. But other Americans and NATO leaders might well do so, and the terms of the security order should explicitly allow it.

Remaining resolute

It could be that Moscow has no interest in this kind of proposal. Or it might agree to it, then seek to subvert it. As such, any vision for a new security order in Eastern Europe needs to be pursued with NATO's many eyes wide open – and with ongoing resoluteness in the defence of all 29 member states. This goes well beyond the issue of verification and compliance.

To begin with, the United States and NATO allies should not dismantle any existing weapons or bases under an EESA regime. In that sense, the physical steps of creating the new security architecture, and the associated costs and risks, would be quite modest.

Under the proposed architecture, the United States and other NATO member states should continue to implement their plans to station modest amounts of equipment in the easternmost NATO countries under the European Reassurance Initiative and *Operation Atlantic Resolve*. These represent a modest effort involving some 5,000 military personnel (or perhaps as many as a few thousand more), the main effects of which are not to create substantial forward-deployed combat power, but to signal resolve and to create in effect a robust tripwire force. This is not objectionable and should continue. And while I do not support those voices arguing for multiple additional US and other NATO brigades (anywhere from two to six or more),[24] the four-battalion presence in NATO's east might be expanded. For example, the additional US brigade that was deployed this year could be sustained indefinitely. It is at present a complement to NATO's other very modest recent initiatives – the NATO Response Force formed at the 2014 Wales Summit and its newest incarnation as a Very High Readiness Joint Task Force. Another US Army brigade could be stationed back in Germany; the recent American drawdown there probably went too far in any case.

On matters of cyber security, information warfare and efforts to influence the internal politics of other countries through covert means, NATO must be ready, as in the Cold War, to fight fire with fire. Russia's interference in the 2016 American election was egregious. Putin believes that the United States was behind the Rose, Orange, Tulip and Maidan revolutions, but Washington's efforts in those countries were transparent and innocuous, featuring the work of organisations such as the International Republican

Institute and the National Democratic Institute. Covert, and far more calculated, efforts akin to those carried out by Russia in the United States (and various European countries) should be initiated in a proportionate way if need be. Methods could include not only help for reformist political movements and politicians but, if necessary, disinformation efforts as well. One hopes that such efforts will not be needed.

In short, no new security order should be pursued with apologies to or trust in Moscow, or with any expectation that even the successful completion of a new architecture could turn Russia and NATO states into genuine strategic partners. But it would have a real chance of reducing tension, worst-case planning and the risk of war. This chance is ample reason to give it serious consideration.

Notes

1 Not everyone agrees that disputes over future security arrangements are at the heart of the current problems in US–Russia relations, but many do. See, for example, International Institute for Strategic Studies, *Strategic Survey 2016* (Abingdon: Routledge for the IISS, 2016), p. 211.

2 On this general subject, see, for example, Ernst B. Haas, *Beyond the Nation-State: Functionalism and International Organization* (Stanford, CA: Stanford University Press, 1964); Hedley Bull, *The Anarchical Society: A Study of Order in World Politics* (New York: Columbia University Press, 1977); and Strobe Talbott, *The Great Experiment: The Story of Ancient Empires, Modern States, and the Quest for a Global Nation* (New York: Simon & Schuster, 2008).

3 For a related view, see Terry Atlas, 'Brzezinski Sees Finlandization of Ukraine as Deal Maker', Bloomberg.com, 12 April 2014, available at https://www.bloomberg.com/news/articles/2014-04-11/brzezinski-sees-finlandization-of-ukraine-as-deal-maker; and Henry A. Kissinger, 'To Settle the Ukraine Crisis, Start at the End', *Washington Post*, 5 March 2014, https://www.washingtonpost.com/opinions/henry-kissinger-to-settle-the-ukraine-crisis-start-at-the-end/2014/03/05/46dad868-a496-11e3-8466-d34c451760b9_story.html?utm_term=.c6b5992bb0f0.

4 Laurence Norman and Maarten van Tartwijk, 'Dutch Premier's Demands Cast New Doubt Over EU–Ukraine Pact', *Wall Street Journal*, 20 October 2016.

5 For a related view, see General Sir Richard Shirreff (former deputy supreme allied commander Europe), 'Is Armed Conflict with Russia a Real Possibility?', remarks at the Brookings Institution, Washington DC, 19

October 2016, https://www.brookings.edu/events/is-armed-conflict-with-russia-a-real-possibility/.

6 Ian Kearns, Lukasz Kulesa and Thomas Frear, 'Preparing for the Worst: Are Russian and NATO Military Exercises Making War in Europe More Likely?', European Leadership Network, London, 12 August 2015, http://www.europeanleadershipnetwork.org/preparing-for-the-worst-are-russian-and-nato-military-exercises-making-war-in-europe-more-likely_2997.html.

7 Eugene Rumer, Richard Sokolsky and Andrew S. Weiss, 'Trump and Russia: The Right Way to Manage Relations', *Foreign Affairs*, vol. 96, no. 2, March–April 2017, p. 16.

8 See Michael O'Hanlon and Jeremy Shapiro, 'Crafting a Win–Win–Win for Russia, Ukraine, and the West', *Washington Post*, 7 December 2015, available at http://www.brookings.edu/research/opinions/2014/12/07-russia-ukraine-ohanlon-shapiro.

9 NATO, 'Euro-Atlantic Partnership Council', 7 April 2016, http://www.nato.int/cps/en/natolive/topics_49276.htm.

10 Information on this support is available from ForeignAssistance.gov, http://beta.foreignassistance.gov/explore#.

11 US Army Europe, 'Army Strong, Strong Europe!: Exercise Rapid Trident', http://www.eur.army.mil/RapidTrident.

12 See NATO, 'Relations with Georgia', 7 June 2016, http://www.nato.int/cps/en/natohq/topics_38988.htm; and Ian S. Livingston, Heather L. Messera and Michael E. O'Hanlon, *Afghanistan Index* (Washington DC: Brookings Institution, 28 February 2011), https://www.brookings.edu/wp-content/uploads/2016/07/index20110228.pdf.

13 NATO, 'Key NATO and Allied Exercises', July 2016, http://www.nato.int/nato_static_fl2014/assets/pdf/pdf_2016_07/20160704_1607-factsheet_exercises_en.pdf.

14 For background on this issue, see Eoin Micheál McNamara, 'Securing the Nordic-Baltic Region', *NATO Review*, http://www.nato.int/docu/Review/2016/Also-in-2016/security-baltic-defense-nato/EN/index.htm.

15 Statista, 'U.S. Arms Exports, 2015, by Country', https://www.statista.com/statistics/248552/us-arms-exports-by-country.

16 See, for example, F. Stephen Larrabee and Peter A. Wilson, 'NATO Needs a Southern Strategy', *National Interest*, 27 January 2014, http://nationalinterest.org/commentary/nato-needs-southern-strategy-9769?page=3.

17 Richard C. Bush, *Untying the Knot: Making Peace in the Taiwan Strait* (Washington DC: Brookings Institution Press, 2005), pp. 23–4.

18 The terms 'revanchist' and 'revisionist' are often used interchangeably, along with the word 'irredentist' – and while there may be subtle differences, all three words imply a desire to reclaim what is viewed as a nation's rightful possessions or areas of influence.

19 See US Department of State, 'Key Facts About the Open Skies Treaty', 6 June 2016, https://2009-2017.state.gov/t/avc/rls/2016/258061.htm; and Arms Control Association, 'The Conventional Armed Forces in Europe (CFE) Treaty and the Adapted

CFE Treaty at a Glance', August 2012, https://www.armscontrol.org/factsheet/cfe.

20 See David M. Herszenhorn, 'Fears Rise as Russian Military Units Pour into Ukraine', *New York Times*, 12 November 2014, http://www.nytimes.com/2014/11/13/world/europe/ukraine-russia-military-border-nato.html; and Mark Urban, 'How Many Russians Are Fighting in Ukraine?', BBC News, 10 March 2015, http://www.bbc.com/news/world-europe-31794523.

21 Lucien Kleinjan, 'Conventional Arms Control in Europe: Decline, Disarray, and the Need for Reinvention', *Arms Control Today*, vol. 46, no. 5, June 2016, p. 24.

22 Joe Gould, 'Electronic Warfare: What U.S. Army Can Learn from Ukraine', *Defense News*, 2 August 2015, http://www.defensenews.com/story/defense/policy-budget/warfare/2015/08/02/us-army-ukraine-russia-electronic-warfare/30913397.

23 Colonel J.B. Vowell, 'Maskirovka: From Russia, with Deception', *RealClearDefense*, 31 October 2016, http://www.realcleardefense.com/articles/2016/10/31/maskirovka_from_russia_with_deception_110282.html?utm_source=RealClearDefense+Morning+Recon&utm_campaign=2db8be085d-EMAIL_CAMPAIGN_2016_10_30&utm_medium=email&utm_term=0_694f73a8dc-2db8be085d-81835773#!.

24 See, for example, Philip M. Breedlove, 'NATO's Next Act: How to Handle Russia and Other Threats', *Foreign Affairs*, vol. 95, no. 4, July–August 2016, p. 104.

The Secret to North Korea's ICBM Success

Michael Elleman

North Korea's missile programme has made astounding strides over the past two years. An arsenal that had been based on short- and medium-range missiles, along with an intermediate-range *Musudan* that repeatedly failed flight tests, has suddenly been supplemented by two new missiles: the intermediate-range *Hwasong*-12 and the intercontinental ballistic missile (ICBM) *Hwasong*-14. No other country has transitioned from a medium-range capability to an ICBM in such a short time. What explains this rapid progression? The answer is simple. North Korea acquired a high-performance liquid-propellant engine (LPE) from a foreign source.

Available evidence clearly indicates that the new LPE is derived from the Soviet RD-250 family of engines, and has been modified to operate as the boosting force for the *Hwasong*-12 and -14. An unknown number of these engines were probably acquired though illicit channels operating in Russia or Ukraine, or both. North Korea's need for an alternative to the failing *Musudan* and the recent appearance of the modified RD-250 engine, along with other evidence, suggests the transfers occurred within the past two years.

Tests reveal recent technical gains

North Korea ground tested a large LPE in September 2016, which it claimed could generate 80 tonnes' thrust. The same LPE was again ground tested in March 2017. This test included four smaller, steering engines. On 14 May

---

Michael Elleman is IISS Senior Fellow for Missile Defence. An earlier version of this article appeared on the IISS Voices blog.

 DOI 10.1080/00396338.2017.1375218

2017, with Kim Jong-un overseeing test preparations, North Korea launched a new intermediate-range ballistic missile, the *Hwasong*-12. The single-stage missile flew on a very steep trajectory, reaching a peak altitude of over 2,000 kilometres.[1] If the *Hwasong*-12 had used a normal flight path, it would have travelled between 4,000 and 4,500km, placing the American territory of Guam, just 3,400km away, within range.

The success of the *Hwasong*-12 flight in May gave North Korean engineers the confidence needed to pursue a more ambitious goal: the initial flight testing of a two-stage missile capable of reaching the continental United States. On 4 July, less than two months after the *Hwasong*-12 test, the two-stage *Hwasong*-14 was launched. A second *Hwasong*-14 was tested on 28 July. The *Hwasong*-14 launches flew on very steep flight paths, with the first shot reaching an apogee of 2,700km.[2] The second test peaked at about 3,800km.[3]

North Korea's announced results were independently confirmed by South Korea, Japan and the US. In both tests, the mock warheads plummeted towards the East Sea, 900–1,000km from the launch point.[4] If flown on a trajectory that maximises range instead of peak altitude, the two missiles would have reached about 7,000km and 9,000km respectively, well exceeding the 5,500km minimum distance for a system to be categorised as an ICBM. The mock warhead carried by the *Hwasong*-14 during the two flight tests was less than 500 kilograms, perhaps as little as 300 kg,[5] so it is difficult to estimate how far the ICBM can travel if armed with a real nuclear warhead. An authoritative analysis completed by German and American missile experts indicates that *Hwasong*-14 may not be able to reach the lower 48 states of the United States if the nuclear device weighs 500kg or more.[6] The present author's analysis concludes that Seattle, but not San Francisco, could be reached if the *Hwasong*-14 carries a 500kg warhead.

The dimensions and visible features of the *Hwasong*-12 indicate an overall mass of between 24,000 and 25,000kg. The *Hwasong*-12's acceleration at lift-off, as determined by the launch video aired by KCNA, is about 8.5–9.0m/s^2. Assuming North Korea did not manipulate the launch video, the thrust generated by the *Hwasong*-12's complete engine assembly is between 45 and 47 tonnes' thrust; the main engine contributes between 39 and 41 tonnes' force, and the auxiliary engines about six tonnes' force. The *Hwasong*-14 has an estimated mass of 33,000–34,000kg, and an initial acceleration rate of about 4–4.5m/s^2, resulting in a total thrust of 46–48 tonnes' force.

Identifying the new LPE and its origins

The origins of the new engine (see Figures 1 and 2) are difficult to determine with certainty. However, a process of elimination sharply narrows the possibilities.

There is no publicly available evidence to suggest that North Korea successfully designed and developed the LPE indigenously. Indeed, although this is subject to lively debate, available evidence indicates that North Korea has not succeeded in producing its own clones of the *Scud* and *Nodong* engines it imported from Russia during the 1980s and 1990s.[7] Even if North Korea had mastered the production of clones, this does not mean that it could design, develop and manufacture a large LPE from scratch, especially one that uses higher-performance propellants and generates 40 tonnes' thrust.

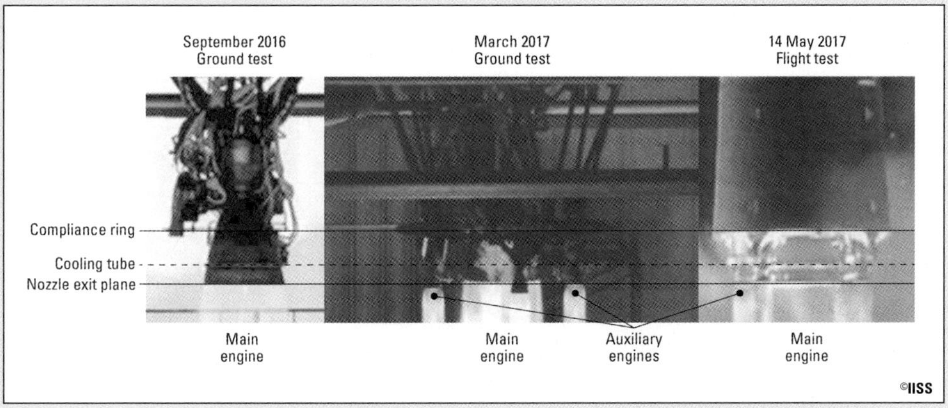

Figure 1. **The liquid-propellant engines ground tested in September 2016 and March 2017 appear to be the same, though only the second ground test and the *Hwasong*-12 flight test operated with four auxiliary or vernier engines, which steer the missile.**

Claims that the LPE is a North Korean product would be more believable if the country's experts had in the recent past developed and tested a series of smaller, less powerful engines, but there are no reports of such activities. Indeed, prior to the *Hwasong*-12 and -14 flights, every liquid-fuelled missile launched by North Korea – all of the *Scud*s and *Nodong*s, even the *Musudan* – was powered by an engine developed and originally produced by the Russian enterprise named for A.M. Isayev; the *Scud, Nodong* and R-27 (from which the *Musudan* is derived) missiles were designed and originally produced by the Russian concern named for V.P. Makeyev. It is, therefore, far more likely that the *Hwasong*-12 and -14 are powered by an LPE imported from an established missile power.

If this engine was imported, most potential sources can be eliminated because the external features, propellant combination and performance profile of the LPE in question are unique. The engine tested by North Korea does not physically resemble any LPE manufactured by the US, France, Japan, India or Iran. Nor do any of these countries produce an engine that uses storable propellants and generates the thrust delivered by the *Hwasong*-12 and -14 LPE. The LPE vaguely resembles the Chinese YF-21 engine, but there are also distinct differences which rule out that possibility. Thus, by a process of elimination, the former Soviet Union is the most likely source.

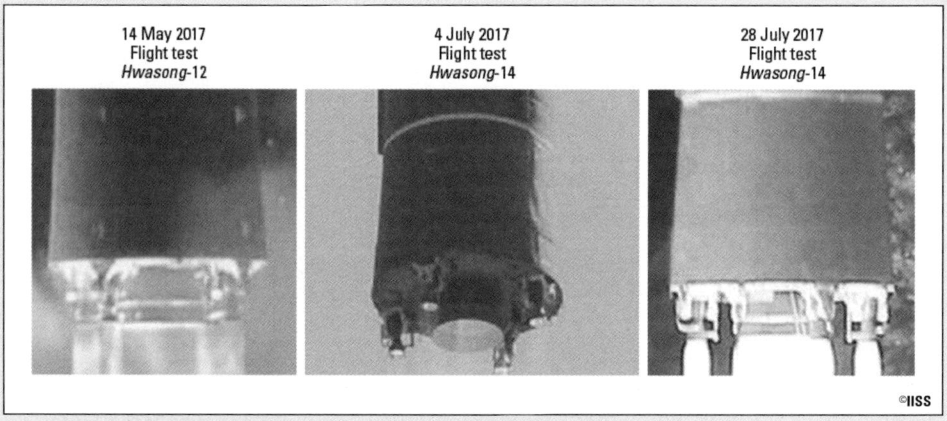

Figure 2. **The three missiles tested by North Korea are powered by the same engine complex, with one main engine and four steering engines.**

Given North Korea's reliance to date on technologies originating with the Isayev and Makeyev enterprises, one might suspect one or both as the probable supplier. However, neither enterprise has been associated with an engine that matches the performance of LPE used by *Hwasong*-12 and -14.

An exhaustive search of engines produced by other manufacturers in the former Soviet Union yields a couple of possibilities, all of which are associated with the Russian enterprise named after V.P. Glushko, now known as Energomash. The RD-217, RD-225 and RD-250 engine families use high-energy, storable-liquid propellants similar to those employed by engines tested by North Korea. Neither the RD-217 nor RD-225 have external features matching those of North Korea's new engine. The RD-250 is the only match.

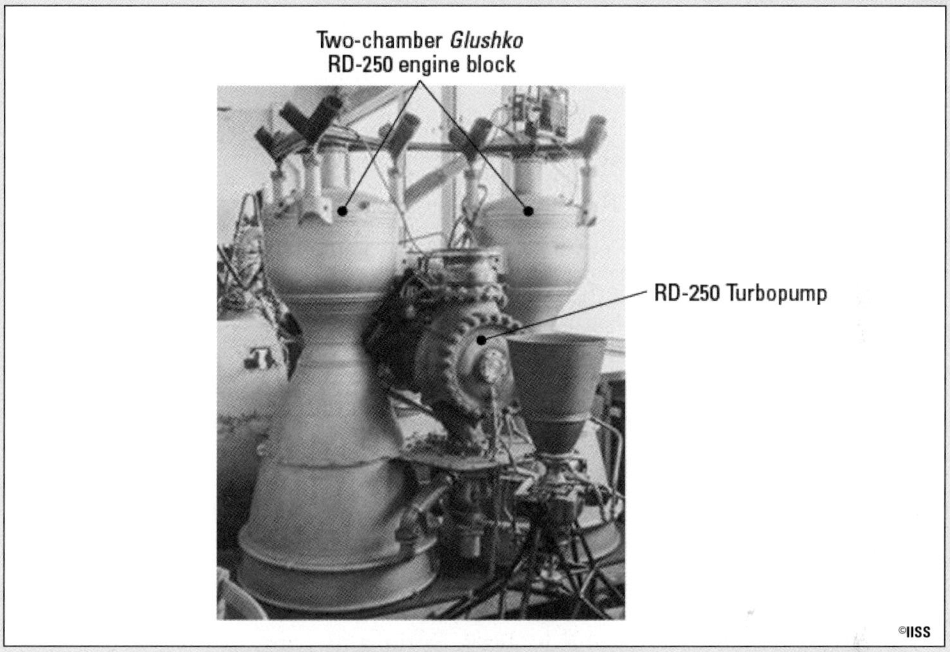

Figure 3. **The RD-250 engine consists of a pair of combustion chambers fed by a single turbopump. Each chamber produces about 394,000 Newtons of thrust, or about 40 tonnes' force, when relying on UDMH as the fuel, and N_2O_4 as the oxidiser. The RD-250's nozzle also features a cooling tube and a compliance ring that resemble those found on the engines tested by North Korea. The small engine with its nozzle pointed upward and displayed in the foreground is not associated with the RD-250 engine.**

The RD-250 engine is normally configured as a pair of combustion chambers, which receive propellant from a single turbopump, as shown in Figure 3. When operated in tandem, the two chambers generate roughly 78–80 tonnes' thrust. This level of thrust is similar to the claims North Korea made when the first ground test was conducted and publicised in September 2016.

It gradually became clear, however, that the *Hwasong*-12 and -14 use single-chamber engines. Note, for example, that Pyongyang claimed that a new pump design was used for the September ground test. This makes sense, because operating the RD-250 as a single-chamber LPE would necessitate a new or highly modified turbopump to deliver propellant for one, not two chambers. Having no demonstrated experience modifying or developing large LPE turbopumps, Pyongyang's engineers would have been hard pressed to make the modifications themselves. Rather, the technical skills needed to modify the existing RD-250 turbopump, or fashioning a new one capable of feeding propellant to a single chamber, would reside with experts with a rich history of working with the RD-250. Such expertise is available at Russia's Energomash concern and Ukraine's KB Yuzhnoye. One has to conclude that the modified engines were sourced from one of those factories.

Engine production is a very different endeavour

The alternative hypothesis, that Russian or Ukrainian engineers were employed in North Korea, is less likely, given the absence of any known production facility in North Korea for large LPEs. This is not to say North Korea does not have missile production and assembly plants. There is plenty of publicly available evidence showing facilities where missile bodies are manufactured and assembled. But airframe-production and missile-assembly facilities are common, and have been seen in Iraq, Syria and Iran. Yet these countries do not produce LPEs. Engine production is a very different endeavour. For example, the *Nodong* engines found on the first stage of the *Unha* launcher, retrieved from the ocean by South Korea in 2012 and 2016 and inspected by international experts, show that they contain foreign-made components, such as ball bearings from the Soviet-produced *Scud*-B missile engine. The *Nodong* engine itself exhibits all the hallmarks of a Soviet-made product, as well. If it had been fabricated in North Korea, by North Korean specialists, one would expect to see minor alterations to the engine's external features. The Soviets produced *Scud* and *Nodong* engines five decades ago, using materials and machine tools unique to Russian manufacturing at the time. North Korea would not have access to precisely the same materials, and would likely opt to use more modern production equipment and make minor adjustments to increase performance and reliability. But these differences are not seen on the retrieved *Nodong* engines. Nor have they been observed on the engines found on *Scud* missiles exported from North Korea.

Further undermining the alternative hypothesis, Western experts who within the past year visited KB Yuzhnoye in Ukraine told the author that a single-chamber version was on display at a nearby university and that a local engineer boasted about producing it. While this does not prove the engine was developed at KB Yuzhnoye, or produced at its machine-building unit, Yuzhmash, it offers strong evidence that the modified RD-250 engine has been seen outside of North Korea.

Why single-chamber engines were transferred rather than the more powerful double-chamber original versions is unclear. One possible hypothesis is that the exporters, for whatever reason, exercised restraint in what they were willing to transfer to North Korea. Combined with a second stage, however, the single-chamber RD-250 engine is powerful enough to send an ICBM armed with a very compact and light warhead to cities on the American west coast.

The RD-250 was originally designed by the Glushko enterprise of Russia, and produced and incorporated into the first stage of the R-36 (SS-9) ICBM and the *Tsiklon*-2 satellite launcher by KB Yuzhnoye of Ukraine. The *Tsiklon*-2 carrier rocket lofted its first satellite into orbit in 1969, with the last of 106 launches occurring in 2006.[8] While Yuzhnoye was responsible for producing the *Tsiklon*-2 rocket, Russian entities launched the satellite. The relationship survived the break-up of the Soviet Union in 1991 primarily because of long-standing institutional linkages, and the commercial interests of both enterprises and both countries. However, despite the *Tsiklon*-2's unsurpassed reliability record, Russia stopped purchasing the Yuzhnoye rocket in 2006 in favour of an indigenous system. KB Yuzhnoye's repeated attempts to market the rocket and related technologies to other potential customers, including Boeing and Brazil, yielded little. The once vaunted KB Yuzhnoye has been near financial collapse since roughly 2015.

The total number of RD-250 engines fabricated in Russia and Ukraine is not known. However, there are almost certainly hundreds of spares stored at KB Yuzhnoye's facilities and at warehouses in Russia where the *Tsiklon*-2 was launched. Spares may also exist at one or more of Energomash's many facilities spread across Russia. Because the RD-250 is no longer employed by operational missiles or launchers, facilities warehousing the obsolete LPEs are probably loosely guarded. A small team of disgruntled employees or underpaid guards at any one of the storage sites, and with access to the LPEs, could be enticed to steal a few dozen engines by one of the many illicit arms dealers, criminal networks and transnational smugglers operating in the former Soviet Union. The engines (less than two metres tall and one metre wide) could be flown or, more likely, transported by train through Russia to North Korea. One cannot exclude the possibility that the engines transited through China on their way to North Korea.

Pyongyang has many connections in Russia, including with the illicit network that funnelled *Scud, Nodong* and R-27 (*Musudan*) hardware to North Korea in the 1980s and 1990s. United Nations sanctions imposed on Pyongyang have likely strengthened the Kim regime's ties to these criminal networks. North Korean agents seeking missile technology are also known to operate in Ukraine. In 2012, for example, two North Korean nationals were arrested and convicted by Ukrainian authorities for attempting to procure missile designs from Yuzhnoye.[9] Today, Yuzhnoye's facilities lie close to the front lines of the Russian-controlled secessionist territory. Clearly, there is no shortage of potential routes through which North Korea might have acquired the few dozen RD-250 engines that would be needed for an ICBM programme.

How did North Korea acquire the RD-250 engine?

When and from where RD-250 engines may have been shipped to North Korea is difficult to determine. It is possible the transfers occurred in the 1990s, when North Korea was actively procuring *Scud*- and *Nodong*-related hardware, as well as R-27 technology and its Isayev 4D10 engine. But this seems unlikely for three reasons.

Firstly, the network North Korea relied on in the 1990s focused on products originating from Russia's Makeyev and Isayev enterprises. Energomash and Yuzhnoye had limited connections to Makeyev or Isayev; indeed, they were rival enterprises competing for contracts as the Soviet

Union crumbled. It is, therefore, a stretch to assume the illicit channels Pyongyang was using in the 1990s had access to products manufactured or used at either Yuzhnoye or Energomash two decades ago.

Secondly, until recently, North Korea appeared to focus on exploiting R-27 hardware for its long-range missile ambitions. Pyongyang's first intermediate-range missile, the *Musudan*, which was first displayed in a 2010 parade, is derived from the R-27 technology acquired in the 1990s. Moreover, until the *Hwasong*-12 launch in March 2017, Pyongyang's design concepts for a prospective ICBM featured a first stage powered by a cluster of two Isayev 4D10 LPEs. Photographs taken while Kim Jong-un toured a missile plant in March 2016 captured the back end of an ICBM prototype that appeared to house a pair of 4D10 engines, not a modified, single-chambered RD-250 LPE. A month later, Kim attended a ground test featuring a cluster of two 4D10 engines operating in tandem,[10] a clear indication that North Korea's future ICBM would rely on this configuration. There is no evidence during this period to suggest that North Korea was developing a missile based on the modified RD-250 engine.

Thirdly, the Isayev 4D10 engine, which relies on staged combustion, is a complicated closed-cycle system that is integrated within the missile's fuel tank. If the open-cycle, externally mounted, single-chamber RD-250 engine had been available in 2015, engineers would have likely preferred to use it to power a new long-range missile, as it shares many features with the engines North Korea has worked with for decades.

However, when North Korean specialists began flight testing the *Musudan* in 2016, the missile repeatedly failed soon after ignition. Only one flight test is believed to have been successful. The cause of the string of failures cannot be determined from media reports. That many failed very early in flight suggests that problems with either the engine itself, or the unique 'submerged' configuration of the engine, were responsible. If this was the case, North Korea's engineers may have recognised that they could not easily overcome the challenges. This might explain why the *Musudan* has not been tested since 2016.

The maiden appearance of the modified RD-250 in September 2016 roughly coincides with North Korea's decision to halt *Musudan* testing. It is reasonable to speculate that Kim's engineers knew the *Musudan* presented grim or insurmountable technical challenges, which prompted a search for an alternative. If North Korea began its quest to identify and procure a new LPE in 2016, the start of the search would have occurred in the same year Yuzhnoye was experiencing the full impact of its financial shortfalls. This is not to suggest that the Ukrainian government was involved, and not necessarily Yuzhnoye executives. In fact, Kiev's 2012 arrest of North Korean agents seeking missile technologies indicates otherwise.

However, workers at Yuzhnoye facilities in Dnipropetrovsk and Pavlograd were likely the first ones to suffer the consequences of the economic misfortunes, leaving them susceptible to exploitation by unscrupulous traders, arms dealers and transnational criminals operating in Russia, Ukraine and elsewhere. The fact that Russian-backed separatists are waging war against the Ukraine government fewer than 200km east of Yuzhnoye's facilities provides ample opportunity and motivation for criminal elements to pilfer facilities containing highly valued hardware. Their connections to illicit-trade networks would seem to make partnerships inevitable.

North Korea's ICBM: still a work in progress

Acquisition of the modified RD-250 engine enabled North Korea to bypass the failing *Musudan* development effort and begin work on creating an ICBM sooner than previously expected. The *Hwasong*-12 and -14 missiles, however, are not yet operationally viable systems. Additional flight tests are needed to assess their navigation and guidance capabilities, determine overall performance under a range of operational conditions and demonstrate their reliability. Empirical data derived from tests to validate the efficacy of warhead re-entry technologies are also needed. Pyongyang could elect to deploy the *Hwasong*-12 and -14 as early as 2018, after only a handful of additional test launches, but at the risk of fielding missiles with marginal reliability. The risks could be reduced over time by continuing flight trials after the missiles are assigned to combat units. But for the immediate future, the *Hwasong*-12 and -14 have limited military value.

For example, consider Kim Jong-un's request for his military to prepare plans for 'enveloping' Guam with a *Hwasong*-12 attack.[11] The attack, according to KCNA, would not target Guam itself. Rather, North Korea would attempt to land the missiles 25 to 40 km from the island's coastline. This would be risky, at best, because Pyongyang has no established measure of the *Hwasong*-12's accuracy, meaning there is a finite possibility that the missiles could overshoot their targets and strike Guam itself. Rough estimates suggest the probability of accidently landing on the island could be greater than 1%.[12]

Perhaps of greater importance is the limited capacity of the *Hwasong*-14 ICBM. The missile's underpowered second stage is sufficient for threatening Hawaii, and possibly Seattle, with a small nuclear warhead, but it cannot target the entire US mainland. Arguably, the *Hwasong*-14 is an interim ICBM that satisfies Kim Jong-un's immediate strategic needs. It seems probable that North Korea will want to field a more capable ICBM in the future. This could be achieved by developing a first stage consisting of two or more modified RD-250 engines, and a second stage powered by either a *Musudan* engine or a single-chamber RD-250. Such a missile could carry larger warheads and simple decoys to render less effective US missile defences deployed in Alaska and California. Developing and testing an improved ICBM, however, will require more time.

It is not too late for the US and its allies, along with China and perhaps Russia, to negotiate an agreement that bans future missile testing, and effectively prevents North Korea from perfecting its capacity to terrorise all of America with nuclear weapons. But it will be very difficult, and the window of opportunity will soon close. Diplomatic action that seeks to freeze North Korea's missile capabilities must be taken immediately.

Notes

1 'North Korea Missile Rose More than 2,000 Kilometers in Altitude: Japan Defense Minister', Reuters, 13 May 2017, http://www.reuters.com/article/us-northkorea-missiles-inada-idUSKBN18A00V.

2 Ankit Panda, 'North Korea Just Tested a Missile that Could Likely Reach Washington DC with a Nuclear Weapon', *Diplomat*, 29 July 2017, http://thediplomat.com/2017/07/north-korea-just-tested-a-missile-that-could-likely-reach-washington-dc-with-a-nuclear-weapon/.

3 *Ibid*.

4 *Ibid*.

5 Author's assessment, based on modelling the performance of the two *Hwasong*-14 flight tests in July 2017.

6 Theodore A. Postol, Markus Schiller and Robert Schmucker, 'North Korea's "Not Quite" ICBM Can't Hit the Lower 48 States', *Bulletin of the Atomic Scientists*, 11 August 2017, http://thebulletin.org/north-korea%E2%80%99s-%E2%80%9Cnot-quite%E2%80%9D-icbm-can%E2%80%99t-hit-lower-48-states11012.

7 For a detailed discussion on the challenges of reverse-engineering sophisticated machinery, such as LPEs, and the evidence indicating that North Korea (and Iran) have failed in such endeavours, see: International Institute for Strategic Studies (IISS), 'North Korean Security Challenges: A Net Assessment', *IISS Strategic Dossier*, July 2011, Chapter Six; IISS, 'Iran's Ballistic Missile Capabilities: A Net Assessment', *IISS Strategic Dossier*, May 2010, Chapter Three; Robert H. Schmucker and Markus Schiller, *Raketenbedrohung 2.0: Technische und politische Grundlagen* (Berlin: E.S. Mittler und Sohn, 2015); and Markus Schiller, 'Characterizing the North Korean Nuclear Missile Threat', RAND Corporation, 2012, p. 77, http://www.rand.org/content/dam/rand/pubs/technical_reports/2012/RAND_TR1268.pdf.

8 See http://www.astronautix.com/t/tsiklon-2.html.

9 'N. Koreans Convicted of Trying to Steal Rocket Technology from Ukraine', Yonhap, 9 June 2012, http://english.yonhapnews.co.kr/national/2012/06/09/91/0301000000AEN20120609000700320F.HTML.

10 John Schilling, 'North Korea's Large Rocket Engine Test: A Significant Step Forward for Pyongyang's ICBM Program', 38 North, 11 April 2016, http://www.38north.org/2016/04/schilling041116/.

11 Ankit Panda, 'Why North Korea Is Planning Long-Range Missile Flight Tests over Japan and Toward Guam', *Diplomat*, 10 August 2017, http://thediplomat.com/2017/08/why-north-korea-is-planning-long-range-missile-flight-tests-over-japan-and-toward-guam.

12 Mark Fitzpatrick and Michael Elleman, 'Deterring North Korea the Wrong Way', Politics and Strategy, 11 August 2017, http://www.iiss.org/en/politics and strategy/blogsections/2017-6dda/august-b877/deterring-north-korea-the-wrong-way-4bd9.

America's Generals Are Out of Ideas for Afghanistan

Christopher D. Kolenda

President Donald Trump's much-anticipated 21 August speech promised to roll out a new strategy for America's 16-year-old war in Afghanistan. (Afghans themselves have been at war for nearly 40 years.) Those hoping for meaningful change were disappointed. The decision to do more of the same and expect different results underscores a broader strategic bankruptcy within the US national-security establishment that is eroding trust in American leadership.

That President Trump agreed to stay engaged in Afghanistan, after previously tweeting that the war is a disaster, is important. He called for stronger counter-terrorism and advisory efforts, and an end to nation-building. He stipulated that Afghanistan do more to fight corruption, and insisted that American involvement is not a blank cheque. He promised an unspecified 'conditions-based' approach to determining when America's involvement in the war would come to a close. He demanded Pakistan turn against the Afghan Taliban, with penalties to follow if Pakistan fails to do so. He insisted that India do more in Afghanistan.

Senators John McCain and Lindsey Graham, long-time advocates of eliminating timelines for withdrawal, praised the approach. General (Retd) John Allen, former US commander in Afghanistan, and expert Michael O'Hanlon commended Trump for making a 'difficult and very presidential

Christopher D. Kolenda, a combat veteran of four tours in Afghanistan, served as senior advisor to three ISAF commanders and two under secretaries of defense. He resigned from the Obama administration in 2014.

Survival | vol. 59 no. 5 | October–November 2017 | pp. 37–46 DOI 10.1080/00396338.2017.1375220

decision' about American policy. Kori Schake, a highly respected thought leader, lauded Trump for changing his mind.[1]

Regional expert Steve Coll, author of *Ghost Wars*, has pointed out that Trump's approach is virtually the same as those tried by George W. Bush and Barack Obama.[2] Those presidents also demanded the Afghan government curb rampant corruption, pressured Pakistan to turn against the Afghan Taliban, ramped up counter-terrorism and advisory efforts, and said America was not in the nation-building business. Obama's 2009 surge-and-withdraw approach has been rightly criticised. By 2015, even he dropped the timelines. The most substantive difference might be the rather crude threat to reduce trade with India if the latter does not increase assistance to Afghanistan.

Will things be different this time?

After nine months in office, and much study of Afghanistan by senior Trump administration officials – including three generals (two retired) serving in traditionally civilian cabinet-level roles – the best that America's professional class could do was to offer two options that guaranteed a loss, and one option that simply kicked the can around the circle again. This is intellectual laziness.

Withdrawal, the first option, would have risked greater instability in Afghanistan and the potential re-emergence of terror safe-havens. Replacing troops with mercenaries, the second option, would have resulted in contractors using lethal force in the name of the United States and against the express wishes of the Afghan government. Anyone who has spent time talking to Afghans understands their deep psychological scars from private companies rampaging along roads and through villages. If ever there was a way to turn the entire Afghan population against the United States, this was probably it.

Still, it seemed a tough job to win a sceptical president over to a continued US presence in Afghanistan. National Security Advisor H.R. McMaster reportedly produced pictures of Afghan women in miniskirts in 1970s Kabul to show that the country was not hopeless.[3] Others cited the myriad terrorist groups in the region. Still others may have calculated that a post-withdrawal catastrophe in Afghanistan would undermine Trump's re-election prospects in 2020.

The president was right to be sceptical. It is probably not lost on him that the same strategic thinking, recycled now for a third time, is unlikely to yield different results.

The implicit theory of success behind the Trump administration's approach, and the ones before it, presumes that more aggressive military action, combined with greater Afghan military and government capacity, will blunt Taliban momentum and enable the Afghan government to regain the battlefield initiative. US pressure on Pakistan, meanwhile, will force the latter to deny sanctuary to the Afghan Taliban. Beaten in Afghanistan and no longer welcome in Pakistan, the Taliban will be forced to sue for peace.

This outcome is highly desirable, but is it feasible? Longitudinal studies on insurgencies and counter-insurgencies show that two factors normally determine the war's outcome. Insurgencies that have maintained tangible local support and external sanctuary have been successful in every such conflict since the Second World War. Counter-insurgency, on the other hand, is a contest for legitimacy. A host-nation government that proves unable to retake and retain insurgent-controlled or contested territory (that is, to win the battle of legitimacy) has lost every time since the Second World War.[4] In no case, according to the RAND study from which these observations are derived, was external military support, of any size, able to create a win if one of these two factors was present.

Both problems exist in Afghanistan. The Afghan Taliban has indigenous support in Afghanistan and external sanctuary in Pakistan. This enables it to control roughly 10% of the 400 districts in Afghanistan and contest nearly 30% more.[5] The Afghan government, meanwhile, has been unable to retake and retain Taliban-controlled or contested territory. The government remains a predatory kleptocracy. Many Afghan forces fight bravely, but have steadily lost ground. For Trump's approach to succeed, both determinative factors must be reversed.

Will Pakistan turn against the Afghan Taliban? Cutting off the Taliban's sanctuary there would be a serious blow – precisely the reason why President Trump and his predecessors have been so adamant about it.

Pakistan has refused. Their national-security establishment fears that India and Afghanistan will team up to dismantle the Pakistani state. The best way to prevent this existential threat, Pakistani leaders surmise, is to invest heavily in the military, develop a nuclear arsenal, court China and foment instability in Afghanistan and Kashmir.

The government in Afghanistan after the fall of the Taliban in 2001 was overwhelmingly dominated by Northern Alliance figures associated with Pakistani rivals India and Iran. Pakistan grew increasingly worried about its lack of influence in Afghanistan, and the perceived growth of Afghan ambitions to eliminate the Durand Line (the internationally recognised border) and claim Pashtun territory in Pakistan. These reflexive fears became self-fulfilling. As the Taliban grew again in strength, abetted by sanctuary in Pakistan, the Afghan government drew closer to India, increased its hostility toward Pakistan, began providing sanctuary and support to the Pakistani Taliban (a designated international terrorist group) and drew the United States into the fray. These developments, in turn, alarmed Pakistan and fed into the national-security establishment's internal logic. Forcing the Afghan Taliban to capitulate, they now believe, is tantamount to national suicide.

Can US coercion work? The United States provides $742.2 million in aid and assistance to Pakistan, and has designated it a major non-NATO ally. These measures are not insignificant, but they are not trump cards. To mitigate the effect of sanctions or cuts in American aid, Pakistan has turned to China – its 'all-weather friend' – for support. Pakistan can also retaliate by shutting down NATO ground lines of communication into land-locked Afghanistan, as it did in 2011–12. Alternative routes would have to pass through Iran or Russia. Strategy cannot wish away geography.

Withholding aid and stripping Pakistan of major non-NATO ally status would be blows. Still, these pale in comparison to the 1990s sanctions that the United States imposed after Pakistan detonated a nuclear device. Even then, Pakistan continued to support insurgencies in Afghanistan and Kashmir, and advanced its nuclear programme. Now, substantial aid and trade from China further offset potential American reductions. In short, American-imposed penalties would be significant, but probably not enough to coerce Pakistan into turning against the Afghan Taliban.

Can the Taliban be deprived of indigenous support in Afghanistan? This was the primary approach adopted by International Security Assistance Force (ISAF) commander General Stanley McChrystal in 2009–10, when NATO forces began surging into Afghanistan with the aim of reversing Taliban momentum and helping the Afghan government win the battle of legitimacy in the eyes of the Afghan people. As the surge reached 140,000 troops and 350,000 Afghan forces, the immediate security gains were impressive.

Legitimate and effective governance was the strategy's Achilles heel. The Afghan government had, by 2006, become thoroughly corrupt. Many positions within the Afghan government and security forces were sold to office-seekers at increasingly exorbitant prices. The payments went to warlords and kleptocratic officials, who, in turn, gave the office-seekers license to do whatever was needed to keep the money flowing upward and to turn a personal profit.[6] Misappropriation of international aid and development assistance, land theft, kidnapping for ransom, extortion of customs revenues, and engagement in the opium trade and other illicit markets were common means of enriching the corrupt class. When people fought back against such extortion, Afghan officials and power-brokers often reported them as al-Qaeda or Taliban members to international forces. ISAF finally grew wise to the practice in 2009, a full eight years into the conflict. People savaged by their own government in this way often turned to the Taliban for protection. 'Ordinary Afghans don't like the Taliban', long-time war correspondent Dexter Filkins told Fareed Zakaria recently. 'But they dislike the Afghan government even more.'[7]

> *The government had become thoroughly corrupt*

The security forces, with some exceptions, participate in the kleptocracy. Those forces, according to the International Crisis Group, remain riven by corruption, factionalism and nepotism – all of which undermine their ability to combat the Taliban.[8] Corruption and poor leadership are eroding Afghan military readiness faster than international advisers can build it.[9]

The consequences of this situation became apparent as international forces withdrew. The Afghan government was unable to retain hard-fought gains. The overall result has been the steady expansion of Taliban territorial control. The face of the Afghan government that Americans see (hard-working westernised technocrats) is not the same face many Afghans see. To date, the United States has been unwilling to confront this dark reality.

Part of the problem is the double-edged sword of placing conditions on aid and assistance. Afghanistan is the most aid-dependent country in the world. Significant penalties would shut down major parts of the government and security forces. Thus, the United States always blinks when the Afghan government fails to meet agreed anti-corruption benchmarks. Warlords and officials know this. They resist reforms that President Ashraf Ghani wants to make. Every time an American president says that there is no blank cheque, the warlords and kleptocrats laugh all the way to the bank.

Successive US administrations have been unable to cope with these problems, which have undermined American national-security interests, bled taxpayer dollars and created an unstable security situation that has claimed the lives of American troops. The Trump administration might be more serious about addressing these issues, but the looming 2019 elections in Afghanistan mean that the likelihood of Afghans enacting painful reforms is nil. Coalition-building, bargaining for patronage and political brinksmanship are already under way. Winning the 2019 elections will top the calculations of Afghan political elites – far more important than acceding to American demands.

The best use of conditionality in these circumstances is to sanction individual spoilers and blockers rather than curtail aid budgets. The best leverage the Trump administration had was to make the president's announcement of support contingent upon specified actions from the Afghan government and various warlords. The Trump administration, however, seems to have received no such concessions.

Taliban capitulation seems to be as remote as ever. It is a brutal and adaptive insurgency. The Taliban, though, has its own major challenges. Its senior leadership council has serious disagreements about the strategic direction of the organisation. Mid-level leaders report distrust of the senior leadership, and frustration over the intractable conflict. Still, their Taliban identity is sufficiently strong that defection to the Afghan government remains unthinkable.[10] Their ties with al-Qaeda are strained, as documents from the bin Laden raid attest. Interestingly, the Taliban's Eid messages since 2009 have outlined positions on political and social issues that are in step with those of the Afghan government and more liberal than those of American allies such as Saudi Arabia. The Taliban of 2017 are different, in ways both good and ill, than the Taliban of 2001.

Developing better options

Part of the reason President Trump was given such stale options is the common practice of turning to the Pentagon for war strategies. This might be fine for conventional wars, but it does not work for irregular wars, such as Afghanistan, where the political and diplomatic elements of national power are far more decisive than military force. The generals quietly recognise this dilemma. They offer high, medium and low troop-level options, but can offer nothing that qualifies as a strategy because they cannot speak for other agencies. For conflicts that have no military solution, why turn only to the Pentagon for options?

Trump – the anti-establishment president – should impose a different method. He should have inter-agency teams create options based on different war-termination outcomes. Irregular-war interventions tend to end successfully in one of three ways: a decisive victory, a negotiated outcome, or transition and withdrawal.[11]

A strategy aimed at decisive victory, for instance, might focus on the use of military force. This was the only non-losing option presented to President Trump, and it is unlikely to work in this conflict. This approach could succeed when a reforming host-nation government is taking on a militant group that has no sanctuary.

An irregular-war strategy that seeks a negotiated outcome will look very different. In this case, diplomacy would become the priority, with military, economic, developmental and intelligence efforts in support. In the case of Afghanistan, military and political support would be designed to stabilise the battlefield and prevent further Taliban gains, while a third-party team begins the long and arduous task of constructing a viable peace process. A country such as Norway, with a long-established track record and body of expert knowledge, could lead it. Other actors, such as Colombia (going through its own peace process), Qatar (hosting the informal Taliban political office) and a large Muslim country such as Indonesia, might offer the right balance. As the author of *The Art of the Deal* should know, a negotiated outcome that meets one's interests is a win.

A third option could seek to transition security efforts to the host-nation government. This option would prioritise host-nation political development, with the other elements in support. Anti-corruption efforts, electoral reform, economic reform and professional security forces are far more important to winning the battle of legitimacy than killing insurgents. The major mistake in the past was to believe that international forces could kill enough insurgents to render the groups small and manageable enough for the host nation. The problem, as we have seen in Afghanistan, is that effective insurgencies can ensure that recruiting outpaces attrition.

The National Security Council should evaluate these options and present their analysis and recommendations to the president.

Finally, the president needs to put someone in charge of American efforts on the ground, to help ensure integration and accountability. The bureaucracy will resist this idea tooth and nail. Probably only a President Trump understands the importance of addressing these silos. Trump International reportedly owns 33 properties worldwide. Every one of them has someone in charge. Imagine the absurdity of eliminating the managers at each property, and instead having the human-resources, information-technology, guest-services and logistics directors at each of the 33 properties report directly to an associated senior vice-president in New York City. The likely results, in President Trump's words on 21 August, are both predictable and unacceptable.

The good news is that the president's address was sufficiently vague to leave alternatives open. He can move along a path more likely to produce a win. He should seize control of his Afghanistan policy and demand his team produce integrated options that he can evaluate. In so doing, he might usher in a more effective way of developing strategies, and begin to repair the trust and confidence in America's wartime leadership that has been so badly damaged since 2001.

Notes

1 John R. Allen and Michael E. O'Hanlon, 'Trump Made the Right Move on Afghanistan', Brookings Institution, 23 August 2017, https://www.brookings.edu/blog/order-from-chaos/2017/08/23/trump-made-the-right-move-on-afghanistan/; and Kori Schake, 'Give Trump Credit for his Afghanistan Plan', *Atlantic*, 22 August 2017, https://www.theatlantic.com/international/archive/2017/08/trump-afghanistan-taliban-terrorism/537567/.

2 Steve Coll, 'The Taliban's Response to Trump's Afghanistan Address', *New Yorker*, 23 August 2017, https://www.newyorker.com/news/daily-comment/the-talibans-response-to-trumps-afghanistan-address.

3 Philip Rucker and Robert Costa, '"It's a Hard Problem": Inside Trump's Decision to Send More Troops to Afghanistan', *Washington Post*, 21 August 2017, https://www.washingtonpost.com/politics/its-a-hard-problem-inside-trumps-decision-to-send-more-troops-to-afghanistan/2017/08/21/14dcb126-868b-11e7-a94f-3139abce39f5_story.html.

4 See Christopher Paul, Colin P. Clarke, Beth Grill and Molly Dunigan, *Paths to Victory: Lessons from Modern Insurgencies* (Washington DC: RAND, 2013). Negotiated outcomes were scored as a win for the side that gained more of their core interests.

5 Special Inspector General for Afghanistan Reconstruction, 'Quarterly Report', 30 July 2017, p. 88.

6 According to current and former Afghan and Western officials interviewed in 2015 and 2016, the position of customs officer at a lucrative crossing point could be sold for as much as $5 million; a provincial chief of police for $3m.

7 Fareed Zakaria, 'Trump Locks America into its Forever War', *Washington Post*, 24 August 2017, https://www.washingtonpost.com/opinions/trump-signs-on-to-the-forever-war-in-afghanistan/2017/08/24/64684004-890e-11e7-a94f-3139abce39f5_story.html.

8 International Crisis Group, 'Afghanistan: The Future of the National Unity Government', report no. 285, 10 April 2017.

9 For a more in-depth analysis of the situation in Afghanistan and the region, see Christopher D. Kolenda, 'Focused Engagement: A New Way Forward in Afghanistan', Center for a New American Security, February 2017, https://www.cnas.org/publications/reports/focused-engagement.

10 See Theo Farrell and Michael Semple, 'Ready for Peace? The Afghan Taliban after a Decade of War', RUSI briefing paper, 31 January 2017, https://rusi.org/sites/default/files/201701_bp_ready_for_peace.pdf; and Theo Farrell and Michael Semple, 'Making Peace with the Taliban', *Survival*, vol. 57, no. 6, October–November 2015, pp. 79–110.

11 See Christopher D. Kolenda, 'End-Game: Why American Interventions Become Quagmires', PhD thesis, King's College London, 2017, pp. 21–2.

Rethinking NATO's Tactical Nuclear Weapons

Steve Andreasen

The aftermath of President Donald Trump's first visit to NATO headquarters in May 2017 and the G20 Summit in July might seem an inopportune time to debate the future of US tactical nuclear weapons in Europe. Anxiety in NATO capitals has risen since last November, driven by continuing concerns over Trump's election and the threatening direction of Russian security policy. Against this backdrop, the easy – some would say obvious – conclusion is for NATO to stay on nuclear-policy autopilot. But anxiety should not preclude strategic thinking about NATO's nuclear future. Rather than cling to a preset course, programmed in a different era, NATO should confront three questions:

- Does it make sense for the United States and NATO to store tactical nuclear weapons in locations with increasing vulnerability to an evolving and more deadly terrorist threat, or to domestic unrest?
- Does it make sense for the United States and NATO to invest billions of dollars in maintaining NATO's current nuclear posture if a safer, more secure and more credible nuclear deterrent is available at a far lower cost?
- Given the uncertainty in many NATO capitals of securing political and public support for the costly modernisation of their dual-capable aircraft and continued storage of US nuclear weapons on their soil, shouldn't NATO get out ahead of that debate?

Steve Andreasen was the director for defense policy and arms control on the US National Security Council staff from 1993 to 2001. He is a national-security consultant in Washington DC, and teaches at the University of Minnesota's Humphrey School of Public Affairs.

Survival | vol. 59 no. 5 | October–November 2017 | pp. 47–53 DOI 10.1080/00396338.2017.1375225

The answers should compel NATO to conclude that sustaining its current nuclear posture is an expense beyond what is needed to maintain a credible deterrent; moreover, it will undercut efforts to sustain credible conventional and counter-terror capabilities across NATO. Most urgently, the security risk of basing US nuclear bombs in Europe, highlighted by recent terrorist attacks there and developments in Turkey, underscores the need for NATO to move to a safer, more secure and more credible nuclear deterrent – including withdrawing, and not replacing, US tactical nuclear weapons in Europe.

Sources of anxiety

After NATO summits in 2010 and 2012 pried open the door to a more rational nuclear posture, Russian aggression in Ukraine in 2014 put anxiety – with a distinctly nuclear component – back in the driver's seat. Even before then, Moscow retained tactical nuclear weapons greatly in excess of those stored by the United States in Europe. Russian nuclear capability was alarmingly married, years ago, with the concept of nuclear 'de-escalation' – the deliberate escalation of a conflict through limited nuclear use designed to create a pause in the conflict and open a pathway for a negotiated settlement on Moscow's terms. The reported Russian deployment of nuclear-capable *Iskander* missiles to Kaliningrad, and a new nuclear-capable intermediate-range cruise missile – in violation of the 1987 Intermediate-Range Nuclear Forces (INF) Treaty – has further aggravated the issue.

The result has been a distinctly one-dimensional, almost schoolyard-like, mentality in many NATO capitals. Whatever Russia does, in particular in the nuclear sphere, NATO must do also (witness calls by US Senator Tom Cotton and Congressman Mike Rogers to develop a US intermediate-range missile for Europe as a counter to Russian capabilities).[1] In that context, some view any change to NATO's current nuclear posture, in particular the consolidation of US tactical nuclear weapons back to the United States, as a display of NATO's weakness that might embolden Russian President Vladimir Putin.

And then there is Donald Trump. Since election day in the United States, 'uncertain' is perhaps the best single-word summary of the Trump presidency. It applies broadly, and has continued for a period of months, beyond the norm of any new administration.

Despite recent efforts by President Trump and senior administration officials to reassure NATO regarding the continuing US commitment to the transatlantic alliance, the uncertainty and anxiety run deep through NATO, as expressed in German Chancellor Angela Merkel's declaration that Europe 'really must take our fate into our own hands'.[2]

The direction of US policy towards Russia compounds the uncertainty. On the one hand, President Trump's professed willingness to improve relations with Moscow is one of the few constants that ran through his campaign, the transition and the early months of his presidency. Then, in March, reports began circulating that Trump might shelve his plan to pursue closer ties, due to Russian 'provocations' – including Russia's reported INF violation.[3] The first Trump–Putin meeting in Hamburg, however, seemed to tilt US policy again towards closer ties between Washington and Moscow. Now, congressional sanctions – and Russian retaliation – have pushed the pendulum the other way. This shift will likely be reinforced by congressional and Justice Department investigations into Russian efforts to influence the US election, the outcome of which will – at a minimum – re-emphasise Russian meddling and perhaps uncover Russian ties to members of the Trump campaign.

A costly status quo

Maintaining NATO's nuclear status quo will come at an increasingly high financial and political cost, and high security risk. Most alarming is that the United States will continue to store tactical nuclear weapons in locations with an increasing risk of vulnerability to an evolving and more deadly terrorist threat, as well as domestic unrest. Nowhere is this more evident than in Turkey.

In March 2016, the Pentagon reportedly ordered military families out of southern Turkey, primarily from Incirlik Air Base, due to ISIS-related security concerns. This came shortly after the Brussels terrorist attacks and what appears to have been a credible threat to Belgian nuclear-power plants.[4] In July 2016, the Turkish commanding officer at Incirlik was arrested for his alleged role in the Turkish coup plot. If Incirlik is, as reported, a major NATO installation hosting one of the largest stockpiles of nuclear weapons in Europe, this shows just how quickly assumptions about the safety and security of US nuclear weapons stored abroad can change.[5]

Events in Turkey should then have triggered a withdrawal of any US nuclear weapons stored at Incirlik; nothing that has happened over the past year should yield a different conclusion. Simply stated, Turkey does not provide a safe foundation for basing nuclear weapons. But the anxiety-driven status quo, compounded by concerns that removing nuclear weapons from Turkey would signal a lack of confidence in its stability, have precluded decisive action. Indeed, somewhat unbelievably given the security risks, the US now plans to bring the B61 bombs stored in Turkey back to the United States, replacing them with a modernised version.[6]

The financial and political costs of sustaining NATO's current nuclear posture have the potential to be similarly consequential to the security of the Alliance. The B61 life-extension programme now under way could result in the most expensive nuclear weapon ever built, with the cost now estimated to be $10 billion or more for only 400–480 weapons. Procuring a next generation of dual-capable aircraft (DCA) – both in the United States and in those NATO countries participating in the mission – will significantly add to these costs.[7]

Yet the argument that tactical nuclear weapons play a deterrent role that cannot be filled by strategic or conventional weapons has been refuted by numerous military experts.[8] For any weapon to be credible as a deterrent, its use must be plausible; otherwise, it has no political utility. But it is hard to envision the circumstances under which a US president would initiate nuclear use for the first time in more than 70 years with a NATO DCA flown by non-US pilots delivering a US B61 bomb. It is equally hard to envision host-country governments authorising their aircraft to deliver the weapon, under what would be a sure threat of nuclear retaliation against them. And according to at least one NATO commander, it is hard to envision any such mission succeeding if ordered.[9]

In short, tactical nuclear weapons are a psychological Maginot Line. Like the French defences of that era, tactical nuclear weapons today come with a high price tag, one that will inevitably draw scarce defence resources away from counter-terrorism and NATO's conventional reassurance initiatives designed to deter Russia. In that sense, Russian political leaders and military planners may welcome NATO's commitment to invest in the nuclear status quo for the next decade.

Politically, the issue of tactical nuclear weapons continues to be treated as the Lord Voldemort – 'he who must not be named' – of NATO security policy out of fear that any public mention will bring the issue back to life. The nuclear mission is not popular in many participating countries. Hence, a loud reaffirmation of the status quo may ignite a backlash that threatens its continuation, let alone the planned upgrades of the B61 and DCA. At the same time, a one-dimensional argument for consolidating US nuclear weapons back to the US – in the absence of a vigorous case for why this will lead to a safer, more secure and more credible NATO deterrent – risks exacerbating persistent concerns about Trump's commitment to the defence of NATO allies. Nevertheless, the idea that NATO can silently continue modernisation, effectively ignoring the scepticism of basing countries and their publics, is simply wishful thinking.

A rational choice

Changing policy will be challenging. In particular, political leadership and administrative competence will be required in Washington, at a time when both seem in low supply within the Trump administration.[10] Moreover, congressional hawks are set on further boxing in the president on Russia, including by requiring the Pentagon to begin developing a missile that would violate the INF Treaty in response to Russia's own violation. That said, a US Nuclear Posture Review (NPR) is happening now, which will set a course on these issues that the Alliance may have to live with for seven years. Time and tide wait for no man.

The first step is to prevent the cement of NATO bureaucracy from hardening around Washington's legs, before the Trump administration can conclude its NPR later this year and take the initiative. The good news is that nothing of this sort apparently came out of the 25 May NATO summit.

Secondly, the administration should prepare a comprehensive, as opposed to incremental, initiative. The president and his national-security team must convincingly underscore America's enduring commitment to the

Alliance, and lay out a vision and rationale for moving towards a safer, more secure and more credible nuclear deterrent – explaining why this will improve the security of all NATO members. This should include a commitment to maintain a NATO nuclear deterrent for as long as one is needed, and to sustain conventional reassurance initiatives. Both of these crucial objectives can be better achieved without the expense, opportunity cost and risk of basing US tactical nuclear weapons in Europe. The administration should also commit to working closely with NATO on the restructuring of its nuclear deterrent in line with clear goals. These should include maintaining the strategic nuclear forces of the Alliance – along with a more visible demonstration of their security guarantee to European allies (such as visits of US long-range nuclear-capable bombers to European air bases) – and enhancing information sharing, consultations and planning.

Thirdly, in order to reduce NATO's anxiety, it will be important for the United States to work collaboratively with key allies. This has so far seemed a tall order for this White House, but a collaborative and focused initiative should not be beyond the capabilities of the president's national-security team. A group of NATO states – ideally including a mixture of basing countries, and old and new NATO allies – will need to support the development of this initiative for managed withdrawal of tactical nuclear weapons and advocate for it within the Alliance.

Fourthly, the NATO process should then be used not to review, but rather to implement, this initiative. NATO should be given a clear mandate to develop and recommend to ministers and leaders how existing nuclear sharing, consultations and planning can be enhanced across NATO, and how NATO can visibly and more credibly demonstrate that it remains a nuclear alliance without US nuclear weapons stored on European soil. Congress, too, has a crucial role to play, including by providing continued, predictable funding of conventional reassurance and counter-terror initiatives.

Finally, proponents of changing the nuclear status quo will need to confidently and convincingly make the case that it is important to stop acting on the dangerous idea that mirroring Russian actions, in particular in the case of nuclear weapons, equates to sound security policy. Russia has retained and is now modernising its inventory of tactical nuclear weapons in Europe.

But with the United States, Britain and France, NATO has a robust nuclear deterrent – with around 1,000 warheads on day-to-day alert, a flexible capability well beyond what is needed to deter nuclear use or destroy any potential nuclear adversary – and does not need to invest in tactical nuclear weapons. NATO has a range of other defence priorities – including terrorism, cyber security and migration – that will demand greater attention and effort in the years ahead. That is a message that all NATO countries need to hear – the sooner the better.

Notes

1 Gregory Hellman and Bryan Bender, 'The Other Treaty on the Chopping Block', *Politico*, 24 June 2017

2 Michael Birnbaum and Rick Noack, 'Following Trump's Trip, Merkel Says Europe Can't Rely on "Others." She Means the U.S.', *Washington Post*, 28 May 2017.

3 'Trump Wary of Russian Deal; New Advisers Urge Tougher Stand', Associated Press, 4 March 2017.

4 Simon Lunn, Isabelle Williams and Steve Andreasen, 'NATO's Nuclear Future: Deter, Reassure, Engage?', Nuclear Threat Initiative, June 2016, http://www.nti.org/media/documents/NATOs_Nuclear_Future_FINAL.pdf.

5 Simon Lunn, Isabelle Williams and Steve Andreasen, 'Warning Bells Around Tactical Nuclear Weapons in Europe', Nuclear Threat Initiative, 21 July 2016, http://www.nti.org/analysis/articles/warning-bells-around-tactical-nuclear-weapons-europe/.

6 Steve Andreasen, 'Let's Get Our Nuclear Weapons Out of Turkey', *Los Angeles Times*, 11 August 2016l.

7 Barry Blechman and Russell Rumbaugh, 'Bombs Away', *Foreign Affairs*, July/August 2014.

8 James Cartwright et al., 'Global Zero US Nuclear Policy Commission: Modernizing US Nuclear Strategy, Force Structure and Posture', Global Zero, May 2012.

9 Karl Heinz-Kamp and Robertus C.N. Remkes, 'Options for NATO Nuclear Sharing Arrangements', in Steve Andreasen and Isabelle Williams (eds), *Reducing Nuclear Risks in Europe* (Washington DC: Nuclear Threat Initiative, November 2011).

10 The following section is adapted from Steve Andreasen and Isabelle Williams, 'Bring Home U.S. Tactical Nuclear Weapons from Europe', in Tom Z. Collina and Geoff Wilson (eds), '10 Big Nuclear Ideas for the Next President', Ploughshares, November 2016, http://www.ploughshares.org/sites/default/files/resources/10-big-nuclear-ideas.pdf.

Noteworthy

29

Percentage of Venezuelan households in poverty during the country's 2004–14 oil-price boom

82

Percentage in 2016[1]

State without a state

'I announce from here the end and the failure and the collapse of the terrorist state of falsehood and terrorism which the terrorist Daesh announced from Mosul.'

Iraqi Prime Minister Haider al-Abadi declares victory over the Islamic State (also known as ISIS, ISIL and Daesh) in the battle for Mosul on 10 July 2017.[2]

'Frankly, I'm desperate over the future. ISIS destroyed the people's mentality, and the wars destroyed the infrastructure, and we paid the price. There is no such thing as the phase "after ISIS". ISIS is a mentality, and this mentality will not end with guns alone.'

Marwan Saeed, a Mosul resident, speaks to the New York Times.[3]

'Mosul and Raqqa is not the end of it by any stretch of the imagination.'

Brigadier General Andrew A. Croft, a senior American Air Force officer participating in the task force currently fighting the Islamic State.[4]

Sound and fury

'The American bastards must be quite unhappy after closely watching our strategic decision. I guess they are not too happy with the gift package we sent them for the occasion of their Independence Day. We should often send them gift packages so they won't be too bored.'

Comments attributed to North Korean leader Kim Jong-un by the Korean Central News Agency following the country's successful test of an intercontinental ballistic missile on 4 July 2017.[5]

'Self-restraint, which is a choice, is all that separates armistice and war.'

US General Vincent K. Brooks, commander of the US troops based in Seoul, comments on the test.[6]

'North Korea best not make any more threats to the United States. They will be met with fire and fury like the world has never seen.'

US President Donald Trump.[7]

Better part of valour?

'If we go harsh with everyone, our people will suffer – trade, direct foreign investments, tourism.'

Alan Peter Cayetano, the foreign-affairs secretary of the Philippines, explains why the country has backed down from its insistence that China abandon features in the South China Sea subject to the ruling of an international tribunal in The Hague that found against China.[8]

Survival | vol. 59 no. 5 | October–November 2017 | pp. 54–56 DOI 10.1080/00396338.2017.1375226

Kenya divided

'The 2017 general election was a fraud. The electoral fraud and fabrication of results was massive and extensive.'

Kenyan opposition leader Raila Odinga alleges that the servers of Kenya's electoral commission had been hacked to increase the vote count for incumbent Uhuru Kenyatta in the country's presidential election.[9]

'Your neighbour will always be your neighbour and we cannot fight over an election. Let us shun violence and refuse to be used for short-term political gain which can only cause our country pain and grief ... We have been neighbours, we are brothers, we are sisters ... Kenya belongs to all of us.'

Uhuru Kenyatta calls for calm after he was re-elected as president of Kenya.[10]

Liu Xiaobo, 1955–2017

'Liu Xiaobo will remain a powerful symbol for all who fight for freedom, democracy and a better world. He was truly a prisoner of conscience, and he paid the highest possible price for his relentless struggle.'

Berit Reiss-Andersen, chair of the Norwegian Nobel Committee, comments on the death of Nobel Peace Prize winner Liu Xiaobo, who died on 13 July 2017 after spending nearly ten years in prison for his pro-democracy activism.[11]

'Swift cremation, swift sea burial. Scared of the living, scared of the dead, and even more scared of the dead who are immortal.'

A user of the messaging app WeChat comments on the handling by the Chinese government of Liu's remains.[12]

Emails!

'Emin just called and asked me to contact you with something very interesting. The Crown prosecutor of Russia met with his father Aras this morning and in their meeting offered to provide the Trump campaign with some official documents and information that would incriminate Hillary and her dealings with Russia and would be very useful to your father.'

Excerpt from an email dated 3 June 2016 and sent to Donald Trump, Jr, son of US President Donald Trump, by Rob Goldstone, an entertainment publicist, on behalf of Russian pop star Emin Agalarov.[13]

'If it's what you say I love it.'

Donald Trump, Jr, responds to the email.[14]

Whistling past the graveyard

'I think that the sums that I have seen ... seem to me to be extortionate and I think "go whistle" is an entirely appropriate expression.'

British Foreign Secretary Boris Johnson dismisses the suggestion that the UK will have to pay the EU a large financial settlement to withdraw from the Union.[15]

'I am not hearing any whistling, just a clock ticking.'

EU negotiator Michel Barnier responds.[16]

Sources

1 Mercy Benzaquen, 'How Food in Venezuela Went from Subsidized to Scarce', *New York Times*, 16 July 2017, https://www.nytimes.com/interactive/2017/07/16/world/americas/venezuela-shortages.html?rref=collection%2Fsectioncollection%2Famericas.

2 'Iraqi PM, Coalition Forces Declare Victory over ISIS in Mosul', CBC News, 11 July 2017, http://www.cbc.ca/beta/news/world/mosul-isis-raqqa-1.4197701.

3 Tim Arango and Michael R. Gordon, 'Iraqi Prime Minister Arrives in Mosul to Declare Victory over ISIS', *New York Times*, 9 July 2017, https://www.nytimes.com/2017/07/09/world/middleeast/mosul-isis-liberated.html?rref=collection%2Fsectioncollection%2Fworld&action=click&contentCollection=world&region=rank&module=package&version=highlights&contentPlacement=1&pgtype=sectionfront&_r=0.

4 *Ibid.*

5 Choe Sang-Hun, 'U.S. Confirms North Korea Fired Intercontinental Ballistic Missile', *New York Times*, 4 July 2017, https://www.nytimes.com/2017/07/04/world/asia/north-korea-missile-test-icbm.html.

6 Jon Sharman, 'US Military Says War with North Korea Cannot Be Ruled Out', *Independent*, 5 July 2017, http://www.independent.co.uk/news/world/asia/us-north-korea-war-icbm-test-not-ruled-out-donald-trump-kim-jong-un-nuclear-weapons-missile-launch-a7824101.html.

7 Julian Borger and Justin McCurry, 'Donald Trump Vows to Answer North Korea Nuclear Threats with "Fire and Fury"', *Guardian*, 9 August 2017, https://www.nytimes.com/2017/08/08/world/asia/north-korea-un-sanctions-nuclear-missile-united-nations.html?hp&action=click&pgtype=Homepage&clickSource=story-heading&module=a-lede-package-region&region=top-news&WT.nav=top-news&_r=0.

8 Gardiner Harris, 'Tillerson Hails U.N. Sanctions, as Chinese Minister Rebukes North Korea at Asean Meeting', *New York Times*, 6 August 2017, https://www.nytimes.com/2017/08/06/world/asia/asean-rex-tillerson-north-korea-sanctions.html?rref=collection%2Fsectioncollection%2Fworld&action=click&contentCollection=world&region=rank&module=package&version=highlights&contentPlacement=1&pgtype=sectionfront.

9 Kimiko de Freytas-Tamura, 'Kenya Election Returns Were Hacked, Opposition Leader Says', *New York Times*, 9 August 2017, https://www.nytimes.com/2017/08/09/world/africa/kenya-election-results-raila-odinga.html?rref=collection%2Fsectioncollection%2Fafrica&action=click&contentCollection=africa&region=stream&module=stream_unit&version=latest&contentPlacement=2&pgtype=sectionfront&_r=0.

10 Jason Burke, 'Uhuru Kenyatta Confirmed as Kenyan President', *Guardian*, 11 August 2017, https://www.theguardian.com/world/2017/aug/11/kenyan-opposition-refuses-to-sign-off-on-election-charade.

11 Chris Buckley, 'Liu Xiaobo, Chinese Dissident Who Won Nobel While Jailed, Dies at 61', *New York Times*, 13 July 2017, https://www.nytimes.com/2017/07/13/world/asia/liu-xiaobo-dead.html?action=click&contentCollection=Asia%20Pacific&module=RelatedCoverage&region=Marginalia&pgtype=article.

12 Amy Qin, 'Liu Xiaobo's Death Pushes China's Censors into Overdrive', *New York Times*, 17 July 2017, https://www.nytimes.com/2017/07/17/world/asia/liu-xiaobo-censor.html?module=WatchingPortal&region=c-column-middle-span-region&pgType=Homepage&action=click&mediaId=thumb_square&state=standard&contentPlacement=2&version=internal&contentCollection=www.nytimes.com&contentId=https%3A%2F%2Fwww.nytimes.com%2F2017%2F07%2F17%2Fworld%2Fasia%2Fliu-xiaobo-censor.html&eventName=Watching-article-click&_r=0.

13 'Transcript: Donald Trump Jr's Email Chain About Meeting Russian Lawyer in Full', *Telegraph*, 12 July 2017, http://www.telegraph.co.uk/news/2017/07/11/transcript-donald-trump-jrs-email-chain-meeting-russian-lawyer/.

14 *Ibid.*

15 Dan Roberts and Henry McDonald, 'EU Says Brexit Talks Could Fail After Johnson's "Go Whistle" Remarks', *Guardian*, 12 July 2017, https://www.theguardian.com/politics/2017/jul/12/eu-warns-brexit-talks-could-fail-after-johnsons-go-whistle-remarks.

16 *Ibid.*

The Evolution of Autocracy: Why Authoritarianism Is Becoming More Formidable

Erica Frantz and Andrea Kendall-Taylor

Globalisation, shifting power dynamics and the growing availability of the internet and other communication technologies have significantly changed the environment in which autocrats operate. Some observers have concluded from these changes that citizens now hold the upper hand, and that dictators' days are numbered.[1] The centralisation of power, according to this argument, is a requisite of dictatorship. In a world in which power is diffusing across NGOs, corporations, and wealthy and technology-empowered individuals, dictators will soon find themselves unable to build and maintain the power needed to uphold their repressive systems of rule.

Although twenty-first-century autocrats face more – and increasingly complex – challenges to their rule, the adaptability and resilience of authoritarian systems should not be underestimated. Since the end of the Cold War, dictators have evolved to survive and even thrive amid changes in their domestic and international environments. Even a casual scan of international news headlines – featuring stories of Russian President Vladimir Putin's latest international feats, the political hardening under Egypt's Abdel Fattah Al-Sisi, Iran's attempts to reassert its regional influence, and Turkish President Recep Tayyip Erdogan's consolidation of power – reinforces the notion that today's autocrats are not waning, but making a comeback.

Erica Frantz is an Assistant Professor at Michigan State University. **Andrea Kendall-Taylor** is Deputy National Intelligence Officer for Russia and Eurasia at the National Intelligence Council and Adjunct Professor at Georgetown's School of Foreign Service.

Survival | vol. 59 no. 5 | October–November 2017 | pp. 57–68 DOI 10.1080/00396338.2017.1375229

How did we get here? After all, for the last 25 years, momentum has been on democracy's side. In 1991, there were just 70 democracies representing about 45% of the world's population. The Soviet Union's collapse, however, set in motion a number of changes to the international environment that put many authoritarian governments on the defensive. Not only did democracy become the standard of political legitimacy, but the absence of a geopolitical alternative also meant that Western democratic states gained new-found leverage to encourage democratic reform. In the immediate aftermath of the Cold War, autocracies struggled to adapt to these changes and their numbers declined. By 2014, the number of democracies had surged to 115 countries comprising approximately 65% of the world's population. Democracy, it seemed, had triumphed and secured its status as the world's preferred form of governance.

Fast-forward to 2017 and a very different picture emerges. Although the number of democratic countries in the world remains near its all-time high, several trends are shifting the momentum in the dictators' favour. Faced with what looked like slow but certain extinction in the 1990s and early 2000s, dictators have adapted. Learning from the mistakes – and successes – of their predecessors and peers, many autocrats have altered their tactics in ways that increase the resilience of their regimes.

The notion that autocracy is resurgent is not new. A number of important books, journal articles and op-eds over the last few years have drawn attention to the mounting challenges democracies face.[2] Most of these accounts, however, focus on trends in the world's democracies. Existing analysis has examined the deterioration of democracy in new or weakly institutionalised democratic states, the erosion of the efficacy and self-confidence of the world's established democracies, and the ways that shifting geopolitics are affecting democracy's march. Little attention has been paid to changes taking place within autocracies themselves.

Authoritarian regimes are evolving. The twenty-first-century autocrat is not the same as his Cold War predecessor. Although certain similarities endure and tried-and-true tactics persist, authoritarian regimes are learning and adapting in ways that warrant our attention. Without an appreciation of authoritarianism's changing dynamics, Western actors interested in supporting democracy will be hobbled by an outdated and inaccurate model of authoritarian politics. Staying abreast of what makes contemporary autocrats – both those in power and those aspiring to it – behave as they do is fundamental to developing strategies to engage and interact with such regimes, and to counter autocracy's resurgence.

Autocracy is evolving

Politicians tend to value the maintenance of their power above all else. Faced with new challenges, leaders are willing to shift and recalibrate strategies to maximise their prospects for staying in office. Vladimir Putin, whose approach to governing has evolved since he came to power in 1999, is a case in point. In his first two terms (1999–2008) Putin benefited from oil-driven economic growth, and had significant success in containing insurgency in the volatile North Caucasus. Russia's relative economic stability and much-improved internal security, especially relative to the tumultuous 1990s, allowed Putin to rule with a lighter touch than he is using today. Even as he worked to establish executive control over the judiciary, legislature and regions, Putin relied less on the repressive tactics he has since come to rely on. He was even confident enough in his authority to step out of the limelight in 2008 and allow a titular transition in power as he switched roles with then-prime minister Dmitry Medvedev.

The Putin who emerged following his re-election in 2012, however, had dramatically changed his approach to maintaining power. Just before he returned as president, Russia experienced its most significant protests since the collapse of the Soviet Union. They occurred in the wake of the Arab Spring, which toppled four of the world's longest-serving dictators, reinforcing Putin's anxiety about the threat of Western-backed attempts to unseat unfriendly regimes. Moreover, low oil prices and economic stagnation, and a more adversarial relationship with NATO after Russia's invasion of Georgia in 2008, strengthened Putin's sense of insecurity and led him to adopt a tougher, more brutal brand of leadership. As Russia experts Fiona Hill and Cliff Gaddy write, 'Vladimir Putin's behavior is driven by the imperative to adapt and respond to changing – especially unpredicted – circumstances'.[3]

It is clear that dictators such as Putin can adapt to changes in their environment. What is less obvious is that there are general and consistent patterns in how autocrats are adapting across countries. In particular, widespread and fundamental changes concerning the ways in which autocrats come to power – and lose it – have altered the incentive structure, decision-making and behaviour of twenty-first-century autocracies since the end of the Cold War. These shifts have been associated with behavioural changes in dictatorships that make today's authoritarian political systems a more formidable challenge to liberal democracy than at any time in the last 25 years.

Changes in the way autocrats come to power

Historically, the onset of autocracy has been sudden and decisive. Military or civilian leaders made clear-cut decisions to suspend democratic rules and engineer authoritarian rule. This is how the authoritarian regimes of interwar Europe, and of Latin America and sub-Saharan Africa in the 1960s, were born. In fact, from 1940–89, almost half of all dictatorships emerged through a *coup d'état*.

Today, the initiation of authoritarianism is far less definitive. Contemporary autocrats are coming to power through a process of 'authoritarianisation', or the gradual erosion of democratic norms and practices. Democratic leaders, elected at the ballot box through reasonably free and fair elections, are slowly undermining institutional constraints on their power, gradually marginalising the opposition (and watchdogs such as the press) and eroding civil society in ways that make it difficult to pinpoint the moment at which the break with democratic politics occurs. For years, academics and political observers debated whether Turkey should be considered a dictatorship. At what point did President Erdogan cross the threshold into authoritarianism? And how should we think about moves by Hungarian Prime Minister Viktor Orbán and Poland's ruling Law and Justice party (PiS) to undermine respect for democratic principles in the heart of Central Europe?

An analysis of how autocracies have emerged over the last 75 years shows that authoritarianisation has been on the rise since the end of the Cold War. In the 1970s and 1980s, only about 10% of autocracies emerged via authoritarianisation, compared with around 60% of regimes that began via coups.[4] By the 2000s, the proportion of autocrats who came to power as democracies decayed had tripled. The trend is even more striking if we examine just those authoritarian regimes that emerged from the breakdown of a democracy (rather than a transition from one authoritarian regime to another, as in the case of Iran in 1979, when the country's monarchy gave way to the theocracy in power today). From 2000–10, authoritarianisation accounted for 40% of all democratic failures, matching coups in frequency. If current trends persist, authoritarianisation will soon become the most common pathway to autocracy.

Turkey's slide into dictatorship is the most recent example of this trend, the country's regime having taken a page out of the modern-day dictators' playbook. When Erdogan was elected in 2003, he and his Justice and Development Party (AKP) enjoyed strong public support. Erdogan tamed inflation, ushered in economic growth and took a stand for working-class, religious conservatives who had been locked out of power for decades.

Because he was elected on a platform of change, observers dismissed the opening salvos of his effort to consolidate control. In 2009, for example, Erdogan fined Dogan Media Group – a collection of newspapers and television channels critical of the president that were owned by one of Turkey's biggest media tycoons – $2.5 billion for alleged tax evasion. At the time, public opinion was divided over whether Erdogan was dutifully punishing a tax evader or intent on muzzling the press. Many also downplayed his early efforts to enhance executive control over the country's military, which historically played an outsized role in politics. With each power grab, however, members of the Turkish political system increasingly understood that their attempts to resist Erdogan's efforts would cost them their jobs and the perks of power. Since 2009, Erdogan has undermined all institutional constraints on his power, including the media, judiciary and security services, and marginalised all significant critics within the AKP.

A similar story is unfolding in Poland. Like Erdogan, the ruling PiS fuelled its popularity by tapping into domestic grievances. Just as Erdogan harnessed discontent among Turkey's religious conservatives, the PiS used a nationalist–populist agenda to appeal to public disenchantment.

Jaroslaw Kaczynski, the co-founder and chair of the PiS, interpreted his party's majority win in the October 2016 elections as a mandate to consolidate power – something he claimed was necessary to deliver on electoral promises. In particular, the PiS has expanded its control over the judiciary. These moves have paved the way for the party to pass legislation that curbs political and civil liberties and makes it more difficult to remove the regime from power. For example, the PiS has enacted changes to media laws that promote government messaging; has sought to regulate NGOs; and, in March 2017, passed legislation limiting rights to assembly. The party is likely to seek to change electoral laws in ways that could give it enough seats to amend the constitution and solidify its control – just as Erdogan did in April 2017.

Erdogan, the PiS and other leaders are following the path blazed by once democratically elected leaders such as Putin and former Venezuelan president Hugo Chavez. Along the way, leaders seek to grab power from the courts or local elected leaders such as governors; shut down the legislature or banish opposition parties from policymaking; silence opposition journalists and media firms while creating new media organisations under direct regime control; and, ultimately, change the rules governing elections. In Hungary, for example, Orbán's party, Fidesz, saw its vote share decline from 52.7% in 2010 to 44.9% in 2014, yet its majority in parliament increased, largely because of its establishment of an electoral system that favours the winning party and its gerrymandering of electoral districts. Leaders implement such changes slowly, often under the guise of reform. They have learned that ambiguity and plausible deniability hinder domestic backlash, mute international criticism, and generally make it difficult for the opposition to mount a decisive response.

This slow dismantling of democracy is producing a particular brand of autocracy, one in which power is highly concentrated in the hands of a single individual.[5] From 2000–10, 75% of authoritarianisation cases led to personalist (as opposed to other forms of) dictatorship. Leaders who come to power via authoritarianisation are well positioned to expand personal control because they eliminate most other constraints on their power in the process of emerging as autocrats. In contrast to the sudden and decisive breaks with democracy that result from coups, which often leave intact many governing institutions, leaders who practise authoritarianisation have already eliminated potential rivals and autonomous centres of power.

There is a tendency to assume that all dictatorships fit the strongman mould. But reality is more nuanced. From the end of the Second World War to the fall of the Soviet Union, most dictatorships have been run not by strongmen, but by strong political parties, such as the Institutional Revolutionary Party (PRI) in Mexico, or by military juntas, as in much of Latin America in the 1970s and 1980s. Since the end of the Cold War, however, highly personalised dictatorships have become the most common form of authoritarianism.[6] In 1988, personalist regimes comprised just 23% of all dictatorships. Today, 40% of all autocracies are ruled by strongmen.

The changing face of autocracy is creating a number of challenges for US foreign policy. Consider today's most belligerent autocrats: North Korea's Kim Jong-un, Syria's Bashar al-Assad, Russia's Vladimir Putin and, increasingly, China's Xi Jinping. These are just a few examples of today's personalist dictators. Because these leaders face few constraints on their decision-making, they often produce unpredictable and aggressive foreign policies, including a greater propensity to fight inter-state wars.[7] Political-science research affirms that leaders' decisions and policymaking are strongly influenced by whether they rule largely at their own discretion or face institutional constraints from a powerful party or military. Not only do unconstrained leaders produce more hostile and volatile foreign policies, but they are also more likely to espouse anti-Western rhetoric, mismanage foreign aid and obliterate their countries' domestic institutions in ways that make it more difficult to establish democracy, even in the longer term.[8] The rise of authoritarianisation, therefore, is likely to fuel the proliferation of the most problematic regimes.

Changes in how autocrats exit power

Not only are twenty-first-century autocrats coming to power differently, but they are also exiting office in new ways. Consider, for example, Blaise Compaoré, who resigned as president of Burkina Faso and fled the country on 31 October 2014 after ruling for 27 years. Just days before his resignation, women took to the streets armed with wooden spoons to protest the government's announcement that the legislature would vote on – and likely pass – a constitutional amendment to extend presidential term limits. The protesters' ranks rapidly swelled, and ultimately tens of thousands of Burkinabe citizens forced one of Africa's longest-serving leaders from office. Although the events in Burkina Faso received a fraction of the media attention dedicated to the Arab Spring uprisings that occurred just a few years earlier, the storyline was much the same. Citizens who had endured decades of repression, corruption and poor living standards took to the streets, often at great personal risk, to demand change.[9]

Protests have rarely been effective

These events present a contrast with the demise of past autocracies. The ability of the people to force autocracies to moderate their behaviour, let alone overthrow them, has historically been limited. Analysis of leadership turnover in autocracies reveals that protests have rarely been an effective mechanism for change. From 1950 to 2012, only 7% of dictators were deposed through popular revolt. Instead, elite supporters posed the greatest danger to a leader's survival in office. From 1950–89, for example, 41% of all autocrats who lost power were ousted by a coup.[10] In the post-Cold War era, the picture has been different. The proportion of autocrats ousted via coup has fallen to only 12%. Meanwhile, popular revolts have become a far more common form of leadership turnover. The percentage of autocrats ousted in such revolts tripled from 4% during the Cold War period to 12% since. From 2010 to 2012 (the most recent year for which data are available), revolts accounted for 25% of all autocratic-leader ousters, while coups accounted for only 6%. Since the Arab Spring began in 2011, for example, protests have brought down five of the world's longest-standing leaders: Tunisia's Zine al-Abidine Ben Ali in January 2011, Egypt's Hosni Mubarak in February 2011, Libya's Muammar Gadhafi in October 2011, Yemen's Ali Abdullah Saleh in February 2012 and Burkina Faso's Blaise Compaoré in October 2014. Less than a decade earlier, the Colour Revolutions swept through the former Soviet Union and dislodged the authoritarian systems of Georgia's Eduard Shevardnadze in 2003, Ukraine's Leonid Kuchma in 2005 and Kyrgyzstan's Askar Akayev in 2005.

The growing vulnerability of autocrats to revolts reflects a pronounced rise in the threat the public poses to a dictator's survival in office, and autocrats are modifying their strategies accordingly. Given the historical prevalence of coups, autocrats have traditionally used survival tactics aimed at countering threats emanating from the elite, such as elite rotation, or coup-proofing strategies, such as overpaying the security services or creating rival services or praetorian guards.

As more dictators fall to protests, however, leaders are increasingly targeting the citizenry. This shifting threat perception explains the dramatic rise in restrictions on political and civil liberties in autocracies. Autocrats are cracking down on the opposition, restricting assembly and choking off civil society to make it harder for citizens to mobilise against their regimes. Freedom House has recorded a rise in these restrictions over the last 11 years, with a majority occurring in countries that are already authoritarian.[11]

This hardening points to a resurgence in authoritarianism. As a growing number of the world's 'hybrid regimes' – countries that mix authoritarian practices with democratic traits – respond to the threat of citizen protest by repressing political and civil liberties, the likelihood that any of them will someday transition to democracy diminishes. Academic research suggests that once countries become full autocracies, they are less likely to democratise than their hybrid counterparts, raising the risk that the ranks of authoritarian states will grow.

Shifting geopolitical trends also appear to be facilitating this authoritarian hardening. Savvy incumbents are learning to more effectively leverage the weaknesses of today's multipolar world order by playing great powers off each other in ways that mitigate Western pressure on their regimes. The foreign assistance, trade, investment and military cooperation that non-Western powers such as China and Russia provide give authoritarian leaders a new source of external legitimacy, and enable them to credibly threaten to downgrade relations with the United States if Washington pressures them too much on democracy and human rights. In Egypt, for example, President Abdel Fattah Al-Sisi can use Cairo's military and economic ties with Russia to offset Western human-rights pressure. The availability of alternatives to the West will make repression a more viable solution to autocrats' rising fears of popular protest.

* * *

So far, Western approaches have been slow to take into account the ways in which autocracies are evolving and their internal dynamics changing. As a result, today's autocracies have become more durable, lasting significantly longer than their predecessors. From 1946 to 1989, the average lifespan of an authoritarian regime was 12 years. Since the end of the Cold War, this number has almost doubled, to 20 years. As of 2012, the typical authoritarian regime had been in power for 25 years. This being the case, what might the future hold for democratic governance?

It is true that democracy still reigns as the most prevalent form of government worldwide. And the findings of multiple surveys suggest that many citizens across the globe prefer it to the alternatives. Yet, should current trends continue, we could witness a disconcerting reversal. If democracies do not respond to the challenges of contemporary authoritarianism, both in terms of their domestic affairs and in countering trends abroad, new autocracies will continue to outpace new democracies and become the international norm. Democracies, therefore, cannot afford to be complacent. To remain dominant, they must engage in the same process of learning and adaptation as their autocratic peers. Countering the twenty-first-century autocrat requires a twenty-first-century democrat.

Notes

1 See, for example, Moises Naim, *The End of Power: From Boardrooms to Battlefields and Churches to States, Why Being in Charge Isn't What It Used to Be* (New York: Basic Books, 2013); and William J. Dobson, *The Dictator's Learning Curve: Inside the Global Battle for Democracy* (New York: Doubleday, 2012).

2 See, for example, Larry Diamond, 'Facing Up to the Democratic Recession', *Journal of Democracy*, vol. 26, no. 1, January 2015, pp. 141–55; Joshua Kurlantcik, *Democracy in Retreat: The Revolt of the Middle Class and the Worldwide Decline of Representative Government* (New Haven, CT: Yale University Press, 2013); and Robert Kagan, 'The Weight of Geopolitics', *Journal of Democracy*, vol. 26, no. 1, January 2015, pp. 21–31.

3 Fiona Hill and Cliff Gaddy, *Mr. Putin: Operative in the Kremlin* (Washington DC: Brookings Institution Press, 2013), p. 6.

4 These statistics, and those that follow

(unless otherwise noted), are based on data that classify the start and end dates, regime type, and entry and exit modes of all authoritarian regimes that held power between 1946 and 2014. See Barbara Geddes, Joseph Wright and Erica Frantz, 'Autocratic Breakdown and Regime Transitions: A New Data Set', *Perspectives on Politics*, vol. 12, no. 2, 2014, pp. 313–31.

5 For more on this finding, see Andrea Kendall-Taylor, Erica Frantz and Joseph Wright, 'The New Dictators: Why Personalism Rules', *Foreign Affairs*, 26 September 2016, https://www.foreignaffairs.com/articles/2016-09-26/new-dictators.

6 Erica Frantz and Andrea Kendall-Taylor, 'Pathways to Democratization in Personalist Dictatorships', *Democratization*, vol. 24, no. 1, 2016. pp. 20–40.

7 Jessica Weeks, 'Strongmen and Straw Men: Authoritarian Regimes and the Initiation of International Conflict', *American Political Science Review*, vol. 106, no. 2, May 2012, pp. 326–47.

8 See Erica Frantz and Natasha Ezrow, *The Politics of Dictatorship: Institutions and Outcomes in Authoritarian Regimes* (Boulder, CO: Lynne Rienner, 2011); Christopher Way and Jessica Weeks, 'Making it Personal: Regime Type and Nuclear Proliferation', *American Journal of Political Science*, vol. 58, no. 3, July 2014, pp. 705–19; Mark Peceny, Caroline C. Beer and Shannon Sanchez-Terry, 'Dictatorial Peace?', *American Political Science Review*, vol. 96, no. 1, March 2002, pp. 15–26; Jessica Weeks, *Dictators at War and Peace* (Ithaca, NY: Cornell University Press, 2014).

9 See Marie-Soleil Frère and Pierre Englebert, 'Briefing: Burkina Faso – The Fall of Blaise Compaoré', *African Affairs*, vol. 114, no. 455, April 2015, pp. 295–307.

10 Data for this analysis come from Milan Svolik, *The Politics of Authoritarian Rule* (New York: Cambridge University Press, 2012), who identifies the manner through which all leaders left office through 2008. We updated Svolik's data set through 2012, using two coders to ensure accuracy. The updated data are available upon request. To classify countries as autocratic, we relied on the classification system found in Geddes, Wright and Frantz, 'Autocratic Breakdown and Regime Transitions: A New Data Set'.

11 Freedom House, 'Populists and Autocrats: The Dual Threat to Global Democracy', 2017, https://freedomhouse.org/report/freedom-world/freedom-world-2017.

Ideology and Strategy in the Middle East: The Case of Iran

Walter Posch

The West's dealings with Iran are characterised by confusion. The greatest challenge stems not so much from Iran's political and military behaviour in the Middle East, or even its nuclear programme, as from uncertainty about Iran's ultimate goals. Tehran maintains diplomatic relations with all the Western democracies except for the most important, the United States. Yet Iran is an ideologically governed political system,[1] widely believed to be motivated by an anti-Western and anti-imperialist view of the world. The key to understanding the problem of Iran thus lies in the relationship between ideology and strategy.

Surprisingly little has been written about the nexus of ideology, on the one hand, and strategy and war, on the other.[2] This may be because authors either take the link for granted or, alternatively, do not consider it a topic worth studying. The 'end of ideology' has been proclaimed and rejected at least twice before.[3] Ideology was declared to have been exhausted by the political consensus of the 1950s, a proposition opposed vociferously by Niklas Luhmann,[4] and then declared to have been abolished by the discourse analysis of Jürgen Habermas, Jean-François Lyotard and, especially, Michel Foucault in the 1970s.[5] The Marxist literary critic Terry Eagleton spoke out forcefully at the beginning of the 1990s against giving up the idea of ideology, but his influence was restricted to academic circles and his argument

Walter Posch is a Middle East security expert and historian at the National Defense Academy of the Austrian Army in Vienna.

Survival | vol. 59 no. 5 | October–November 2017 | pp. 69–98 DOI 10.1080/00396338.2017.1375256

was given scant consideration in strategic studies. Something similar happened to Alan Cassels, who penned the best overview of the role of ideology in international relations.[6]

Francis Fukuyama had greater influence on strategic thought, but more in the sense of grand strategy and global order than of military strategy itself.[7] After the collapse of the Soviet Union, Fukuyama famously proclaimed the end of history, and with it the end of ideologies. There has since been an erroneous, but persistent, Western belief that the end of the Cold War signified the end of big, ideological confrontations. This, in due course, led to the belief that Western concepts of governance and power projection in the Middle East were free of ideology. From a Middle Eastern perspective, however, Western hegemony and resistance to it are both deeply ideological and interlinked.

Ideology and strategy in the West: hegemony

In a 1993 article, and later in his 1996 book, Samuel T. Huntington challenged Fukuyama's thesis, discerning a looming clash of civilisations.[8] This was a partial reintroduction of aspects of culture and cultural geography to the debate on international relations,[9] and did not shy away from questions of ideology and policy. Huntington's thesis was taken up in public debate, just like Fukuyama's. Unfortunately, Huntington's arguments were quickly misused: in Europe, and especially in Germany due to an infelicitous translation, the idea was misrepresented as a 'war' between cultures and religions, making Huntington the alleged intellectual witness for an ongoing, religiously grounded war between the West and Islam, Occident and orient. Both authors, however, took the 'benign' nature of US hegemony for granted. As Bill McSweeney notes:

> strategic thinking in post-Cold War foreign policy was couched in less altruistic terms in the Pentagon's [1992 draft] 'Defence Planning Guidance'. The United States, it claimed, must continue to dominate the international system; it must 'discourage' the 'advanced industrial nations from challenging our leadership or … even aspiring to a larger regional or global role'.[10]

America's global leadership was accepted in (western) Europe without any objection, and either sheepishly cloaked in the oxymoron of a 'benign' or 'liberal' hegemony, or historicised as *pax americana,* and exalted to the status of a global public good.[11] Rather than challenging US hegemony, transatlantic relations were conducted, by way of NATO, as a way of placing European security interests at the centre of US strategic thinking, defence planning and military expenditure. Europe would compete with the US for global markets; the old continent's defence, however, would still be NATO's domain, so that the definition of an independent security and defence policy or the creation of an independent military wing was, in essence, limited to the gesture politics of the European Common Security and Defence Policy (CSDP).[12]

Soft power: hegemony in culture and academia

Joseph S. Nye's seminal work on soft power cites a wide array of non-military factors such as pop culture and the economy, and describes them as elements of 'globalisation'.[13] Others, however, are more candid. In a short and succinct article, John Mearsheimer observes that chairs in international relations, and similar institutions at which international elites are trained, are usually located in the US – consequently the theory of American 'benign hegemony' rules.[14] The political and ideological discourse of the so-called Third World[15] is regarded, if it is discussed at all, as the domain of intellectuals or political activists – that is, not the domain of political decision-makers, who relegate such issues to the context of foreign aid or neo-colonialism.[16]

It is in recognition of this underlying logic that conservative scholars such as William S. Lind have viewed any political discourse emanating from the Third World as a threat. More than anyone else, Lind clearly understands the consequences of allowing American benign hegemony to be questioned. He warns of the presence of anti-imperialist discourse and argument among the US public, and speaks of an ideological struggle against 'cultural Marxism',[17] fearing that such ideas will dilute American cultural identity, and thus diminish America's capacity to project power.[18] In other words, once benign hegemony in the field of theory is gone, political and military hegemony will follow suit. Lind was perhaps the first scholar of standing to warn against multiculturalism and political correctness as threats to US hegemony. It has often been said that he and his academic and intellectual disciples are only marginal, right-wing intellectuals. Be this as it may, their influence is not negligible: firstly, they figure prominently among the advisors of President Donald Trump.[19] Secondly, their views are not new; they stem from a tradition linking security and American identity, and which, in contrast to the tradition of the liberal foreign-policy community, is concerned equally with external military threats and domestic cultural and political threats.[20]

Military superiority

The United States' hegemonic view of itself after the Cold War – an ideology with global implications – was reflected in a military strategy based on military and economic superiority. The so-called revolution in military affairs, and new information-strategy concepts such as the OODA loop (observe, orient, decide, act – an idea developed by John Boyd) made possible a clean war, after the politicians' fancy. In this type of war, there would be fewer battles, or battles themselves would become obsolete, as cognitive confusion would paralyse the enemy at all levels (tactical, operational and strategic).[21] The concept may have been criticised for its disavowal of the physical aspects of the military – the art of war – but it dominated the subsequent decade.

US military strategists further concluded that, because of the United States' military superiority, enemies had very little choice other than to react asymmetrically – by way of irregular warfare or the development of weapons of mass destruction – or capitulate. The future of warfare thus lies in asymmetry. Lawrence Freedman, however, has quite rightly pointed out that the term asymmetry is now used for every type of military resistance and has thus lost its analytical value.[22] By contrast, Lind's theory of 'fourth-generation warfare' has proven far-sighted, developing and refining Boyd's technology-driven approach.[23] Just like Boyd, Lind stressed the increased use of technology on the battlefield and the central importance of the media front; however, he also drew attention to the combination of these two aspects with terrorism and classic forms of warfare. Lind's concept found its most acerbic critic in Antulio J. Echevarria, who saw these new forms of war as nothing more than classic revolutionary movements.[24] It must be noted, however, that in 1989 Lind was able to predict the type of warfare that would be employed by ISIS almost 30 years later. (In reality, the gap between Lind and Echevarria is far less wide than either is willing to accept, especially if 'terrorism' and 'revolutionary movement' are interpreted as amounting to roughly the same thing.[25])

But just like asymmetry, the term terrorism lacks analytical clarity, because any international attempt to define it has proven politically unviable. Originally, terrorists were those who committed acts of terrorism, such as indiscriminate killings of civilians for ideological or political ends. Yet a tendency persists to apply the term to any violence committed by or on behalf of an actor that embraces a hostile ideology – regardless of the nature of the conflict, its root causes or the means employed. As a result, the enemy is denied legitimacy (because terrorists are inherently illegitimate), and political solutions, which always entail painful compromises, are made impossible (because terrorists are not to be negotiated with). In military terms, the 'global war on terror' declared by George W. Bush after 9/11 brought few innovations, and in 2005 the Bush administration reformulated it as an ideological struggle.[26] As a consequence, state sponsors of terrorism – often but not always 'rogue states' – would also become targets of US counter-terrorism efforts. This has applied, for many years, to the Islamic Republic of Iran.

Ideology and strategy in the Middle East: resistance

From the point of view of the so-called Third World, Western ideas of global order and governance are nothing more than a variation on imperialism, a nineteenth-century concept which led to the formation of anti-colonial and anti-imperialist movements all around the world. Some American scholars concur with this analysis. According to Eric Carlton, 'like the British, French, and other colonizing European powers the Americans may be regarded as the quintessential military imperialists. Their actions ... are strangely reminiscent of those of the Athenians who created an empire ostensibly to impose democratic forms on sometimes unwilling states.'[27] Military superiority is the key to this effort, as Huntington puts it:

> The West won the world not by superiority of its ideas or values or religion ... but rather by its superiority in applying organized violence. Westerners often forget this fact; non-Westerners never do.[28]

As a result, the ideologies developed in the Middle East during the twentieth century were – and remain – anti-colonialist and anti-imperialist in nature. This applies to nationalists, such as the Kemalists in Turkey and the Nasserites in Egypt, as well as to movements inspired by socialism, such as the Algerian National Liberation Front, the Ba'ath Party in Syria and Iraq, and the Islamists in Iran and Sudan. Even al-Qaeda and ISIS can be seen within these parameters. The political and analytical characteristics of anti-imperialism were created during the decolonisation of the 1950s and 1960s, and formulated as 'Third-Worldism'. Intellectuals such as Frantz Fanon[29] adapted Marxist and Maoist ideas and set them in the context of the anti-colonial wars of liberation, sometimes with extreme consequences for Europe.[30] At the level of realpolitik, states organised themselves in the Non-Aligned Movement (NAM) which developed out of the 1955 Bandung Conference, as well as in the Marxist-revolutionary Organization of Solidarity with the People of Asia, Africa and Latin America (OSPAAAL), founded in Cuba in 1965. Muslim thinkers and movements, from the Egyptian Sayyid Qutb to the Iranian Ayatollah Khomeini and the strategic schools taught in the Islamic Republic of Iran, have drawn on the secular anti-imperialist tradition and made use of its lines of argument,[31] often in Islamic rhetorical disguise.

Robert Cooper, drawing on controversies spanning EU integration and the 2003 Iraq War, attempted a new interpretation of the relationship between the first and third worlds. In his essay, 'The Breaking of Nations', he classified states as post-modern, modern and pre-modern.[32] Post-modern states have left the wars of the modern world behind them and developed new, pacifist models of cooperation among themselves (like the EU); modern states, by necessity, still rely on force in international relations, and pre-modern states have only weakly developed political systems and often cannot assert state authority. Pre-modern thus became an umbrella term for both failed and rogue states, and is today primarily used for Muslim countries. The academic world took hardly any notice of Cooper's attempt at a definition; it is, however, often employed by European diplomats as an interpretive model for a chaotic world. In the Third World, and especially by Muslim intellectuals, this concept is flatly rejected.

In Muslim countries, the ideological tradition of anti-colonialism, anti-imperialism and Third-Worldism has generated a fundamentally positive view of anti-Western insurgencies. After all, almost all Muslim countries fought wars of liberation or could look back on a tradition of guerrilla movements, some of which were successful and others heroic failures. Resistance per se is part of the Middle East's political identity. Nye missed this point totally, calling anti-imperialism simply anti-Americanism and predicting its quick downfall.[33] Yet anti-imperialism is an ideological constant, opposing US hegemony. The fact that jihadis allegedly hate the Shi'ites more than the Americans does not devalue their core message, for in the end, 'Islamic rule', however it is defined, is directed against US hegemony.

Yet the terms 'resistance' (*muqavamah*) against and 'liberation' (*tahrir*) from Western usurpers are used so often that they, like 'terrorism' and 'asymmetry' in the West, have little value, and can be applied to a whole range of military actions: as a rule, they imply guerrilla activities, but also operations carried out by regular armed forces, as well as bomb attacks. In any case, resistance carries positive connotations with the broader public, and is always read in the context of a corresponding ideology. In 2008, Arnaud de La Grange and Jean-Marc Balencie drew attention to the combination of ideology and military resistance.[34] Their proof of the Lind approach is a jihadi strategy paper, penned by Abu Musab al-Suri in 2005.[35] For the Muslim world, al-Suri had formulated exactly the type of war which Lind predicted:[36] total warfare, waged in a decentralised manner, strongly ideological, and combining guerrilla operations, operational-level warfare and terrorism. A decade later, and as part of the French debate on terrorism and jihad, Gilles Kepel took up al-Suri's strategy paper in order to draw attention to the importance of jihadi ideology and strategy – in this case, the inclusion of the front in Europe.[37] In the final analysis, developments in Iraq were instrumental in the acceptance of the interpretation of Sunni Muslim jihad as a global insurgency.[38] French publications on strategy argued this point early on; in the US, former CIA agent Michael Scheuer was the first to formulate a similar view, and found his thesis supported by none other than Osama bin Laden.[39] Applied to the region, this means that America's 'benign' hegemonic ambitions are faced with a globally conceived Sunni Muslim insurgency (or jihad) originating in the Middle East. Jihadism thus is a free-for-all strategy aiming not so much to hold territory but to create a condition of violent anarchy, something the Western hegemon cannot control, at least not without a strong, legitimate and indigenous pro-Western actor on the ground.

The Western military reaction to jihadism is counter-insurgency. This explains the great interest among non-military circles in military counter-insurgency concepts which, under General David Petraeus and on the basis of French examples, were turned into a new doctrine in 2006.[40] However, interpreting fourth-generation warfare as a global insurgency has two consequences. Firstly, it illustrates the discrepancy between military reality (counter-insurgency) and political perception (terrorism). As much as al-Qaeda fighters and those of the Taliban or ISIS are internationally regarded as terrorists – they do, after all, indubitably commit acts of terrorism – they cannot be stopped with counter-terrorism means alone, because terrorism, as predicted by Lind, has become a part of the way war is waged.[41] Secondly, employing a counter-insurgency strategy amounts to a victory of Islamist discourse (*muqawamah, tahrir*) over that of the West (global war on terror, terrorism). Insurgencies, just like liberation movements, are legitimate in the eyes of most Muslims. Even if the vast majority rejects the methods used by al-Qaeda and similar groups, the goal of shaking off Western hegemony over the Middle East is deemed legitimate. This is one reason, among others, why experts conclude that the jihadi threat will neither decrease nor disappear, even after a military victory over ISIS.[42]

The Islamic Republic of Iran is thus in an awkward position. On the one hand, its ideology is firmly rooted in Oriental anti-imperialism; on the other hand, it is not part of the global jihadi insurgency that wages fourth-generation warfare in the region – against Iran, and ultimately against the West. The new strategic reality for Iran has been called the 'greater Middle Eastern crisis' by Fred Halliday, who, using post-2003 Iraq as a point of reference, was among the first to recognise the new triangular confrontation between Iran, the US and jihadism.[43] Following simple strategic logic, this should make the West and Iran partners. Before deciding whether this is possible, however, we must turn to the nexus of ideology and strategy.

Islamic Republic of Iran: ideology and strategy

The idiosyncrasies and contradictions of Iran's security policy and power projection have ideological and historical roots.[44] One of the functions of ideology in general, according to Luhmann, is 'to integrate contradictions and to coordinate actions based on different values'.[45] One of these idiosyncrasies in the case of Iran is the careful reading of Western strategic and ideological literature, including Nye, Fukuyama and Huntington, which led to the adoption of 'soft power' and cultural politics as elements of Iranian strategy. In general, Iran is not only aware of but actively employs Nye's concept of soft power (*qodrat-e narm*), which Iranian diplomacy applies to almost all fields of foreign policy and strategy.[46] For instance, Iran freely embraces secular pan-Iranian nationalism and Muslim solidarity to woo the Kurds, but at the same time views the existence of the autonomous Kurdistan region in Northern Iraq and its promotion of Kurdish nationalism (*kurdayeti*) as a soft security threat.[47] In a similar vein, Iranian security elites view Western soft power as a 'cultural onslaught of the West' (*hojum-e farhangi-ye gharb*) against Iran's national and Islamic traditions, mores and identity:

> The main function of the Western cultural threat is the 'soft war' (*jang-e narm*) and the main aim of this is the weakening of national culture and identity of Islamic societies. This is why the presence of NATO in the region poses various serious threats for the Islamic Republic of Iran. In this context the spread of liberal and western values around Iran must be stressed.[48]

This concept comes very close to Lind's 'cultural Marxism', although there is no proof that the Iranians have actually read Lind. Many of Iran's security elites are convinced there is a 'cultural NATO' (*nato-ye farhangi*): media and other tools employed by NATO states directing a soft war against Iran in order to weaken the Islamic Republic; they consequently attach great importance and apply great vigilance to the alleged role of Western intelligence services in the fields of culture and academia.[49]

From an institutional and historic perspective, a revolutionary, underground Islamist movement, which took power in 1979, has been merged with a functioning modern state and security apparatus. One obvious consequence of this combination is subsequent institutional splitting, such as the existence of an ideological military force – the Islamic Revolutionary Guard Corps (IRGC) – alongside the regular army.[50] Another is the application of varying ideologies or ideological traditions according to geography.

Ideology and geography

Iran's security and military elites employ contradicting ideologies – or elements of ideology – and apply them to areas where Iran has strategic interests, or which are important for Iran's security. This is nothing special; Arab regimes use pan-Arab (*qaumi*) and pan-Islamic arguments alongside national (*qutri,* that is, Iraqi, Syrian, Yemeni) ideas and identities depending on circumstances and political opportunities.[51] In the Iranian case, Tehran uses a logical pattern of when and how to apply elements of its ideology depending on geography. Four ideological pillars are applied, with different levels of emphasis, to three geographic areas. The four ideological pillars can be explained with reference to the history of Iran and of the Islamic movement in Iran, and they are, in some respects, contradictory. They are: Iranian nationalism, traditional Shi'ism, *tiers-mondialisme* (or Third-Worldism), and non-confessional, revolutionary Islamism (or Khomeinism). The three regions are the immediate neighbourhood, the Islamic world (especially the Middle East) and the wider international community of the so-called Third World. The ideological pillars are not of equal importance to each region: 'global' Shi'ism does not play a role in Iranian Third World policy, while Third-Worldism carries no relevance in Iran's immediate neighbourhood. Often, a number of ideological approaches are resorted to in order to justify the same policy, as in the case of Syria. As a rule, the boundaries between the ideological approaches and the regions are blurred.

Strategic principles and their implementation

The security–political and strategic derivations[52] of ideology are reflected in the Iranian constitution: Article 3/16 requires that the principles of Islam be observed in foreign policy; Article 11 stresses the brotherhood of Muslim nations; and Articles 152–54 prohibit any membership of military alliances and the creation of international military bases on Iranian territory – and, at the same time, codify the support of the 'oppressed' (*mostaza'fin*), that is, revolutionary movements worldwide. The US interprets the latter as support for international terrorism and Iranian meddling in the region.

As far as I am aware, however, these constitutional articles have never been expounded in a national strategy document, such as a White Paper. What is available is a binding, 25-year plan, published in 2005, which is little more than an economic and development strategy, and to which Western observers generally do not attach much importance.[53] According to this paper, the Islamic Republic of Iran will develop into an energy and traffic hub between Central Asia and the Arab region, as well as between India, Russia and Europe. This includes the planned construction of the Nabucco pipeline, which was to transport Iranian gas to European markets, as well as the harbour project in Chah Bahar and railway projects from there to Afghanistan, Central Asia and Russia.[54]

The Iranian nuclear programme is a special case: it can be interpreted both nationalistically (in terms of sovereignty and national pride) and via Third-Worldism (nuclear justice, technological progress),[55] and it promotes Iran's prestige in all geographic areas – hence Iran was prepared to endure heavy sanctions for it. That said, Tehran remains within the framework of the Non-Proliferation Treaty (NPT), the precise interpretation of which was one of the points of contention during the negotiations with the EU/E3+3 (Great Britain, France, Germany, China, Russia and the United States).[56]

However, there are currently no indications that Iran's non-nuclear status is now permanently settled, nor that the neighbouring states are realigning their foreign policy accordingly. Israel certainly does not feel compelled to sign the NPT, and thus give up its strategic ambiguity, simply because the Islamic Republic abides by it.

Ideological pragmatism and expedient interests

The four ideological pillars appear contradictory: Iranian nationalism and traditional Shi'ism are, in principle, introspective and conservative; in contrast, global Islam and the ideology of the Third World are revolutionary and expansive. Interestingly, the Iranian elites do not even attempt to solve these contradictions; instead, they have made pragmatism the guiding factor in foreign policy and strategy: the principle of *maslahat-e nezam*, the 'expediency of the system', means that ideological purity takes a back seat when it comes to the survival of the state and the regime.[57] Stressing expediency means compromising on ideological purity, which in turn leads to political pragmatism (or, indeed, opportunism). Undoubtedly, the main expedient interest of the system is to stay in power. Nor is there anything special or new about such an attitude – other ideologies have similarly sacrificed ideological purity upon coming to power.[58]

Pragmatism is often understood as the beginning of the post-revolutionary phase, a feature not unique to the Iranian regime. But the roots of the Iranian regime's ideological pragmatism, and especially the easy way the Iranians deal with apparent contradiction on an institutional level, lie also in the experience of the Iranian clergy, who established the principle of 'order in disorder' (*nazm dar bî-nazmî*) over a century ago. This, in turn, means that the clergy can handle different interpretations of, and views on, theological and religious topics very well, and have applied this relative openness to politics within the multifaceted Islamist spectrum. Ayatollah Khamenei, the Supreme Leader of the Islamic Revolution, whose programmatic speeches set out the correct interpretation of the ideology and the nature of its strategic derivations,[59] does not act in a vacuum, but heads a broad, consensual and national decision-making process, supported by a powerful security–political and strategic research environment.[60]

On domestic policy, an elaborate system of political officers (representatives of the Supreme Leader, the political and ideological bureaus, and so on) similar to the old Soviet *politruk* system, as well as efficient censorship, ensure that diversity of opinion does not stray outside the Islamist spectrum. On foreign policy, pragmatism means, firstly, that Tehran avoids getting bogged down in fruitless conflicts over the 'politically correct' ideological approach to policy.[61] This not only saves energy, but makes it possible to communicate policy changes to the population more easily, without contravening ideology and thus robbing the regime of legitimacy. There are numerous examples of ideological pragmatism to be found in Iran's foreign and security policy, the most important being the ceasefire with Iraq in 1988, the decision not to intervene in Afghanistan in 1998 and current Iranian policy vis-à-vis Syria. The concept of expedient interests also makes it easier to prioritise conflicts: Iran and Russia have left unaddressed their opposing positions concerning the legal status of the Caspian Sea, out of consideration for shared interests elsewhere.

There are limits to flexibility, which apply not only to anti-Americanism and 'anti-Zionism', but also to the constitutional articles quoted above. Arms shipments from Israel and later the United States (in the Iran–Contra affair) in the 1980s were always officially denied by Iran, and thus never led to the change of direction in Tehran's foreign policy Washington and Tel Aviv had desired.[62] A more recent example concerns Iranian–Russian relations: when Russian media reported on Russia's use of Hamadan Air Base, it immediately became a political issue, and led to the Iranian government denying Russia further use of the base. Neutrality, as laid down in the constitution, was thus stronger than the military benefit of cooperation with Russia, despite a comprehensive convergence of interests, especially regarding Syria.

Ideological vision and reality

If Iran were to give ideology absolute priority in its strategy and foreign policy, Tehran would have to pursue an aggressive foreign policy which would massively exceed the country's military and economic capabilities. In general, Tehran's political pragmatism prevents such a course. Yet events in the region have created new challenges for Iran.

Iran's strategic vision and the axis of resistance

The focus of Iranian foreign policy and strategic interests is on the Middle East. Put differently, Iran wants to be a regional power. At first glance, this is nothing new, as the previous Iranian regime was involved, for the same reasons, in Lebanon from the 1950s onwards.[63] The revolution of 1979, however, changed the Iranian rationale for this claim, as Tehran was no longer looking for consensus with the international community. This is why the break with Israel occurred, and why the liberation of Palestine became the focus of the debate on foreign policy.

There were a number of reasons for this. Among others, an aggressively pro-Palestinian foreign policy was in keeping with the zeitgeist. The Palestinian struggle against Israel, which Iran (like most Muslim states) regards as an illegitimate, alien presence in the region, was, at that time, approved by all political groups. The Iranian Islamists and leftists have had contacts with Palestinians since the 1940s, and in the 1960s Palestinian groups in Lebanon trained hundreds of young political activists, many of whom were to rise to command functions in the Revolutionary Guard.[64] Iranians were also among the first to interpret the Palestinian question in religious and not nationalist terms – that is, as a struggle between indigenous Muslims and non-Muslim European colonists. In this way, the Iranians not only wrested the prerogative of interpretation, as regards the Palestinian question, from the hands of the Marxist groups, but by stressing the pan-Islamic nature of Palestine, they also compensated for the shortcoming of being, as Shi'ites and Persians, outsiders in the region.

The Iranian role of the outsider led, immediately after Saddam Hussein's attack on Iran, to the creation of close strategic ties with the ideologically distant, Ba'athist–secular Arab Republic of Syria.[65] Once Iraq ceased to be a threat, this alliance had to be reinterpreted: Syria, according to Iran, became a part of the 'Axis of Resistance' (*mehvar-e moqavemat*) against Israel. The Lebanese Hizbullah, a part of Hamas (especially the group of Khaled Meshal) and the Palestinian Islamic Jihad were incorporated into this axis. The lowest common denominator of these ideologically divergent players was the question of Palestine and enmity towards Israel.[66] The alliance against Saddam Hussein, originally of a purely military–strategic nature, thus became an ideological alliance against Israel, which achieved its greatest success when, in 2006, Hizbullah managed to repel an Israeli attack. At that time, Iran, Hizbullah and Syria enjoyed great prestige among the ordinary Sunni populace of all important Arab states, which was highly disquieting to the Arab elites.

Support for the Palestinian liberation movement and the creation of the so-called Axis of Resistance also played a role in the context of an Iranian revolutionary strategic vision. Following Khomeini, the Iranian elites are convinced that the question of Palestine is of central importance to the Muslim population of the Arab states (the so-called Arab street),[67] whereas the Arab elites, in many places westernised or secular, view the Palestinians critically and Israel pragmatically. Starting from its own experience, Tehran assumes that, in the long term, tensions between the secular and culturally westernised elites and the broader Muslim population are bound to lead to revolutionary upheaval all across the Middle East: these regimes will either be swept away by a revolution or, as part of a possible democratisation, voted out of office. This is why Tehran regarded the so-called Arab Spring as an Islamic awakening and as a repetition of its own historic experience. According to Iranian logic, after the departure of the old elites, Islamic–populist or even revolutionary governments would assume power and reassess their relationship with Iran in the light of Muslim brotherliness and community, which would mean the end of Tehran's isolation – something that did occur briefly in Egypt under Muhammad Morsi. Trusting its economic and military strength, and buoyed by its nuclear programme, the Iranians would have no problem winning the struggle for regional hegemony against Saudi Arabia and exerting pressure on Israel. In 2006, and again in 2012, the year when Morsi visited Tehran, the Iranians came tantalisingly close to realising this strategic vision. In the end, it was Saudi Arabia which put paid to Tehran's (pan-Islamically inspired) claim to be a regional power.

Arab elites view Israel pragmatically

Since the end of the Second World War, periods of tension between Riyadh and Tehran have alternated with periods of detente. The tensions are rooted in a strategic rivalry with Saudi Arabia which reaches back to the time before the revolution and which became worse after 1979, but which was overshadowed for a long time by the tensions between Iran and Iraq.[68] Apart from the immediate Middle East, it was Afghanistan, in particular, which stood at the centre of the competition. There, both states sponsored hostile Sunni and Shia groups and militias, which meant that their antagonism was realised in a religious war. With the victory of the Taliban in 1998, Tehran had to accept defeat at the Hindu Kush, and only returned to the country in 2001, with the Americans. Tensions between Iran and Saudi Arabia also exploded in Pakistan in the shape of violent sectarian conflicts; these, however, were repeatedly de-escalated.

From the Iranian point of view, sectarianism constitutes a strategic catastrophe. There are numerous reasons for this. The attempt to move the region's Shi'ites to revolution failed in the 1980s, which is why Iran has wanted to prevent itself being seen in the region as a Persian Shia state, but rather as a Muslim power. Arab Shi'ites are differently organised, and most networks of the high Shia clergy in Najaf and Kerbala are critical of the Iranians.[69] Lastly, Iran has been unable to help its fellow Shi'ites in the face of threats to life and limb: Tehran remained silent during the Shia uprising in Iraq in 1991; decided not to come to their aid by intervening militarily in Afghanistan in 1998; limited its protests against the 2011 Saudi intervention in Bahrain to, for the most part, notes of protest; stood idly by as Nigerian Shi'ites became victims of Sunni attacks between 2014 and 2016; and generally ignores the plight of Pakistani Shi'ites, who are often victims of indiscriminate sectarian hatred.

Iran's deafening silence concerning the fate of fellow Shi'ites is a product of relative powerlessness: Iran is unable to help them through military, humanitarian or diplomatic efforts. Iranian strategists also did not want to be forced into conflicts where there was little to be gained. This, for example, is the case in Yemen, where Iran is much less involved because, unlike in Iraq and Syria, no vital interests are at stake.

Despite this, sectarianisation was irresistible. Saudi Arabia's public relations initially played an important role, as the kingdom managed to reinterpret the Axis of Resistance, after the 2003 Iraq invasion and the

2006 Lebanon War, as a Shia Crescent, and to degrade Iran and Hizbullah in the eyes of the Arab public. The Saudi success would not have been so striking if the situation in Iraq and Syria had remained stable, and if al-Qaeda and later ISIS had not appeared on the scene. The end of Ba'athist hegemony in Iraq, the crisis in Syria and, most importantly, the decision of Hizbullah to join the Syrian civil war, made sectarianism the predominant template when it comes to explaining almost all conflicts in the Middle East.[70]

Iran and Syria: from nationalism to nationalism

To Tehran, however, the reality in Syria looks rather more complex than simply sectarian. Ironically, the Arab Spring at first confirmed the Iranian point of view, as some of the insurgents really did come from Islamist circles, revolting against a secular regime. Tehran, however, quickly realised that it had no contacts in the Syrian opposition, not even with those hailing from the Muslim Brotherhood, Iran's preferred partner. And due to Iran's many years of cooperating with the regime, it was not only tarnished as far as the political representatives of the insurgency were concerned, but also loathed by swathes of the population.

This, alongside other reasons – keeping up the pressure on Israel, as well as the rivalry with Saudi Arabia – led Khamenei to decide in favour of military support for Syria as part of the Axis of Resistance, knowing full well that there was little enthusiasm on the part of the Iranian public for this undertaking. With ISIS's power increasing and the battle continuing, the cost in lives among Iranian or Iranian-led volunteer units rose, and Tehran no longer justified its involvement in the country with revolutionary rhetoric, but stressed the necessity of fighting ISIS and similar groups in Syria and Iraq, before they became a danger inside Iran itself.

To put it another way: vis-à-vis the population, the government uses a nationalist line of argument; in the region, it is restricted to Shia foreign policy. This will change Tehran's relationship with the Arab Shi'ites. Hizbullah has already become an equal partner rather than a proxy, given its important role in training Shia insurgents. And the relationship to the Grand Ayatollahs in Iraq has changed, since it was they who allowed the creation of Shia volunteer units. In both cases – stressing nationalism and Shia Islam – this was a setback for the pan-Islamic, Khomeinist ideology.

From the point of view of Tehran, however, this hardly seems relevant anymore; what counts is how Syria can be stabilised, given its myriad militias and millions of refugees. Apart from its behaviour driven by realpolitik, such as cooperation with Russia and – depending on circumstances – Turkey, there are reports that Tehran wants to change the religious landscape in its favour. There are also Syrian opposition reports of Iranian plans to move Iraqi Shi'ites to Syria and to convert the Syrian Alawites to Shia Islam.[71] But in order to convince the Iranian population, the government used another argument: that it is better to fight ISIS in Syria with Shia volunteers from Iraq and Afghanistan than with drafted Iranian soldiers. So, Tehran employed different ideological approaches to justify the Iranian–Syrian alliance: nationalistically in the first phase, when it was a case of defending against an Iraqi invasion, and pan-Islamically in the second, with the Axis of Resistance (which, especially in South America, president Mahmoud Ahmadinejad described in Third-World terms, as a kind of global revolutionary project). Finally, in the last years of its Syria policy, Iran was reduced to its Shia identity, which prompted Tehran again to use nationalist arguments to justify its commitment to its own population.

Tehran and the West in a fourth-generation war?

In the decade after 9/11, many observers were surprised to find a number of instances where the strategic interests of the United States and Iran converged: the Afghan Taliban, Saddam Hussein in Iraq and al-Qaeda were regarded as common enemies, fuelling Sunni conspiracy theories that Iran and the US, supported by Israel, were planning the destruction of the Sunni world. In reality, only in Afghanistan was there any form of intelligence and military cooperation established. In Syria, Iran and the US originally had opposing goals, and in Iraq, direct cooperation was neither possible nor desired, although both sides were at pains to avoid any direct confrontation. The fact that Iran had long-standing relations with political and military groups in Iraq which would later become partners of the US, though known in expert circles, had little effect on political planning in Tehran or Washington. There were subsequent informal meetings between the Iranians and the US, about which all that is known is that they were arranged by the Iraqis. It is not clear how far Iraqi military operations against ISIS were co-ordinated between Washington and Tehran via Baghdad.

Military means

Given that the Iran–Iraq War was waged conventionally, the identification of Islamist revolutionaries with anti-imperialist resistance movements had little influence on the military doctrines of the Iranian Army and the IRGC. Even the religious and ideological fervour of the human waves employed against Iraqi positions contributed nothing of value to Iranian tactics or strategy; the world had witnessed something similar, albeit on an even larger scale, in the First World War. One exception could be Iran's naval doctrine, which was referred to as guerrilla war at sea. The Iranian assumption since 1989 is that the US Navy intends to enter Iran's shallow, strongly indented coastal waters, and that Iran must fight back with guerrilla tactics.[72] Numerous reports suggest that this is more a matter of propaganda than of standing, implemented doctrine. If it applies at all, the guerrilla-war-at-sea doctrine only applies to the navy of the Revolutionary Guard, which, for the most part, consists of fast-attack craft.[73] The regular navy, as opposed to the IRGC navy, attaches great importance to its military respectability on the international stage. The second exception concerns the ideologically motivated international operations of Revolutionary Guard units in Lebanon and Sudan.

The Revolutionary Guard

The creation of the IRGC successfully gathered the numerous, spontaneously created Islamist militias under a single command.[74] Its original mission was to preserve domestic security and to implement Islamic rule. During the long war with Iraq, the IRGC created military divisions, which were maintained until 2009. In that year, the divisional structure was abandoned and, instead, 31 regional commands were created, which was a return to the organisational structure of the period immediately after the revolution. One special characteristic of the Revolutionary Guards is the creation of mission-specific HQs (*qarargah*, or QG). During the war, QG Ramazan was tasked with the military training and equipment of Kurdish and Shia Iraqi groups, and QG Baqerzade with pursuing People's Mujahedin on Iraqi territory, while QG Sarollah coordinated the security of Tehran between 1999 and 2009, QG Hamza coordinated the suppression of the Kurdistan Free Life Party (PJAK), a Kurdistan Workers Party (PKK) offshoot, and so on. Two units were especially important for the developing relationship with Iraq: Badr and Quds.

The Badr unit in Iraq

The Badr Brigade (*faylaq/sepah-e Badr*) was created as a Shia militia for Iraqi prisoners of war. From 1982 to 2011 it served as the military arm of the Supreme Council for the Islamic Revolution in Iraq (SCIRI). But in contrast to SCIRI, and despite their Iraqi nationality, Badr members were part of the IRGC.[75] During the Iran–Iraq War, Badr was commanded by Iranian officers; Iranian-trained officers of Iraqi descent were only entrusted with command functions after the war. One of them was Hadi al-Amiri, the current commander. In 2003, after the fall of Saddam Hussein, SCIRI and Badr returned to Iraq and soon joined the government. Following his return, Amiri transformed the Badr Brigade into the Badr Organisation (*Munzammat Badr*) for reconstruction. Aside from American pressure, one of the reasons for the change was a fatwa issued by Grand Ayatollah Sistani forbidding the creation of militias. Badr members soon applied for positions in the Iraqi security establishment, and Amiri began his political career; inter alia, he served for four years as minister for transport. Amiri was active on three levels: in active politics, both in parliament and in the ministry, where he gained valuable experience in administration; in reconstruction; and in the security services. Tehran thus not only managed to get elements friendly to Iran into important positions in Baghdad, which in itself must be regarded as a success, but also to insert an element into the Iraqi security establishment which was a part of the chain of command of the Revolutionary Guard, and whose command echelon is familiar with Iranian security interests and the responsible commanders in the Iranian security community.

It is not clear whether the Badr returned to Iraq with weapons, and if so, with how many. From the available open sources, it is also not possible to judge whether and how Badr members retained their military skills, or in what form they took part in combat operations during the civil war. What is clear, however, is that in summer 2014, and faced with a possible ISIS breakthrough to Baghdad, when Sistani issued his now famous fatwa on self-defence,[76] Badr was already playing a central role in the creation of the Popular Mobilisation Units (*Hashd al-Shaabi*). Since then, Badr has participated in a number of important battles as a part of these forces (the last instance being in Mosul). The ultimate legal status and organisational design of the *Hashd al-Shaabi*, of which also some Sunni units are a part, has not yet been decided. It must, however, be assumed that Amiri and other Badr commanders will have a say.

The Quds Force and army special forces

In contrast to Badr, the Quds Force[77] is a central element of Iranian power projection. Quds was founded at the beginning of the Iran–Iraq War at the instigation of commander Mohsen Rezai. Its first commander was today's Head of the Revolutionary Guards, Major-General Mohammad Ali Jaafari. It was originally planned as a kind of commando unit, to carry out acts of sabotage behind enemy lines, or to be used for critical reconnaissance. This explains the high percentage of Arabic-speaking and culturally aware members involved from an early stage. Quds had obviously recognised the importance of the 'strategic corporal' – that is, a non-commissioned officer who can communicate with the population in the area of operations, a function the US only introduced later via its Human Terrain System.[78] Later, Quds was also employed in Lebanon, Syria and, apparently, in Afghanistan. In 1989, after the war, Khamenei defined Quds' mission more precisely: it is primarily an ideological unit whose task it is to create indigenous revolutionary cells (*hezbollahi*) and to train them ideologically and militarily, and thus contribute to the Islamic Revolution as defined by Khomeini.[79]

Until Saddam Hussein's fall, Quds was mainly active in Lebanon, in close coordination with Hizbullah and its military wing under Imad Mughniya, who was assassinated in 2008. The US and Israel have also accused Quds of international attacks outside the Middle East, although its main area of operations clearly remains the Middle East. In 2009, Quds, up to then a special-forces unit within the land forces of the Revolutionary Guard, was made a service in its own right (*niru-ye Qods*).[80] Soon after, it won fame in Iraq and Syria under the command of Major-General Qasem Soleimani. Given the primacy of politics, Soleimani became indispensable in Iraqi intra-Shi'ite politics. He also coordinated Iran's military support for the Iraqis and for the Syrian government, whose survival has become Tehran's declared goal. In Syria, losses must have been especially heavy. Many of the first Iranian volunteers to arrive in Syria were members of the war generation and belonged to the IRGC. (After suffering heavy losses, Iranian volunteers in Syria serve in the ranks of the Basij Fatehin unit or in the IRGC's Saberin special-forces unit.[81]) At about the same time, Iraqi Shi'ites followed. As time went on, Tehran began to focus its recruitment drive on Afghan Shi'ites and deployed them too to the Syrian theatre of war.[82] Arab Shi'ites were organised into the Abu Fadhl al-Abbas brigade, Afghans in the Fatemiyun brigade and Pakistanis in the Zeynabiyya brigade; all these nominal brigades are coordinated by the Quds Force. A detailed analysis and assessment of the various militias and the role of Quds still remains to be done.[83] It should be noted, however, that permanent military and political pressure has almost exhausted Quds' resources. It is thus not surprising that almost concurrently with the change in the political discourse – that is to say, turning away from Khomeinism and towards a nationalist justification of the operations in Syria – other military units from Iran appeared on the battlefield: namely, the *takavoran* (commando units of the regular army), in this case the 65th Airborne Brigade, which had fought in the war in Oman in the 1970s.[84]

* * *

The situation has thus come full circle: the Islamic Republic of Iran, which began its operations in Iraq and Syria with ideologically drilled special-forces units tasked to create Islamist militias, has had to fall back, after years of fighting, on classic army special forces trained in counter-insurgency.

Thanks to its cultural affinity and knowledge of the terrain, Iran may have fewer problems than other countries with a stake in Iraq and Syria; however, it finds itself playing a role similar to that of Western states or Russia, rather than that of an anti-Western resistance force. This role is now inseparably connected with Iran's sworn enemies: internationally operating Sunni jihadi groups such as al-Qaeda and ISIS.

Unlike those jihadi groups, the Islamic Republic of Iran will not be in a position to wage fourth-generation warfare against the West. Iran is a state with an ideology, not an ideology with fighters. The most important difference between ISIS and the Islamic Republic is that in Iran a revolutionary movement took control of a functioning state with its institutions, whereas ISIS arose from the ruins of a nation-state that had eroded in its civic functions under the brutalising rule of Saddam Hussein and was further devastated by foreign intervention.[85] Even defeated, post-ISIS jihadi groups will further destabilise the region and spread anarchy. On the international stage, Iran thus acts as a nation-state, even if Tehran itself, as well as its adversaries in the West, do not cease to stress the revolutionary nature of Iranian politics and policy. In this context, the existence of special military units, especially Quds, is used as proof of its revolutionary identity. This is countered by the need to fall back on an elite unit, in a military tradition stretching back to the US Green Berets, which has been trained in counter-insurgency.

Iran's military normalisation is therefore happening concurrently with a change in its ideological justification. For now, this shift in ideology remains part of the pragmatism described above, whilst its foreign and security policy regarding Syria remains unchanged. Yet, whatever happens to President Bashar al-Assad himself, the Syrian crisis will most likely drag on for decades to come as a triangular confrontation between Iran and Russia, the West, and ISIS and post-ISIS forces. Based on a new, almost nihilistic radicalism, these forces exercise anarchic anti-Western strategies – such as their strikes in Europe – with greater vigour and radicalism than Iran. The US is in a much better position to weather disorder created by jihadi anarchy in its present form than Europe, which is faced with direct terrorist spillover effects and an almost unsolvable refugee problem. Compared with the challenge of fourth-generation warfare, the Islamic Republic of Iran constitutes a much smaller military and conceptual challenge for Western strategists, as well as for Western strategic interests. In other words, potential jihadi anarchy – not the state of Iran – is the greater security risk for the West. This insight is not new; abhorrence of anarchy and disorder has been an American strategic principle from Truman to Reagan. As McSweeney puts it, 'the Soviet Union was a threat but it was not the primary threat. That was disorder.'[86] It is within this strategic logic that president Obama had pushed for the nuclear deal, which apart from closing Iran's nuclear file in the eyes of the international community, should also allow for broader cooperation against ISIS in all relevant theatres of war.[87]

Against this backdrop, one has to ask strategists in Tehran and Washington whether ideological hostility and mutual demonisation is worth the cost, or whether a rapprochement would better serve both their own interests and the region's. After all, Iranian military and political success in a vital theatre such as Iraq depends largely on the coordination of interests and forces with the United States. Ideological idiosyncrasies and pragmatism aside, of course, Iran's revolutionary language and anti-imperialist identity, along with America's hegemonic identity, makes normalisation of relations highly unlikely. Identity and interests are intimately related, both in defining oneself and in defining the enemy.[88] For Iran, the enemy is the United States and Israel; for the United States, it is Iran, playing the role of an ersatz Soviet Union, despite having the political and military capabilities of the former Yugoslavia. Yet identities, interests and perceptions of security derive from political choices, not objective criteria – and this means they can change.

Notes

1 On this, see Mehrdad Haghayeghi, 'Politics and Ideology in the Islamic Republic of Iran', *Middle Eastern Studies,* vol. 29, no. 1, 1993, pp. 36–52.

2 Arthur Schweitzer approaches the topic using National Socialism and Communism as examples, but does not address the nexus between ideology and military strategy explicitly. See Arthur Schweitzer, 'Ideological Strategy', *Western Political Quarterly,* vol. 15, no. 1, 1962, pp. 46–66. For an explicit treatment of the topic, see Eric Carlton, *War and Ideology* (Washington DC: Barnes and Noble Books, 1990), and especially his introduction to the topic, pp. 18–28. For an excellent analysis of modern ide-

ologies, both political and religious, see Fred Halliday, *The Middle East in International Relations: Power, Politics and Ideology* (Cambridge: Cambridge University Press, 2005), pp. 193–228.

3 Kathleen Knight, 'Transformation of the Concept of *Ideology* in the Twentieth Century', *American Political Science Review*, vol. 100, no. 4, 2006, pp. 619–26.

4 Niklas Luhmann, 'Wahrheit und Ideologie', in Niklas Luhmann, *Soziologische Aufklärung 1. Aufsätze zur Theorie sozialer Systeme* (Opladen: Westdeutscher Verlag), 1970, pp. 54–65.

5 Terry Eagleton, *Ideology: An Introduction*, second extended edition (London: Verso, 2007).

6 Alan Cassels, *Ideology and International Relations in the Modern World* (Abingdon: Routledge, 1996).

7 Francis Fukuyama, *The End of History and the Last Man* (New York: Free Press, 1992).

8 See Samuel T. Huntington, 'The Clash of Civilisations', *Foreign Affairs*, Summer 1993; and Samuel T. Huntington, *The Clash of Civilizations and the Remaking of World Order* (New York: Simon & Schuster, 1996).

9 Robert D. Kaplan, *The Revenge of Geography: What the Map Tells Us About Coming Conflicts and the Battle Against Fate* (London and New York: Random House, 2013).

10 Bill McSweeney, *Security, Identity and Interests: A Sociology of International Relations* (Cambridge: Cambridge University Press, 1999), p. 188.

11 See Peter Rudolf, 'Rückkehr des liberalen Hegemon. Warnungen vor Überdehnung und Isolationismus sind unangebracht', *Internationale Politik*, January 2006, pp. 6–15; and Jens van Scherpenberg, *Pax Americana als globales öffentliches Gut*, SWP discussion paper, Berlin, 2003. Americans are less cautious about their country's 'imperial' role in the world; see Jackson Lears, 'How the US Began Its Empire', *New York Review of Books*, 23 February 2017, pp. 37–40. The most elaborate study on US imperialism to date is Kees van der Pijl, *The Discipline of Western Supremacy*, vol. III, (London: Pluto Press, 2014).

12 See Robert Cooper, *The Breaking of Nations: Order and Chaos in the Twenty-First Centrury*, paperback edition (London: Grove Press, 2004), pp. 160–72.

13 Joseph S. Nye, *Soft Power: The Means to Success in World Politics* (New York: PublicAffairs, 2004).

14 John J. Mearsheimer, 'Benign Hegemony', *International Studies Review*, vol. 18, no. 1, March 2016, pp. 147–9.

15 For a political history of the Third World, see Vijay Prashad, *The Darker Nations: A People's History of the Third World* (London and New York: Free Press, 2007). See also Christian Caryl, *Strange Rebels: 1979 and the Birth of the XXIst Century* (New York: Basic Books, 2013).

16 For a typical example, see William Easterley, *The White Man's Burden: Why the West's Efforts to Aid the Rest Have Done So Much Ill and So Little Good* (Oxford: Oxford University Press, 2006).

17 William S. Lind, 'What is Cultural Marxism?', http://www.marylandthursdaymeeting.com/Archives/

SpecialWebDocuments/Cultural. Marxism.htm. For the current public debate about neo-Marxism in the US, see Samuel Freeman, 'The Headquarters of Neo-Marxism', *New York Review of Books,* 23 March 2017, pp. 63–5.

18 Lawrence Freedman, *Strategy: A History* (Oxford: Oxford University Press, 2013), p. 226.

19 Arthur S. Bloom, 'William S. Lind's Way of War: Meet the Field Marshal of Military Reform and Cultural Conservativism', *American Conservative,* 17 October 2016. Lind is also an important contributor to Breitbart, whose executive chairman, Stephen K. Bannon, was White House chief strategist.

20 McSweeney, *Security, Identity and Interests*, pp. 121f.

21 Freedman, *Strategy*, pp. 218, 219. See also the remarks on the OODA loop and strategic paralysis in Hervé Coutau-Bégarie, *Traité de Stratégie*, fifth extended edition (Paris: Economica, 2006), pp 655–62. The debate on John Boyd and the OODA loop continues. Boyd, an air-force officer, had a negative attitude towards ideologies and strategic schools. Too much had changed since Clausewitz, and even more since the days of Sun Tzu. See Frans Osinga, *Science, Strategy and War: The Strategic Theory of John Boyd*, dissertation, Delft, 2005.

22 Freedman, *Strategy*, p. 221.

23 William S. Lind et al., 'The Changing Face of War: Into the Fourth Generation', *Marine Corps Gazette*, October 1989, pp. 22–6.

24 Antulio J. Echevarria II, *Fourth Generation War and Other Myths*, Strategic Studies Institute, June 2008, http://ssi.armywarcollege.edu/pdffiles/pub632.pdf.

25 Ironically, the difference between Lind and Echevarria seems to be ideological; the latter apparently concedes some understanding, perhaps even legitimacy, to 'revolutionary movements', whereas Lind rejects them outright for ideological reasons.

26 Eric Schmitt and Tom Shankar, 'U.S. Officials Retool Slogan for Terror War', *New York Times,* 26 July 2005.

27 Carlton, *War and Ideology*, p. 30.

28 Huntington, *Clash of Civilizations*, p. 51.

29 Frantz Fanon, *Die Verdammten dieser Erde* (Munich: Suhrkamp Taschenbuch, 1969), translated from the French (Paris, 1961).

30 Fanon's justification and systematisation of political violence and the revolutionary subject he postulated fascinated European intellectuals and made them 'politically aware', sometimes leading to terrorism. See Sabine Kebir, 'Revolutionäre Subjekte bei Frantz Fanon', *Politik und Zeitgeschichte*, 14–15/2008; and Butz Peters, *Tödlicher Irrtum. Die Geschichte der RAF* (Frankfurt am Main: Fischer Verlag, 2007).

31 Cassels, *Ideology*, pp. 227–39; Halliday, *The Middle East,* pp. 197 and 213–28.

32 Sir Robert Francis Cooper is a British diplomat and public intellectual who served from 2002–10 as Director-General for External and Politico-Military Affairs at the General Secretariat of the Council of the European Union. He developed his thesis of the 'post-modern state' as early as 2000. See Robert Cooper, *The*

Post-Modern State and the World Order (London: Demos, 2004), available at https://www.demos.co.uk/files/post-modernstate.pdf.

33 Nye, *Soft Power*, pp. 35–43.

34 Arnaud de La Grange and Jean-Marc Balencie, *Les Guerres Bâtardes: Comment l'Occident perd les baitailles du XXIe siècle* (Paris: Perrin, 2008).

35 Abu Musab al-Suri (born Mustafa Setmaryam Nasar) figures prominently in Ahmed Rashid, 'Seeing the Despair of Jihad', *New York Review of Books*, 24 November 2016, pp. 51f.

36 La Grange and Balencie, *Guerres Bâtardes*, pp. 31–7.

37 Gilles Kepel, *Terreur dans l'Hexagone: Genèse du djihad français* (Paris: Gallimard, 2015), pp. 49–51, 156.

38 See Max Boot, *Invisible Armies: An Epic History of Guerrilla Warfare from Ancient Times to the Present* (New York: Liveright, 2013), pp. 547ff.

39 Anonymous [Michael Scheuer], *Imperial Hubris: Why the West is Losing the War on Terror* (Lincoln, NE: Potomac Books, 2005).

40 'Counterinsurgency', FM 3-24, June 2006, https://fas.org/irp/doddir/army/fm3-24fd.pdf. The doctrine directly refers to Galula in the preface; for an analysis of this tradition, see Cahier de la recherche doctrinale (ed.), *From Galula to Petraeus. The French Legacy in the US Counterinsurgency Doctrine*, Paris 2010. In the revised version of the field manual in force now, no mention is made of Galula or Petraeus. See 'Insurgencies and Countering Insurgencies', FM 3-24, MCWP 3-33.5, May 2014, https://fas.org/irp/doddir/army/fm3-24.pdf. See also Fred Kaplan, 'The End of the Age of Petraeus', *Foreign Affairs*, vol. 92, no. 1, January/February 2013, pp. 75–90; and Dirk Freudenberg, 'Aufstandsbekämpfung im Lichte des bevölkerungszentrierten Ansatz', *Zeitschrift für Außen- und Sicherheitspolitik*, 9/2016, pp. 477–88.

41 See http://www.indianstrategicknowledgeonline.com/web/baylis3e_ch09.pdf.

42 See Basma Salama, *The Resilience of the Islamic State*, Publications of the Austrian National Defence Academy, May 2016, pp. 82–91; and Guido Steinberg, *Kalifat des Schreckens: IS und die Bedrohung durch den islamistischen Terror* (München: Droemer und Knaur, 2015).

43 Fred Halliday, 'Iran's Regional and Strategic Interests', in Walter Posch (ed.), *Iranian Challenges*, Chaillot paper no. 89, Paris, 2006, p. 59.

44 This analysis relies on the author's own studies based on original documents used in Walter Posch, T'he Third World, Global Islam and Pragmatism: The Making of Iranian Foreign Policy', SWP Research Paper no. 3, Berlin, 2013, https://www.swp-berlin.org/fileadmin/contents/products/research_papers/2013_RP03_poc.pdf.

45 See Luhmann, 'Wahrheit und Ideologie', p. 62; and Knight, 'Transformation of the Concept of Ideology in the Twentieth Century', p. 619, and the sources quoted there.

46 For a representative, but by no means comprehensive, sample of Iranian writing on soft power, see Ebrahim Hajiyâni and Hamed Iranshahi (eds), *Dar-amadi bar diplomasi-ye farhangi-ye Jomhuriye- Eslami-ye Iran* [Introduction

to the cultural diplomacy of the Islamic Republic of Iran] (Tehran, 1393/2014); and Ja'far Haqq-Panah, Simin Shirazi-Mougui and Shiva Alizadeh, *Qodrat-e Narm-e Iran dar Asya-ye markazi va Qafqaz* [Iranian soft power in Central Asia and the Caucasus] (Tehran, 1393/2014). For a general overview on Iranian soft power, see Ruholamin Sa'idi, *Diplomâsiy-e omumi-ye Jomhuri-ye Eslâmi-ye Irân: motâle'eh-ye mouredi-ye Lobnân* (Tehran, 1393/2014), pp. 161–80.

47 Walter Posch, 'Fellow Aryans and Muslim Brothers: Iranian Narratives on the Kurds', in Gareth Stansfield and Mohammed Sharif (eds), *The Kurdish Question Revisited* (London: C. Hurst & Co., 2017), p. 345.

48 Ali Ja'afari, *NATO dar Khâvarmiyâne va Khalij-e Fârs, manâfe' va amniyat-e melli-ye Irân* (Teheran, 1393/2013), pp. 208–9.

49 Asghar Eftekhari and Alireza Qodratabadi, 'Naqsh-e sazemanha-ye ettelaati dar ta'min-e amniyat-e narm' [The role of intelligence services in securing soft security], in *Faslname-ye Pazhuheshha-ye hefazati-amniyati* [Journal for security and intelligence research of the Imam Hosein University], vol. 5, no. 17, Spring 1395/ Spring 2016, pp. 23–40. The Imam Hossein University is the IRGC's university.

50 This situation is comparable to the ideological context of the creation of the Waffen-SS. See Schweitzer, 'Ideological Strategy', p. 55, a point largely overlooked by Moises Graduno Garcia, in 'Le modèle des Pasdaran-Artesh: préoccupations internes et défis externs dans le cadre du printemps arabe', in Jean-François Daguzan and Stéphane Valter (eds), *Les forces Armées arabes et moyen orientales après les printepmps arabes* (Paris: Editions Eska, 2014), pp. 273–98.

51 Halliday, *The Middle East*, pp. 210–11.

52 The following is derived from Posch, 'Third World', pp. 14–17.

53 A critical analysis of this programme is offered by Jahangir Amuzegar, 'Iran's 20-Year Economic Perspective: Promises and Pitfalls', in *Middle East Policy*, vol. 16, no. 3, 2009, pp. 41–57. The original document quoted in Posch, 'Third World', p. 20, footnote 72 is no longer available on the internet.

54 Iran's Central Asian and Afghanistan strategy should be analysed from this perspective. See Posch, *Third World*, pp. 19–21 and the sources quoted there.

55 Posch, *Third World*, pp. 22–4.

56 See Bernard Hourcade, *Géopolitique de l'Iran* (Paris: Armand Colin, 2010), pp. 125–34.

57 On this term, see Posch, 'Third World', pp. 17–18 and the sources quoted there.

58 See the important chapter on power and ideology in Schweitzer, 'Ideological Strategy', pp. 49–54.

59 It is worth comparing Khamenei's role with leadership principles in Nazi Germany, or the party line and personality cult in Stalin's Soviet Union. *Ibid.*, p. 53.

60 Posch, 'Third World', pp. 10–11.

61 This does not mean that Iranian foreign and security policy is formulated by the clergy, but the latter defines the ideological frame. On the consultation process, see Posch, 'Third World',

pp. 7–13 and Mehran Kamrava, 'Iranian National-Security Debates: Factionalism and Lost Opportunities', *Middle East Policy*, vol. 14, no. 2, 2007, pp. 84–100.

62 Much has been written on this episode. See, for instance, Trita Parsi, *Treacherous Alliance: The Secret Dealings of Israel, Iran and the U.S.* (New Haven, CT: Yale University Press, 2007), pp. 114–21; and Ronen Bergman, *The Secret War with Iran: The 30-Year Covert Struggle for Control of a Rogue State* (London: OneWorld, 2008), pp. 118–20 and 125–30. For the Iranian side of the Iran–Contra affair, see Ulrich von Schwerin, 'Mehdi Hashemi and the Iran-Contra-Affair', *British Journal of Middle Eastern Studies*, vol. 42, no. 4, 2015, pp. 520–37; on Iranian–Israeli oil deals from the revolution to the mid-1990s, see Daniel Ammann, *The King of Oil: The Secret Lives of Marc Rich* (New York: St Martin's Press, 2009), pp. 92–104.

63 William A. Samii, 'The Security Relationship Between Lebanon and Pre-revolutionary Iran', in Houchang Chehabi (ed.), *Distant Relations: Iran and Lebanon in the Last 500 Years* (London: I.B. Tauris, 2006), pp. 162–80.

64 For one example of many, the former commander of the Revolutionary Guard, see Majid Najafi (ed.), *From South Lebanon to Southern Iran: Memoirs of Commander Seyyed Rahim Safavi* [Persian] (Teheran, 1383/2004).

65 Jubin Goodarzi, *Syria and Iran: Diplomatic Alliance and Power Politics in the Middle East*, (London: I.B. Tauris, 2006).

66 Posch, 'Third World', pp. 27–8.

67 For a good analysis of this term see David Pollock, *The Arab Street: Public Opinion in the Arab World*, WINEP Policy Paper no. 32, 1992, http://www.washingtoninstitute.org/uploads/Documents/pubs/PP_32_TheArabStreet.pdf.

68 See Farzad Cyrus Sharifi-Yazdi, *Arab–Iranian Rivalry in the Persian Gulf: Territorial Disputes and the Balance of Power in the Middle East* (London: I.B. Tauris, 2015); Michael P. Colaresi, Karen Rasler and William R. Thomason, *Strategic Rivalries in World Politics: Position, Space and Conflict Escalation* (Cambridge: Cambridge University Press, 2007), pp. 14, 92, 106, 199; and Abdolrezâ Hushang Mahdavi, *Iranian Foreign Policy in the Time of Pahlavi (1922–1979)* [Persian] (Tehran, 1386/2008).

69 Laurence Louer, *Chiisme et politique au Moyen-Orient, Iran, Irak, Liban, Monarchies du Golfe* (Paris: Editions Autrement, 2008). For a good analysis of Arab Shia, see Graham Fuller and Rend Rahim Francke, *The Arab Shi'a: The Forgotten Muslims* (New York: Palgrave Macmillan, 1999).

70 This was predicted in, for example, Vali Nasr, *The Shia Revival: How Conflicts Within Islam Will Shape the Future* (New York: W.W. Norton, 2006).

71 Marti Chulov, 'Iran Repopulates Syria With Shia Muslims to Help Tighten the Regime's Control', *Guardian*, 14 January 2017.

72 It should be noted in this context that the regular army is only used for national defence and border protection, and that Iran lacks deep-water ports, so that until recently even container ships destined for Iran had

to be moored in the UAE. See Meir Javedanfar, 'Iran's Weakness? Its Ports', *Diplomat*, 9 July 2010.

73 Ashkbus Danekar, 'Special Operations in the Persian Gulf', Persian Gulf Study Centre, Tehran, 1367/1989, pp. 267–84. On the numerous confrontations between the Navy of the Revolutionary Guard and the US Fifth Fleet, see Walter Posch, 'Provoking an Agreement? The Hormuz Incident Revisited', in Harald Haas, Franz Kernic and Andrea Plaschke (eds), *Leadership in Challenging Situations* (New York: Peter Lang, 2012), pp. 267–75. See also Sascha Albrecht and Walter Posch, 'Sabre-Rattling in the Persian Gulf: Legal and Military Aspects of the Ideological Confrontation Between Iran and the United States', *SWP Comments*, no. 4, Berlin, April 2012, https://www.swp-berlin.org/fileadmin/contents/products/comments/2012C14_alr_poc.pdf.

74 On the Iranian security establishment, see Walter Posch, 'Der iranische Sicherheitsapparat', in *Handbuch der Iranistik* (Hamburg, 2017, forthcoming); and Hourcade, *Géopolitique de l'Iran* , pp. 102–9.

75 Faleh A. Jaber, *The Shiite Movement in Iraq* (London: Saqi Books, 2003), p. 153.

76 Rachel Kantz Feder, 'A Call to Arms: What Lies Beneath Sistani's Potent Fatwa', Open Democracy, 10 July 2014.

77 On Quds, see Walter Posch, 'Politische Gewalt in der Islamischen Republik Iran', in Jasmina Rupp (ed.), *Der (Alb) Traum vom Kalifat* (Vienna: Böhlau Wien, 2016), pp. 211–36.

78 De La Grange and Balencie, *Les Guerres Bâtardes*, pp. 50–6.

79 He did so at the occasion of the staff course at Emam Hossein University on 20 November 1989; for the speech, see http://farsi.khamenei.ir/speech-content?id=11062.

80 The Revolutionary Guard is formed of five services (*niru-ye panjgane*): air, sea, land, Quds and Basiji.

81 'The Zaynabiyun, Fatemiyun and Fatehin Have Destroyed the Balance' [Persian], Mashreqnews, 18 Azar 1395/8 December 2016.

82 On Afghan Shia Hazaras fighting in Syria on behalf of Iran, see Christoph Reuter, 'Der Krieg der anderen', *Der Spiegel*, 9 May 2015.

83 For a preliminary study on Shia militias in Iraq and Syria, see Walter Posch, 'Schiitische Milizen in Irak und in Syrien: Volksmobilsierungungseinheiten und andere', Vienna National Defense Academy, August 2017.

84 Abbas Qaidaari, 'Who Sent Iranian Green Berets to Syria?', *Al-Monitor*, 28 April 2016.

85 The erosion of state institutions, sectarianisation and ethnification as well as the impoverishment of the Iraqi population under Saddam Hussein have been known to scholars such as Pierre-Jean Luizard, *La question irakienne* (Paris: Fayard, 2004), pp. 166–72, 352–4.

86 McSweeney, *Security, Identity and Interests*, p. 120.

87 Adam Chandler, 'The President's Pen Pal in Tehran', *Atlantic*, 6 November 2014.

88 McSweeney, *Security, Identity and Interests*, pp. 215–19.

Donald Trump's Status-Driven Foreign Policy

Reinhard Wolf

Ever since Donald Trump won the US presidential election, governments and pundits all over the world have been agonising about the direction American foreign policy will take under his watch. Is he a traditional 'America First' isolationist who fears 'entangling alliances' and therefore wants to soften commitments to Europe and East Asia? Is he bent on a clash of civilisations with the Muslim world? Does he want to team up with Russia in order to contain China's rise? Or is he, above all, a mercantilist who sees trade restrictions as the only way to improve the lot of the American working class?

In fact, the new president lacks any clear sense of direction concerning the substantive goals of American foreign policy. Trump has no *Weltanschauung*. He has never subscribed to a consistent ideology and has rarely committed to a doctrinaire party line. He has changed his party registration at least five times since registering as a Republican in New York in 1987.[1] It is no surprise that pundits are at a loss in looking for a coherent international programme, let alone a grand strategy which would systematically match means and ends.[2]

Instead, the key to understanding Trump's foreign-policy outlook lies in his extreme attention to symbolism. Questions of substance are eclipsed by an obsession with status and respect. His well-known fixation with personal prestige also shapes his view of America's place in the world. His life-long desire to look like a 'winner' who enjoys the respect of his peers

Reinhard Wolf is Professor of Political Science at Goethe University, Frankfurt am Main, Germany.

Survival | vol. 59 no. 5 | October–November 2017 | pp. 99–116 DOI 10.1080/00396338.2017.1375260

has always figured prominently in Trump's take on American external relations. It is a constant theme, illustrated with changing examples of alleged US mistreatment. It is the one feature common to both his earliest statements on American foreign policy and his most recent speeches. To this day, he abhors supposed national humiliations and the idea that foreigners might be 'laughing at us' as a result of America's 'stupid deals'. In his view, making America great again should always have been the ultimate goal of US policymakers. So, for Trump, America First is not so much about advancing the national interest measured in terms of material wealth or physical survival. It is, first and foremost, about the United States becoming the undisputed 'number one' again, and being treated with due respect. Trump is, in fact, deeply worried about global order. Yet his concerns are greatly at odds with those of the liberal internationalists.

Trump's international outlook bears some unsettling parallels with the domestic grievances voiced by the white supremacists whom the former propagator of 'birtherism' is so reluctant to criticise, as well as with a broader population of white Americans whose support for the president appears linked to their anxieties about deteriorating racial status. Similarly, Trump himself strongly resents what he perceives as an ongoing demotion of his country. In his eyes, global history has been moving in the wrong direction for quite some time: foreigners have been taking advantage of the United States, while America's cosmopolitan elites have been too weak to defend their nation's rightful position – with potentially fatal consequences for the country's long-term prospects. As he told *Playboy* in 1990: 'Our country is right now perceived as weak ... as being spit on by the rest of the world ... Weakness always causes problems ... If this country gets any kinder or gentler, it's literally going to cease to exist.'[3] The United States needs Trump's personal toughness if the clock is to be turned back. Restoring the natural international hierarchy is Trump's ultimate mission.

A personal fixation

By way of definition, respect is an attitude that conveys recognition of an actor's social status. Consequently, actors experience insufficient status recognition as disrespect.[4] An actor's status depends on its standing in two hierarchies. In the hierarchy of prestige, actors gain or lose status to the extent they possess widely valued attributes (such as wealth, beauty and power), glory (due to great deeds and accomplishments) and honour (based on their compliance with a code of conduct encompassing cultural notions of actors' integrity). Perhaps more importantly, actors also attain status through advancing in the hierarchy of deference which is based on bilateral or multilateral patterns of deference between dominant and subordinate actors (leaders vs followers, patrons vs clients).

Trump's preoccupation with his personal standing in social hierarchies need only be briefly summarised because it has already been covered elsewhere. Even before his entry into politics, Trump stimulated a degree of interest in his personal character like few other presidents, and this has only increased since the election.[5]

By almost all accounts, Trump is a narcissist who has long wanted to be a celebrity.[6] Since his high-school days, when his performance in baseball earned him a favourable mention in a local newspaper, Trump has been obsessed with publicity. Even as an ostensibly busy entrepreneur, he used to begin his morning routine with a scan of his personal media coverage.[7] He has always been especially keen on reports of his accomplishments as a builder, as well as on his private fortune. Trump's countless attacks on journalists and biographers who have supposedly lowballed his wealth and achievements attest to the enormous importance he accords to a good reputation. This includes repeated phone calls to journalists, usually under the aliases of 'John Barron' and 'John Miller', to talk himself up.[8] Further proof lies in his endless self-promotion in interviews and his own (or his ghostwritten) publications. And, as Michael Barbaro notes, accompanying his preoccupation with personal status in American society, Trump has developed a 'deep-seated fear of public embarrassment'.[9]

The roots of this fixation can probably be traced to Trump's hyper-competitive worldview. Beginning in childhood, when his entrepreneur father Fred urged him to become a 'winner' and a 'killer', Trump has divided society into winners and losers – a Darwinian world where success breeds success, and losers fall to the wayside.[10] According to Trump, one either has the winner's instinct, or is doomed to recurrent failure.[11] Not surprisingly,

Trump insists – even in background interviews – that he himself has always been a winner.[12]

Toughness with rivals and opponents is the key to advancing in such a world. Accommodation paves the road to failure because it shows a lack of resolve: 'If you take the first step backward, you might as well just keep going. To put it in another way: If you can accept losing, then you have already lost.'[13] By his own account, Trump told his future lawyer, former Joseph McCarthy aide Roy Cohn, at their first meeting: 'I'd rather fight than fold, because as soon as you fold once, you get the reputation of being a folder.'[14] Forceful retaliation and swift counter-attacks are key elements of this approach: 'When a person screws you, screw them back fifteen times harder.'[15] Trump and Cohn became notorious for their habit of responding to lawsuits by upping the ante, suing their opponents for even greater sums.[16] The same retaliatory pattern characterises Trump's attitude to perceived slights – for instance, his Twitter wars with Cher and Bette Midler, or his public spat with Meryl Streep, 'one of the most over-rated actresses in Hollywood'. Tellingly, Trump's verbal counter-attacks are regularly aimed at tarnishing his opponent's public prestige.[17]

This, according to Trump, is how one wins respect. 'My father was one tough son-of-a-gun', he once told an interviewer. 'My father respects me because I stood up to him.'[18] The alternative is to take a subordinate position in a hierarchy of deference: 'You just can't let people make a sucker out of you.'[19] Even in his school years, Trump reportedly went to great lengths to prove his mettle.[20] He apparently believes this trait distinguishes people like him from most other people: '[for] the most part, you can't respect people because most people aren't worthy of respect'.[21]

Trump worries about the position he occupies in the hierarchy of prestige. Time and again, he has shown himself to be extremely concerned about his public image, and has made a great effort to correct what he sees as inadequate accounts of his successes. This is only reinforced by the need to boost the Trump brand, which has become vital to his business success.[22] In one of his books, he explicitly advises his readers against personal modesty: personal achievements need to be publicly advertised.[23] Trump has always chased press coverage for his supposed accomplishments in business – and with women. He is obsessed with numbers, which he interprets as evidence of his achievements.[24] Recent examples include his angry reaction to coverage of the relatively paltry turnout at his inauguration, as well as his false claim that he had defeated Hillary Clinton not just in the electoral college, but also in terms of the popular vote. Earlier indications of this trait can be seen in his fixation with the viewing figures for *The Apprentice*, and, even more so, in his notorious arguments over his net worth. While it may be an exaggeration to say he is interested in money primarily as a 'way to keep score',[25] he clearly values money not just for its own sake, but as a mark of his public standing. Unusually for a supposed member of the super-rich class, Trump has repeatedly contacted the editors of *Forbes* magazine to argue that he is actually far wealthier than they would have their readers believe.[26] He has sued journalists whom he accuses of underreporting his true wealth.[27] These disputes apparently lie at the bottom of his long-standing ire at the 'tremendous dishonesty, tremendous dishonesty, in the press'.[28]

Foreign relations: 'Number one, they have to respect you'

More than anything else, this personal obsession with winning and gaining respect has shaped Trump's thinking on foreign policy. In essence, he is applying his personal dispositions and goals to the collective persona of the United States. He seems personally embarrassed by America's fading prestige, and annoyed by what he sees as insufficient recognition of its place in the world. This is not only to be inferred from what is known about his personal character; it is the most reliable theme in his foreign-policy statements, consistent over time and before differing audiences. In speeches and background interviews, in his books and on television – throughout his life in the public eye, Trump has complained about the supposed erosion of America's status. There is every reason to assume that Trump's anger about foreign disrespect is not just political rhetoric, but truly reflects his basic ideas and feelings.

Long before he started to complain about immigration, international terrorism and the loss of industrial jobs to foreign competitors, Trump was voicing his frustration with America's loss of status. As early as 1980, when he gave his first TV interview to a national audience, Trump saw disregard for America as the country's key foreign-policy problem. The country needed 'proper leadership' in order 'to become what it once was'. When asked to explain what exactly the United States should become again, Trump responded that 'it should really be a country that gets the respect of other countries'.[29] As he told interviewer Rona Barrett, 'I just don't feel the country is going forward in the proper direction … We just sit back and take everybody's abuse.'[30] He saw evidence for this claim in the United States' shrunken influence in the Gulf:

> I think this country is responsible for that war by its own weaknesses. I don't think you'd have this [Iran–Iraq] war if they – again using the other word, if we were respected, properly respected as a country and as a people, and as a nation. I don't think that you would have the war going on right now between Iran and Iraq. I don't think that Iran would have our hostages for 10 minutes if they respected this country.[31]

The same idea – that America was no longer 'great', and was certainly not being treated with the respect a great country deserves – motivated Trump's first personal statement of his political views to a national audience. In 1987, he placed a full-page ad in the *New York Times*, framed as a letter 'To The American People'. Under the caption 'There's nothing wrong with America's Foreign Defense Policy that a little backbone can't cure', Trump aired a complaint that would sound familiar to current leaders in Tokyo, Paris and Berlin: US allies, specifically Japan and Saudi Arabia, were 'taking advantage of the United States' by failing to pay their fair share for their protection. This was all the more scandalous when America's 'vast' trade deficits with these allies were taken into account. The world was 'laughing at America's politicians' who tolerated the exploitative relationship. Fittingly, Trump concluded the letter with an appeal to his compatriots not to allow 'our great country to be laughed at anymore'.[32] The letter fails to address the social consequences of the 'vast deficits' which figure so prominently in his more recent statements – that is to say, it does not mention possible impacts on industrial jobs and wages, but only suggests that Saudi and Japanese reimbursements should be used to 'help our farmers, our sick, our homeless'.

The same theme is present in Trump's most recent statements. As he put it in a 2016 interview with *Washington Post* journalists Bob Woodward and Robert Costa, 'there is a tremendous lack of respect for our country. And I think for our leader.'[33] He continued:

> Yeah, I don't want people to be afraid. I want them to respect our country. Right now, they don't respect our country ... People have respected me. My life has been a life where I've been respected. I want them to respect our country. I want them to respect our leader. But I want them to respect our country.[34]

Similarly, when asked in a Republican primary debate about his ideas for getting Russian forces out of Syria, Trump restated his conviction that reasserting the status of America and its leaders would be essential for reaching any equitable understanding: 'So, number one, they have to respect you. He [Vladimir Putin] has absolutely no respect for President Obama. Zero.'[35]

In line with the logic of his views about business, Trump believes America's problem is its lack of victories: 'respect is about winning. We don't win anymore.'[36] Trump has made this grim assertion in numerous statements and publications;[37] in fact, it is the very theme with which he began the speech that launched his candidacy: 'Our country is in serious trouble. We don't have victories anymore. We used to have victories, but we don't have them.'[38] Trump sees the US as a country enduring constant defeat. It suffered 'tons of humiliations' during the Obama administration,[39] is 'pushed around, used by other countries',[40] is losing ground to its enemies,[41] and is constantly 'getting beaten in trade agreements'.[42]

To substantiate these claims, Trump has a litany of alleged reverses: the US has rolled over to China, enabling it to potentially become the world's largest economy,[43] has been taken advantage of by a disrespectful China in the South China Sea,[44] has concluded an embarrassing trade deal with South Korea,[45] has been beaten economically by Japan and Mexico,[46] has been disrespected by Pakistan,[47] has been humiliated by Iran's capture of US sailors,[48] has been blatantly ignored by Putin and the warring factions in Syria,[49] and, again and again, has been taken advantage of by free-riding allies which do not treat the US with respect.[50]

What makes all these defeats even more shameful in Trump's eyes is the fact that they easily could have been avoided, and thus seem partly self-inflicted. In many instances, Washington supposedly held the best cards, yet US officials failed to defend America's status.[51] It was beaten only because its 'globalist' leaders, particularly Barack Obama, were lacking in toughness and competence. America, Trump asserts, could only be 'taken to the cleaners' and 'ripped off' by China and other nations because its leaders showed weak resolve or acted stupidly.[52] This inadequacy in negotiations, candidate Trump contended – just as he had done in his 1987 *New York Times* ad – prevents others from taking America seriously. Foreign nations and their leaders are laughing at the way the US government handles its external affairs.[53] All this, according to Trump, has led to a situation in which US citizens can no longer be proud of their nation: 'We've become an embarrassment to ourselves and to our history.'[54] As he told Woodward and Costa, 'more than anything else, the stupidity of the trade deals we have with China, with Japan, with Mexico' made him angry and kindled his interest in running for president.[55]

Arguably, Trump cares more about the symbolic effects of material issues such as infrastructure and trade than about tangible impacts on US citizens. Trump not only laments the economic losses caused by America's 'crumbling' infrastructure, he also sees it as a national embarrassment. 'Our airports? Are you kidding me? A disgrace ... I fly in from China or Qatar, and it's as if I've come from a different world.'[56] Similarly: 'You come to LaGuardia Airport, it's like a third world country',[57] and 'Our country has been allowed to languish and become a tarnished, second-class place in the eyes of the world'.[58]

Likewise, Trump sees trade, above all, as an international contest in which countries running a surplus emerge as 'winners' while the nations in deficit 'are losing' and 'get beaten'.[59] Trade statistics are his way of keeping score, just like the balance sheets of private companies.[60] A trade deficit indicates either a backward economy or, as in the case of the US, the incompetence of a country's trade negotiators and their alarming inability to make 'good deals'. By 'rolling over to China', America risks the People's Republic soon replacing it as the world's largest economy, thus compromising its position as 'number one'.[61] This focus on the symbolic meaning of bilateral trade statistics may go a long way in explaining Trump's transactional approach to foreign policy. It also sheds light on his low interest in bolstering multilateral institutions, which might prevent the US from bringing its full economic power to bear.[62]

All this leads to the inevitable conclusion that 'the brand of the United States' is no longer great. 'Sadly, the American dream is dead',[63] and something has to be done to 'make America proud again'.[64]

'They will respect us like never before'

Donald Trump has come to see himself as the person most qualified to change this state of affairs, 'someone who can truly lead America back to what has made us great in the past'.[65] To restore its pride, he asserts, 'our country needs a truly great leader … a leader who wrote *The Art of the Deal*'.[66]

While promising many initiatives to 'fix the mess' the country has supposedly got itself into, Trump rarely explains what exactly is to be understood by American greatness. He comes closest to doing so in *Great Again*, in which he equates the idea of American greatness with the United States being 'the leader of the free and unfree world'.[67] This implies that Trump does not exactly favour a retreat into isolationism; rather, he wants to restore America's role as number one in the global deference hierarchy. In his announcement speech, he presented this in materialist terms, promising to 'make our country so rich again, and therefore make it great again. Because we need money. We're dying.'[68] In a similar vein, during a primary debate, Trump vowed to 'make this country greater than ever before. We'll have more jobs. We'll have more of everything.'[69] But whatever his precise vision of American greatness may be, it is clear that Trump measures it in terms of status recognition: 'If I'm president … the world will respect us. They will respect us like never before.'[70] This helps explain the mission of America First: as long as America adheres to the credo of globalism, 'other nations will not treat America with respect'.[71]

Not surprisingly, this is to be achieved by shows of toughness and the building of a reputation for success. As he told *Playboy* in 1990, 'People need ego, whole nations need ego. I think our country needs *more* ego, because it is being ripped off so badly.'[72] A 'rougher', less accommodating stance, backed by military strength, can make America richer and respected again.[73] A more competitive approach will focus on the relative outcome of negotiations or conflicts, restore to the US the aura of a winner lost on the watch of previous administrations,[74] and 'turn bad trade agreements into great ones'.[75] This applies to both partners and opponents.[76] In particular, he has promised that he will make China 'behave properly' on trade and with regard to its support for North Korea.[77]

No doubt, Trump favours a very selfish approach to foreign policy. But the egotistical transactionalism he brings to the international arena is not just a tactic for improving America's economic well-being; Trump is not an amoral cynic, a New York Machiavelli. At the heart of his foreign-policy views lies a normative conviction. Fundamentally, Trump is – and has always been – driven by a moral grudge, his deep-seated belief that brazen upstarts have treated his country unfairly for far too long. He is wholeheartedly convinced that his nation is great, and deserves to be treated accordingly.

Implications

The implications for foreign governments are obvious: they should anticipate that the new administration will pursue policies that seek to restore what Trump perceives as America's proper status. Firstly, we will see a greater focus on the symbolic aspects of negotiations. Short-term appearances will gain in importance, while the substantial outcomes, especially long-term material consequences, will count for less.[78] Whatever the issue, Washington will try to look like a 'winner'. Secondly, and relatedly, it will become harder to strike bargains with an administration that is more committed to zero-sum thinking and toughness for toughness' sake. Concessions will be made more reluctantly, and only when they are clearly and immediately reciprocated by the other side. Washington will insist on perceptible quid pro quos and not wait for diffuse benefits that might materialise in the long run.

Finally, and most ominously, America's rivals and possible opponents should expect from Washington a greater willingness to incur risks, especially when America's status is involved. This prediction follows not only from the president's prickly temperament and his proven willingness to make hazardous business deals (such as the acquisition of the New York Plaza, the Eastern Air Lines shuttle, the New Jersey Generals and three casinos in Atlantic City), but also from Trump's staunch conviction that the United States is *entitled* to the number-one position in the global status order. This top rank functions as the reference position to which he baselines his understanding of overall gains and losses. Accordingly, it is to be expected that he will take far greater chances to ensure American pre-eminence.[79] This could well complicate relations with Russia, whose president shows a similar preoccupation with status. However, it seems most perilous in the field of American–Chinese relations. In Trump's dealings with Beijing, dangerous confrontations seem almost inevitable as long as a continuously rising China deems itself entitled to an ever-increasing say in East Asia and beyond.

Coping with these shifts will be challenging for America's partners and opponents, especially for those who are not prepared to indulge the Trump administration's heightened status sensitivity by making it feel somewhat more respected. Understandably, many non-Americans (and, indeed, Americans) will abhor the idea of accommodating the status aspirations of an American president who has repeatedly shown that he himself deems few people worthy of respect. And it is hard to dispute that Trump's America is less deserving of respect than the United States under Barack Obama, when Washington was more willing to advance global interests (and to combat bigotry at home). Nevertheless, foreign decision-makers cannot wish away the fact that the leader of the world's most powerful nation is driven by a visceral feeling that his country cannot take any more abuse. Nor can they ignore their own citizens' expectation that they uphold the national interest and protect the international order as best they can under these unpleasant circumstances.

Foreign leaders will face a difficult balancing act in seeking a modus vivendi, both to avoid escalation and to improve the prospects for future moral suasion. Appeasement of an erratic bully is always distasteful, and often too costly: to begin with, foreign leaders have their own constituents for whom national dignity and status are important. Still, symbolic accommodation is sometimes the most sensible course. The crucial thing to bear in mind is that, for some time to come, foreign decision-makers must deal with a powerful actor who strongly resents 'unfair upstarts' and claims an unquestionable right to redress what he considers a disgraceful historical trend.

For those willing to take such a pragmatic stance, there are some principles which might help to preserve a degree of cooperation and avoid the most dangerous conflicts. Firstly, wherever possible, America's friends and allies around the world should try to satisfy the new administration's commitment to American greatness by casting the US in the role of a respected and responsible leader. Rather than resigning themselves to the coming of an isolationist and utterly selfish America, they need to remind the Trump administration that true and lasting number-one status can only be obtained when America's partners freely recognise it as the paramount actor in the deference hierarchy, which in turn requires substantial US contributions to the provision of collective goods. Secondly, in their future dealings with Washington, foreign decision-makers need to pay much closer attention to possible symbolic aspects, even when the issue at hand appears rather straightforward. This includes, of course, a close eye on status perceptions among Trump's domestic base. Otherwise, Washington's interlocutors run an increasing risk both of aggravating the White House and of missing an opportunity to gain its goodwill. Thirdly, foreign capitals could look for opportunities to easily satisfy Trump's heightened status aspirations. Where neither important values nor substantial interests are on the line, they might want to make some visible concessions or respectful gestures to let Trump enjoy one of his much-cherished victories. Given the immense importance he attaches to respect and winning, such initiatives might achieve far more with his administration than in other diplomatic settings.[80] Fourthly, where concessions are out of the question, foreign decision-makers should try to de-emphasise the status aspects of the issue at hand, thereby making it easier for the Trump administration to accept an impasse. And by standing its ground without appearing disrespectful, a foreign government might also improve its chances of earning the respect of Trump himself.

Finally, and this refers especially to America's rivals and opponents, it certainly pays to treat the 45th president with caution. With a thin-skinned and highly status-sensitive commander-in-chief, violent escalation will be more difficult to forestall than under Trump's predecessors. We might count ourselves lucky to survive the Trump years without a major war.[81] If this requires accommodating the president's insistence on foreign respect, it might be worth the price.

Acknowledgements

The author would like to thank Markus Liegl and Christian Tuschhoff for helpful comments on an earlier version of this article.

Notes

1 See Michael Kranish and Marc Fisher, *Trump Revealed: An American Journey of Ambition, Ego, Money, and Power* (New York: Scribner, 2016), p. 290; and Joshua Gillin, 'Bush Says Trump Was a Democrat Longer than a Republican "in the Last Decade"', Politifact, 24 August 2015, http://www.politifact.com/florida/statements/2015/aug/24/jeb-bush/bush-says-trump-was-democrat-longer-republican-las/.

2 See Stephen M. Walt, 'America's New President Is Not a Rational Actor', *Foreign Policy*, 25 January 2017, http://foreignpolicy.com/2017/01/25/americas-new-president-is-not-a-rational-actor/; and Jon Finer, 'Trump Has No Foreign Policy: There's No Such Thing as a Trump Doctrine, Folks – Just an Incoherent Mess', *Politico*, 18 February 2017, http://www.politico.com/magazine/story/2017/02/trump-has-no-foreign-policy-214797.

3 Glenn Plaskin, 'Playboy Interview: Donald Trump (1990)', *Playboy*, http://www.playboy.com/articles/playboy-interview-donald-trump-1990.

4 Reinhard Wolf, 'Respect and Disrespect in International Politics: The Significance of Status Recognition', *International Theory*, vol. 3, no. 1, February 2011, pp. 105–42.

5 See Beth A. Visser, Angela S. Book and Anthony A. Volk, 'Is Hillary Dishonest and Donald Narcissistic? A HEXACO Analysis of the Presidential Candidates' Public Personas', *Personality and Individual Differences*, vol. 106, 1 February 2017, pp. 281–6; Anton Ashcroft, 'Donald Trump: Narcissist, Psychopath or Representative of the People?', *Psychotherapy and Politics International*, vol. 14, no. 3, 2016, pp. 217–22; and Dan P. McAdams, 'The Mind of Donald Trump', *Atlantic*, June 2016, https://www.theatlantic.com/magazine/archive/2016/06/the-mind-of-donald-trump/480771/.

6 See McAdams, 'The Mind of Donald Trump'; Michael D'Antonio, *The Truth About Trump* (New York: St Martin's

Press, 2015), pp. 17–18, 250, 280; Susan B. Glasser and Michael Kruse, 'Trumpology: A Master Class', *Politico Magazine*, May/June 2016, http://www.politico.com/magazine/story/2016/04/donald-trump-2016-campaign-biography-psychology-history-barrett-hurt-dantiono-blair-obrien-213835; and Susan B. Glasser and Michael Kruse, 'I Think He's a Very Dangerous Man for the Next Three or Four Weeks', *Politico*, 12 October 2016, http://www.politico.com/magazine/story/2016/10/donald-trump-2016-biographers-214350.

7 D'Antonio, *The Truth About Trump*, pp. 18, 61.

8 Kranish and Fisher, *Trump Revealed*, pp. 118–20.

9 Michael Barbaro, 'What Drives Donald Trump? Fear of Losing Status, Tapes Show', *New York Times*, 25 October 2016, https://www.nytimes.com/2016/10/26/us/politics/donald-trump-interviews.html?_r=0.

10 See D'Antonio, *The Truth About Trump*, pp. xxi, 57–9, 424–5; Kranish and Fisher, *Trump Revealed*, pp. 145, 175; and Donald Trump and Meredith McIver, *Think Like a Champion: An Informal Education in Business and Life* (Boston, MA: Da Capo Press, 2010), p. 23.

11 D'Antonio, *The Truth about Trump*, p. 425; Donald Trump, interview with Rona Barrett, *Washington Post*, 6 October 1980, p. 20, https://www.washingtonpost.com/wp-stat/graphics/politics/trump-archive/docs/rona-barrett-1980-interview-of-donald-trump.pdf.

12 Trump, interview with Bob Woodward and Robert Costa, *Washington Post*, 31 March 2016, pp. 13, 44, https://www.washingtonpost.com/wp-stat/graphics/politics/trump-archive/docs/donald-trump-interview-with-bob-woodward-and-robert-costa.pdf.

13 Donald Trump, *Great Again: How to Fix Our Crippled America* [formerly titled *Crippled America*] (New York: First Threshold editions, 2015), p. 138.

14 Donald Trump and Tony Schwartz, *Trump: The Art of the Deal* (New York: Ballantine Books, 1987), p. 98.

15 Kranish and Fisher, *Trump Revealed*, p. 260.

16 *Ibid.*, Chapter 4.

17 See D'Antonio, *The Truth about Trump*, pp. 14, 432; and Jasmine C. Lee and Kevin Quealy, 'The 319 People, Places and Things Donald Trump Has Insulted on Twitter: A Complete List', *New York Times*, 27 February 2016, https://www.nytimes.com/interactive/2016/01/28/upshot/donald-trump-twitter-insults.html?_r=0.

18 See Jerome Tuccille, *Trump: The Saga of America's Most Powerful Real Estate Baron* (Washington DC: Beard Books, 1985), p. 38; and Glasser and Kruse, 'Trumpology: A Master Class'.

19 D'Antonio, *The Truth about Trump*, p. 202.

20 *Ibid.*, p. 14. See also Kranish and Fisher, *Trump Revealed*, p. 42; and Glasser and Kruse, 'Trumpology: A Master Class'.

21 D'Antonio, *The Truth About Trump*, pp. 424, 57.

22 Glasser and Kruse, 'Trumpology: A Master Class'.

23 Trump and McIver, *Think Like a Champion*, p. 77.

24 Kranish and Fisher, *Trump Revealed*, p. 215.

25 See Trump and Schwartz, p. 63; and D'Antonio, *The Truth About Trump*, pp. 14, 438.

26 D'Antonio, *The Truth About Trump*, pp. 312–13.

27 *Ibid.*, pp. 355–9; and Kranish and Fisher, *Trump Revealed*, pp. 294, 299–304.

28 See D'Antonio, *The Truth about Trump*, p. 421; Kranish and Fisher, *Trump Revealed*, p. 304; Trump, *Great Again*, Chapter 15; Donald Trump, interview with Shawn Boburg, Robert O'Harrow, Drew Harwell, Jerry Goldstein and May Markon, *Washington Post*, 18 May 2016, pp. 20–1, https://www.washingtonpost.com/wp-stat/graphics/politics/trump-archive/docs/donald-trump-interview-with-shawn-boburg-robert-oharrow-drew-harwell-amy-goldstein-jerry-markon-may-18-2016.pdf.

29 Trump, interview with Barrett, pp. 33–4.

30 *Ibid.*

31 *Ibid.*, p. 36.

32 Donald Trump, 'There's Nothing Wrong With America's Foreign Defense Policy That a Little Backbone Can't Cure', *New York Times*, 2 September 1987, available at https://www.reddit.com/r/The_Donald/comments/4521em/theres_nothing_wrong_with_americas_foreign/. See also D'Antonio, *The Truth about Trump*, pp. 237–9; and Plaskin, *Playboy* interview.

33 Trump, interview with Woodward and Costa, p. 39.

34 *Ibid.*, p. 38.

35 'CNN Live Event/Special GOP Presidential Debate', CNN, 16 September 2015, http://transcripts.cnn.com/TRANSCRIPTS/1509/16/se.02.html.

36 Trump, interview with Woodward and Costa, p. 38.

37 Trump, *Great Again*, pp. x–xi, 9, 33–4, 42–3, 133; Plaskin, *Playboy* interview; Donald Trump, 'Remarks by President Trump and First Lady Melania Trump at Make America Great Again Rally', Melbourne, Florida, 18 February 2017, https://www.whitehouse.gov/the-press-office/2017/02/18/remarks-president-trump-and-first-lady-melania-trump-make-america-grea-0.

38 Donald Trump, 'Donald Trump's Presidential Announcement Speech', *Time*, 16 June 2015, http://time.com/3923128/donald-trump-announcement-speech/.

39 See Donald Trump, *Time to Get Tough: Making America Great Again!* (Washington DC: Regnery Publishing, 2011), p. 90; and Donald Trump, 'Donald Trump 2016 RNC Draft Speech Transcript', http://www.politico.com/story/2016/07/full-transcript-donald-trump-nomination-acceptance-speech-at-rnc-225974.

40 Trump, *Great Again*, pp. 7, 23; Plaskin, *Playboy* interview.

41 Trump, announcement speech.

42 See Trump, announcement speech; and Trump, *Great Again*, p. 87.

43 Trump, *Great Again*, p. 43.

44 Trump, interview with Woodward and Costa, p. 39.

45 Trump, *Time to Get Tough*, p. 5.

46 Trump, announcement speech.

47 Trump, *Time to Get Tough*, p. 100.

48 Trump, RNC draft speech.

49 *Ibid.*; and Trump, *Great Again*, p. 137.

50 See Trump, *Great Again*, pp. 34–5, 162; Plaskin, *Playboy* interview; Trump,

interview with Woodward and Costa, p. 37; Donald Trump, inaugural address, Washington DC, 20 January 2017, https://www.whitehouse.gov/inaugural-address; and Donald Trump, interview with Marc Fisher and Michael Kranish, *Washington Post*, 9 June 2016, https://www.washingtonpost.com/wp-stat/graphics/politics/trump-archive/docs/donald-trump-interview-with-marc-fisher-and-michael-kranish-june-9-2016.pdf.

51 See Trump, *Great Again*, pp. 43, 136; Trump, *Time to Get Tough*, p. 14; and Trump, announcement speech.

52 See Trump, interview with Woodward and Costa, pp. 6, 27–8, 38, 43; D'Antonio, *The Truth about Trump*, p. 420; Kranish and Fisher, *Trump Revealed*, p. 365; Trump, *Time to Get Tough*, p. 4; Trump, *Great Again*, p. 43; Trump, announcement speech; Trump, interview with Fisher and Kranish, p. 42; and Plaskin, *Playboy* interview.

53 See Trump, *Great Again*, pp. 63, 105, 137; Trump, *Time to Get Tough*, pp. 2, 91–9; Kranish and Fisher, *Trump Revealed*, pp. 275, 292; Plaskin, *Playboy* interview; and Jonathan Swan, 'Exclusive: Trump Vents in Oval Office: "I Want Tariffs. Bring Me Some Tariffs!"', Axios, 27 August 2017, https://www.axios.com/exclusive-trump-vents-in-oval-office-i-want-tariffs-bring-me-some-tariffs-2478121273.html.

54 Trump, *Great Again*, p. 137; Trump, *Time to Get Tough*, pp. 5, 96.

55 Trump, interview with Woodward and Costa, p. 6.

56 Trump, *Great Again*, p. 121.

57 Trump, announcement speech.

58 Trump, *Great Again*, p. 161.

59 See Trump, announcement speech; and Trump, *Great Again*, pp. 87–8.

60 See Steven Horwitz, 'Countries Are Not Companies', Foundation for Economic Education, 5 January 2017; and Edward Alden, 'The Roots of Trump's Trade Rage', *Politico*, 16 January 2017, http://www.politico.com/magazine/story/2017/01/the-roots-of-trumps-trade-rage-214639.

61 See Trump, *Great Again*, p. 43; and Trump, *Time to Get Tough*.

62 Trump, RNC draft speech.

63 Trump, announcement speech.

64 Trump, RNC draft speech; Trump, inaugural address.

65 Trump, *Great Again*, p. xi.

66 Trump, announcement speech.

67 Trump, *Great Again*, p. x.

68 Trump, announcement speech.

69 'CNN Live Event'.

70 *Ibid.*

71 Trump, RNC draft speech.

72 Plaskin, *Playboy* interview (emphasis in original).

73 Trump, *Time to Get Tough*, pp. 2, 4–5; Trump, *Great Again*, pp. 32–3, 137–8; Kranish and Fisher, *Trump Revealed*, p. 365; Plaskin, *Playboy* interview.

74 Trump, interview with Woodward and Costa, pp. 38–9, 41–2.

75 See Trump, RNC draft speech; Trump, interview with Woodward and Costa; and 'remarks by President Trump and First Lady Melania Trump'. Many years ago, Trump even announced that, if he ever became president, he would appoint himself United States Trade Representative. See D'Antonio, *The Truth about Trump*, p. 323.

76 See Trump, *Time to Get Tough*; and Trump, announcement speech.

77 See Trump, announcement speech; and Nolan D. McCaskill, 'Trump: China Should Make Kim Jong Un "Disappear"', *Politico*, 10 February 2016, http://www.politico.com/story/2016/02/trump-kim-jong-un-219068.

78 '"This Deal Will Make Me Look Terrible": Full Transcript of Trump's Calls With Mexico and Australia', *Washington Post*, 3 August 2017, https://www.washington-post.com/graphics/2017/politics/australia-mexico-transcripts/?utm_term=.0754b229b52c.

79 See Richard N. Lebow, *A Cultural Theory of International Relations* (Cambridge: Cambridge University Press, 2008), pp. 365–9; Tudor A. Onea, 'Between Dominance and Decline: Status Anxiety and Great Power Rivalry', *Review of International Studies*, vol. 40, no. 1, 2014, pp. 125–52; and David A. Welch, *Justice and the Genesis of War* (Cambridge: Cambridge University Press, 1993), pp. 23–4.

80 Perhaps this great responsiveness to respectful treatment explains why president-elect Trump seems to have had such a constructive meeting with his predecessor at the White House. After all the scorn he had heaped on the 'weak' and 'incompetent' Obama, he suddenly praised the outgoing president as a 'very good man', whose counsel he would seek again. See Domenico Montanaro, 'In Meeting at White House, President-Elect Trump Calls Obama "Very Good Man"', National Public Radio, 10 November 2016, http://www.npr.org/2016/11/10/501566466/in-surreal-moment-president-elect-donald-trump-meets-with-president-obama. At their first summit, mutual back-patting between Trump and Chinese president Xi Jinping may also have eased some tensions between Washington and Beijing. See Chris Buckley, 'A Spring Thaw? Trump Now Has "Very Good" Words for China's Leader', *New York Times*, 29 April 2017, https://www.nytimes.com/2017/04/29/world/asia/trump-xi-jinping-china.html?mcubz=1.

81 Philip Gordon, 'A Vision of Trump at War: How the President Could Stumble into Conflict', *Foreign Affairs*, vol. 96, no. 3, May/June 2017, pp. 10–19.

Autonomous Weapon Systems and Strategic Stability

Jürgen Altmann and Frank Sauer

In July 2015, an open letter from artificial-intelligence experts and roboticists called for a ban on autonomous weapon systems (AWS), comparing their revolutionary potential to that of gun powder and nuclear weapons.[1] According to a 2012 Pentagon directive, AWS are weapon systems which, 'once activated … can select and engage targets without further intervention by a human operator'.[2] Proponents of AWS have suggested that they could offer various benefits, from reducing military expenditure to ringing in a new era of more humane and less atrocious warfare. By contrast, critics – some characterising AWS as 'killer robots'[3] – expect the accompanying political, legal and ethical risks to outweigh these benefits, and thus argue for a preventive prohibition.

AWS are not yet operational, but decades of military research and development, as well as the growing technological overlap between the rapidly expanding commercial use of artificial intelligence (AI) and robotics, and the accelerating 'spin-in' of these technologies into the military realm, make autonomy in weapon systems a possibility for the very near future. Military programmes adapting key technologies and components for achieving autonomy in weapon systems, as well as the development of prototypes and doctrine, are well under way in a number of states.

Jürgen Altmann is a lecturer in experimental physics at Technical University of Dortmund, working on the prospective assessment of new military technologies and the analysis of preventive arms-control measures. **Frank Sauer** is a senior research fellow and lecturer in international relations at Bundeswehr University in Munich, working on international security and arms control. He is the author of *Atomic Anxiety: Deterrence, Taboo, and the Non-Use of U.S. Nuclear Weapons* (Palgrave Macmillan, 2015). Both authors are members of the International Committee for Robot Arms Control (ICRAC).

Survival | vol. 59 no. 5 | October–November 2017 | pp. 117–142 DOI 10.1080/00396338.2017.1375263

Accompanying this work is a rapidly expanding body of literature on the various technical, legal and ethical implications of AWS. However, one particularly crucial aspect has – with exceptions confirming the rule[4] – received comparably little systematic attention: the potential impact of autonomous weapon systems on global peace and strategic stability.

By drawing on Cold War lessons and extrapolating insights from the current military use of remotely controlled unmanned systems, we argue that AWS are prone to proliferation and bound to foment an arms race resulting in increased crisis instability and escalation risks. We conclude that these strategic risks justify a critical stance towards AWS.

Defining the debate

It is worth noting that some weapon systems, so far used only for defensive purposes, have long been able to identify, track and engage incoming targets on their own. These systems can already be set up so that humans are cut out of decision-making, a capability deemed necessary because there can be instances in which there is not enough time for humans to react, as during attacks with missiles or mortar shells.

These defensive weapons are stationary or fixed on ships or trailers, and are designed to fire at inanimate targets. They repeatedly perform pre-programmed actions within tightly set parameters and time frames in comparably structured and controlled environments. Consequently, they are commonly thought to be only the precursors to AWS, and might be described as *automatic*, as distinct from the *autonomous* systems currently being developed. The latter will be able to operate without human control or supervision in dynamic, unstructured, open environments, attacking various sets of targets, including inhabited vehicles, structures or even individuals. They will operate over an extended period of time after activation – and will potentially be able to learn and adapt their behaviour.

It can be difficult, however, to differentiate between automatic and autonomous systems in practice, with many systems falling into a considerable grey area. Autonomous functionality in weapon systems develops over a continuum. Some advanced 'automatic' systems are already behaving in ways that might be considered autonomous – for instance, when automatically (autonomously?) targeting the source of incoming fire. Such systems also blur the line between 'defensive' and 'offensive'. Nevertheless, juxtaposing automatic and autonomous systems is a helpful mental exercise to grasp what AWS are going to be like, and what benefits they, according to their proponents, will provide.

Such benefits include the possibility that new systems will combine superior performance with lower costs due to a reduced need for personnel. Moreover, AWS are said to render constant control and communication links obsolete. Daisy-chained, line-of-sight connections can already allow for control and communication without necessarily revealing a system's location. But dispensing with a communications link altogether could offer even stronger insurance against communications disruption or hijacking. Much more importantly, being able to do without an up- and downlink removes the inevitable delay between the human operator's command and the system's response, thus generating a clear tactical advantage over a remotely controlled, 'slower' adversarial system. Finally, some proponents hope that, since AWS experience neither fear nor stress, and do not overreact, they might render warfare more humane and prevent some of the atrocities of war. Not only are machines devoid of negative human emotions, they also lack a self-preservation instinct, so they could well delay returning fire, it is argued. They are supposed to allow not only for greater restraint but better discrimination between civilians and combatants, resulting in an application of force that accords with international humanitarian law.[5]

Critics counter that militarised AI systems are – and for the foreseeable future will be – incapable of distinguishing between combatants and civilians, as well as being unable to assure a proportionate application of military force, which renders the battlefield use of AWS illegal.[6] Also, should an autonomous weapon system nevertheless be fielded and end up causing disproportionate loss of life among (or injury to) civilians, or damage to civilian objects, it is unclear who might be held legally responsible, since machines can obviously not be court-martialled.[7]

Critics concerned with the ethical, rather than legal, implications of AWS argue that such systems are intrinsically amoral because delegating kill decisions to an algorithm in a machine – which is not accountable for its actions in any meaningful ethical sense – infringes on fundamental human values including dignity and the right to life.[8] Such humanitarian concerns are also reflected in public opinion. Representative polling data suggests that a majority of US citizens oppose the use of AWS, with 40% 'strongly opposing' them.[9] An online poll conducted by the Open Roboethics Initiative in 14 different languages supports these findings at the global level.[10]

Finally, operational risks are cause for concern. For instance, the potential of AWS for high-tempo fratricide, way beyond the speed of human intervention, incentivises militaries to avoid full autonomy in weapon systems, and instead to retain humans in the chain of decision-making as a fail-safe mechanism.[11] We argue that concerns of this nature are relevant not just at the operational level, but point to the potentially detrimental impact of AWS on overall strategic stability.

Two dimensions of instability

The goal of upholding stability to prevent a catastrophic nuclear war was a central feature of the Cold War. Destabilisation loomed with the arms build-up, in particular with the development of ballistic missiles carrying multiple independently targetable re-entry vehicles (MIRVs), and of missile defence. The former dramatically increased fears of a first strike and thus the pressure to launch on warning, that is, before the arrival of enemy warheads 10–30 minutes later. 'Accidental nuclear war' scares, fuelled by human and technical errors in early-warning systems, informed the decisions to limit anti-ballistic-missile systems and to preferentially reduce MIRVed missiles and warhead counts.[12] The goal of stability was also taken up in the realm of conventional military armaments, mainly in the Treaty on Conventional Armed Forces in Europe (CFE Treaty).[13]

The lessons of the Cold War are worth remembering. They suggest that instability has two dimensions. The first encompasses military instability with regard to the proliferation of arms and the emergence of arms races. During the Cold War, the perceived risk of 'horizontal proliferation' – that is, the spread of nuclear weapons beyond the existing nuclear-weapons states – gave rise to the Non-Proliferation Treaty and various export-control regimes. The risk of vertical proliferation – that is, an uncontrolled build-up of arms that drives up military expenditure and exacerbates the security dilemma, thus increasing the likelihood of crises – was reflected in the various strategic arms-limitation and -reduction agreements between the US and the Soviet Union. As the US Office of Technology Assessment (OTA) put it in 1985,

> Arms race stability involves the effect of planned deployments on the scope and pace of the arms race … If a deployment on one side is likely to lead to a responding deployment on the other side which is in turn likely to induce a still higher level of deployment on the first side, the first side's deployment might be seen as 'destabilizing' the arms competition.[14]

Generally speaking, any quantitative or qualitative arms race between – in this example – two potential adversaries involves an element of instability. But a race's pace can vary widely. Destabilisation becomes a particular concern when qualitatively new technologies promising clear military advantages seem close at hand. When potential adversaries make special efforts to get ahead themselves, or at least to avoid falling behind, this can trigger a dynamic intensified by mutual observation of – as well as speculation in light of uncertainty about – the other side's advances. If the situation is perceived as urgent, and precedents have been or are about to be set, there are compelling incentives for accelerating the development of technology and incorporating it into militaries, a process that is then more likely to outpace and render moot any attempt at agreement on mutual, preventive prohibitions.

The second dimension of strategic instability is crisis instability and escalation, either across the threshold from peace to war, or, when war has already broken out, to a higher level of violence – in particular from conventional to nuclear weapons. With respect to nuclear weapons, crisis stability during the Cold War was seen, according to the OTA, as

> the degree to which strategic force characteristics might, in a crisis situation, reduce incentives to initiate the use of nuclear weapons … Weapon systems are considered destabilizing if in a crisis they would

> add significant incentives to initiate a nuclear attack, and particularly to attack quickly before there is much time to collect reliable information and carefully weigh all available options and their consequences.[15]

In terms of conventional forces, the preamble of the CFE Treaty encompasses crisis stability in its commitment to 'establishing a secure and stable balance of conventional forces at lower levels ... eliminating disparities detrimental to stability and security [and] eliminating ... the capability for launching surprise attack and for initiating large-scale offensive action in Europe'.[16]

Both dimensions are closely connected. New kinds of weapons, developed as an outcome of an arms race, can increase crisis instability, with MIRVed missiles being a prominent Cold War example. And (perceived) crisis instability can create motives for diversifying weapon carriers and fuel the arms race in turn, as the development of nuclear submarines demonstrates.

Proliferation and arms-race instability

As early as 2007, the US Department of Defense wrote in its Unmanned Systems Roadmap that for processor technology 'the ultimate goal is to replace the operators with a mechanical facsimile [of] equal or superior thinking speed, memory capacity, and responses gained from training and experience'. The document also stated that the 'primary technical challenges for weapon release from unmanned systems include the ability to reliably target the right objective'.[17] The goal of weapon autonomy pervades all subsequent road maps.[18] Autonomous weapon-system functions have since been tested on land, under water, on the sea and, most notably, in the air. In fact, current trends with respect to unmanned combat aerial vehicles (UCAVs or 'combat drones') provide indicators for what to expect with regard to AWS. Unlike today's high-profile UCAVs, such as the *Reaper*, which are propeller driven, slow, carry comparably small payloads and have few to no capabilities for operating in contested airspace, future systems will be less dependent on human control, faster, stealthy and capable of delivering bigger payloads.

The X-47B, for instance, has demonstrated autonomous take-off from and landing on an aircraft-carrier deck, as well as autonomous aerial refuelling.

This technology demonstrator was developed by the US Navy's Unmanned Carrier-Launched Airborne Surveillance and Strike programme (UCLASS). Similarly, the British *Taranis* UCAV was described by the UK Ministry of Defence as 'fully autonomous' and able to 'defend itself against manned and other unmanned enemy aircraft' with 'almost no need for operator input'.[19] However, the ministry also stated that 'the operation of weapons systems will always be under human control'.[20]

While AWS test beds such as *Taranis* and the X-47B rely on familiar designs, in this case the airframes of a fast, stealthy, next-generation drone with substantial payload capabilities, future systems will display an autonomous swarming capability, and thus AWS will also come in much smaller sizes. In October 2016, for instance, the US Department of Defense demonstrated a swarm of 103 *Perdix* micro drones capable of 'advanced swarm behaviors such as collective decision-making, adaptive formation flying, and self-healing'.[21] In the future, such micro drones are to be 3D printed in large batches and deployed from (manned) flying systems. This dispensing method has already been successfully tested at Mach 0.6 speed by two F/A-18 *Super Hornets* releasing a *Perdix* drone swarm. The US Navy's LOCUST programme is also seeking to develop swarming, disposable unmanned aerial vehicles (UAVs).[22]

The overall goal for this new ecosystem of flying assets is to replace not just the old generation of drones but also manned aircraft, thus continuing the trend towards keeping human pilots out of harm's way and providing superior unmanned air-to-ground *and* air-to-air capabilities across the board.[23] In air-to-air combat, the big, fast autonomous drones currently envisioned will be able to fly high-g manoeuvres no human pilot would be able to endure. More importantly, they would ensure much shorter reaction times. On-board sensors combined with artificial 'intelligence' – either located onboard or distributed in the swarm and based on decision-making algorithms endowed with the authority to initiate an attack without awaiting human input – are to make these weapons autonomous and hence provide a decisive edge over remotely controlled and human-piloted adversary systems alike.

While the development of AWS is currently most advanced in the air and under water – that is, in less cluttered environments – the example of autonomous (swarms of) UCAVs demonstrates the generally valid proposition that for future unmanned systems, operational speed will reign supreme, regardless of the domain. In that sense, technological developments in AI and robotics, as well as current expectations regarding future armed conflict (and the need for speed), jointly point towards AWS. In fact, US deputy secretary of defense Bob Work stated in March 2016 that even the final delegation of lethal authority to autonomous systems will inexorably happen as a result of this race for speed.[24] According to Work, the United States 'will not delegate lethal authority for a machine to make a decision … The only time we'll delegate authority is in things that go faster than human reaction time, like cyber or electronic warfare.' Yet, he conceded that such self-restraint may be unsustainable if an authoritarian rival acts differently. 'We might be going up against a competitor who is more willing to delegate authority to machines than we are and, as that competition unfolds, we'll have to make decisions on how we can best compete', Work said. 'It's not something that we have fully figured out, but we spend a lot of time thinking about it.'[25]

Operational speed will reign supreme

To further deepen our understanding of AWS, it is useful to take a step back and underline that they need not necessarily take the shape of a specific weapon system akin to, for instance, a drone or a missile. AWS also do not require a specific military-technology development path, the way nuclear weapons do, for example. As AI, autonomous systems and robot technologies mature and begin to pervade the civilian sphere, militaries will increasingly be able to make use of them for their own purposes, as the development of information and communication technology suggests. Naturally, any military adaptation of a dual-use technology will need to fulfil specific military requirements that do not exist in a civilian environment, or are less relevant for mass markets. Nevertheless, AWS development will profit from the implementation or mirroring of a variety of civilian technologies (or derivatives thereof) and their adoption for military purposes, technologies which are currently either already available or on the cusp of becoming ready for series production in the private sector. This trend is already observable in the case of armed drones. Light detection and ranging (LIDAR) systems are another example. These are the optical sensors used by the automotive industry to give self-driving cars a 360-degree picture of their surroundings. LIDAR prices have recently dropped from five figures to a few hundred dollars. The units have also become more rugged and much smaller.[26] Given that these components, which are necessary for endowing mobile systems with autonomy, are now cheaply and readily available off the shelf, there is every reason to expect the military to adapt, and, if required, adjust and refine, them for their own purposes.[27]

It is clear that the research and development for AWS-relevant technology is well under way and distributed across countless university laboratories and, especially, commercial enterprises that are making use of economies of scale and the forces of the free market to spur competition, lower prices and shorten innovation cycles. This renders the military research and development effort in the case of AWS different from those of past high-tech conventional weapon systems (the F-35 comes to mind), let alone nuclear weapons. So while the impact of AWS might be revolutionary in terms of their implications for warfare, their development within the context of the military is best described as evolutionary: the military is merely continuing and, with outside help and technology lifted from the private sector, accelerating an already existing trend to replace labour with capital and automate dull, dirty and dangerous military tasks.[28] For example, former secretary of defense Ashton Carter sought closer ties with Silicon Valley to hasten the incorporation of technological innovations into the US military after the US officially declared AI and robotics cornerstones of its new 'third offset' strategy to counter rising powers.[29]

Thus, AWS are easy to obtain compared with other paradigm-shifting weapons, such as nuclear weapons, which even now require the Herculean effort of a state-run, focused politico-military effort to produce. AWS do not require ores, centrifuges, high-speed fuses or other comparably 'exotic' components to be assembled and tested in a clandestine manner. Consequently, while nuclear technologies can be – and are – proliferation controlled, AWS are much harder to regulate. With comparatively fewer choke points that might be targeted by non-proliferation policies, AWS are potentially available to a wide range of state and non-state actors, not just those nation-states that are willing and able to muster the considerable resources needed for the robotic equivalent of the *Manhattan Project*.[30] This carries significant implications for arms control.

There will of course be differences in quality. Sophisticated AWS will have to meet the same or similar military standards that current weapon systems, such as main battle tanks or combat aircraft, do. Moreover, technologically leading nations such as the US and Israel are carrying out research to produce autonomous systems that comply with international humanitarian law. Less scrupulous actors, however, will find AWS development much easier. Comparably crude AWS which do not live up to the standards of a professional military in terms of reliability, compliance with international humanitarian law or the ability to go head-to-head with systems of a near-peer competitor could, in fact, be put together with technology available today by second- or third-tier state actors, and perhaps even non-state actors. Converting a remotely controlled combat drone to autonomously fire a weapon in response to a simple pattern-recognising algorithm is already doable. Even the technological edge displayed by sophisticated AWS is unlikely to be maintained over the longer term. While sensor and weapon packages to a large degree determine the overall capabilities of a system, implementing autonomy ultimately comes down to software, which is effortlessly copied and uniquely vulnerable to being stolen via computer-network operations. Thus, while the development of AWS clearly presents a challenge to less technologically advanced actors, obtaining AWS with some degree of military capability is a feasible goal for any country already developing, for example, remotely controlled armed UAVs – the number of which rose from two to ten between 2001 and 2016.[31] Admittedly, the US and Israel are still in the lead with regard to developing unmanned systems and implementing autonomous-weapon functionality – China only recently test-fired a guided missile from a drone via satellite link for the first time.[32] But considering that drone programmes can draw from the vibrant global market for unmanned aerial vehicles of all shapes and sizes,

> *Implementing autonomy comes down to software*

the hurdles regarding AWS are much lower than those of other potentially game-changing weapons of the past.

Proliferation of AWS could of course also occur via exports, including to the grey and black markets. In this way, autonomous systems could fall not only into the hands of technologically inferior state actors, but also those of non-state actors, including extremist groups. Hamas, Hizbullah and the Islamic State have already deployed and used armed drones. As sensors and electronics are increasingly miniaturised, small and easily transportable systems could be made autonomous with respect to navigation, target recognition, precision and unusual modes of attack.[33] Terrorist groups could also gain access to comparably sophisticated systems that they could never develop on their own. Again, autonomy in this context does not necessarily require military-grade precision – a quick and dirty approach would suffice for these actors. In fact, it stands to reason that terrorist groups would use autonomous killing capabilities indiscriminately in addition to using them, if possible, in a precise fashion for targeted assassinations.

It is still unclear how the development of unmanned systems on the one hand and specific countermeasures on the other will play out. Traditional aircraft-sized drones such as the X-47B or *Taranis*, to stick with these examples, are obviously susceptible to existing anti-aircraft systems. As for smaller-sized systems, various tools, from microwaves to lasers to rifle-sized radio jammers for disrupting the control link, are currently being developed as countermeasures. Simpler, less exotic methods such as nets, fences or even trained hunting birds might also prove effective for remotely controlled and autonomous systems alike. It is clear, however, that saturation attacks have been identified as a key future capability for defeating a wide range of existing and upcoming defensive systems – both human-operated and automatic.[34] The latter are a particular focus of research into swarming as a potential solution.[35] And military systems operating at very high speeds and in great numbers or swarms are bound to generate new instabilities, to which we will turn in our next section.

To first sum up our argument so far, there are obvious dual-use problems and an unusually high risk of proliferation when it comes to AWS. Should one of the technologically leading nation-states go forward with the deployment of AWS, it would be comparably easy – and thus very likely – that others would follow suit.[36] In that sense, the development of AWS could well trigger a destabilising arms race.

Crisis instability and escalation

Increasing operational speeds mean that human involvement in AWS would be limited to, at best, general oversight and decision-making in instances where communication delays of up to a few seconds – and thinking and deliberation times of a few minutes – could be deemed acceptable, meaning they would not result in defeat or the loss of systems. Many situations would not allow for the luxury of human pondering, however. In such cases, the actions and reactions of individual AWS, as well as AWS swarms, would have to be controlled autonomously by algorithms – in other words determined only by programming software in advance and possibly through the adaptation and learning of the systems themselves. After all, as Paul Scharre put it, 'winning in swarm combat may depend upon having the best algorithms to enable better coordination and faster reaction times, rather than simply the best platforms'.[37]

One such swarm-combat situation could be a severe political crisis in which adversaries believe that war could break out. With swarms deployed in close proximity to each other, control software would have to react to signs of an attack within a split-second time frame – by evading or, possibly, counter-attacking in a use-them-or-lose-them situation. Even false indications of an attack – sun glint interpreted as a rocket flame, sudden and unexpected moves of the adversary, or a simple malfunction – could trigger escalation.

The nature of military conflict is such that these kinds of interactions could not be tested or trained for beforehand. In addition, it is, technically speaking, impossible to fathom all possible outcomes in advance. Clearly, the interaction of swarms, if fully autonomous, would be unpredictable, and could potentially result in an escalation from crisis to war, or, within armed conflict, to higher levels of violence. This is not a theoretical proposition deduced solely from systems theory and the argument of unavoidable 'normal accidents'.[38] On the contrary, comparable runaway interactions between algorithms are already happening in the civilian sphere on a regular basis. In April 2011, the price of an out-of-print biology textbook rose within weeks to $23.7 million on the Amazon marketplace due to the price-setting algorithms of two vendors interacting with each other.[39] Eventually one of the vendors intervened; no damage was done because nobody purchased the book at this absurd price. Greater havoc was caused in the New York Stock Exchange 'flash crash' of 6 May 2010 in which computerised high-frequency trading played an essential role, and during which stock indices and important industry stocks collapsed.[40] In this case 'circuit breakers' established by monitoring authorities set in, suspending high-speed trading and preventing further avalanche effects. These oversight and intervention mechanisms have been improved since then, but debate continues as to whether they are sufficient to prevent another significant flash crash; mini-crashes and interventions occur daily.[41]

During the Cold War, and even afterwards, both the US and the Soviet Union received erroneous indications of nuclear attack on multiple occasions.[42] These varied from sunlight reflected off clouds to magnetic training tapes fed into the early-warning system by accident. In all these cases, human reasoning led to restraint instead of escalation; double checks revealed that the alarm had been false. At the time, double checking and reconsideration were possible due to flight times of between several hours (in the case of bombers and cruise missiles) and 10–30 minutes (for ballistic missiles launched from submarines or those covering intercontinental ranges), as well as systems for preventing unwanted crisis escalation, such as the 'hotline' for communication between Moscow and Washington established after the Cuban Missile Crisis. Humans, or rapid-reaction mechanisms pre-programmed by humans, can also act as a fail-safe in instances where an overarching authority exists to enforce a shared set of rules, as in the stock-exchange example – unlike in international politics.

With the goal of improved military effectiveness providing a strong incentive to increase operational speeds, and thus to allow AWS to operate without further human intervention, tried and tested mechanisms for double-checking and reconsideration that allow humans to function as fail-safes or circuit-breakers are discarded. This, in combination with unforeseeable algorithm interactions producing unforeseeable military outcomes, increases crisis instability and is unpleasantly reminiscent of Cold War scenarios of accidental war.

Setting aside the increasing risk of unwanted escalation, AWS are also bound to introduce stronger incentives for premeditated (including surprise) attacks. This is because of a combination of three factors: casualty avoidance, cost reduction and, once again, swarming.

Firstly, unmanned systems, generally speaking, keep soldiers out of harm's way – which is positive, but which also reduces the political risk of military endeavours, especially in democracies.[43] Referring to the current generation of combat drones, Christof Heyns, the United Nations Special Rapporteur on extrajudicial, summary or arbitrary executions, put it this way: '[Drones] make it easier for States to deploy deadly and targeted force on the territories of other States.'[44] As unmanned systems become faster and smaller, as well as, eventually, autonomous – which will also make them stealthier due to radio silence, and allow them to become 'swarmier' – the resulting room for manoeuvre in political and military terms increases.

> *Unmanned systems keep soldiers out of harm's way*

Secondly, the example of *Perdix* demonstrates that AWS need not be big, costly or high-tech. Instead, such systems can be cheap and disposable, produced using 3D printers and gaining strength from numbers, their 'intelligence' residing in a distributed fashion in the swarm or, if external communication is an option, at some higher level within the military 'system of systems' at large.

A closely related third consideration is that swarms would make mounting a successful defence especially difficult due to their resilience and their ability to attack from many directions, simultaneously, in an overwhelming fashion. Small and very small AWS (those measuring tens of centimetres at most) would suffer from limited power supply on board, but could be brought closer to the target by riding along on 'motherships', as has been demonstrated with *Perdix*. With payloads weighing a few hundred grams at most, the amount of destructive power of small drones would be limited too. But if directed at political or military leaders or sensitive military infrastructure, they would produce relevant damage and provide entirely new means for carrying out assassinations and decapitation strikes.[45]

None of these points in isolation would introduce a radically novel element to military decision-making. After all, the fact that a weapon is cheap does not necessarily render it more likely to be used.[46] However, the combination of these three factors – brought about mainly by the development of hard-to-defend-against autonomous swarms – presents a strong incentive to seize the advantage of being the first on the offensive.

Considering the current climate between Russia and NATO, it stands to reason that old mechanisms of threat perception and worst-case thinking might see a comeback in the wake of AWS deployment.[47] Russia was reportedly alarmed when the idea of using stealthy drones for missile defence was floated in the US.[48] Swarms of AWS could be used to attack nuclear-weapon delivery systems, command and control systems, and sensitive infrastructure components such as antennas, sensors or air intakes. Even though an attacker might have little interest or confidence in the success of a disarming first strike of this type, the fact that such strikes were now possible would in itself increase nervousness and distrust between nuclear-armed adversaries.

This overlap between the conventional and the nuclear realm is not new, of course. It emerged with precision munitions and bunker-busting (or possibly electromagnetic-pulse) warheads during the 1990s and 2000s,[49] and is also documented in the New START treaty, the preamble of which states that the US and Russia are 'mindful of the impact of conventionally armed ICBMs and SLBMs on strategic stability'.[50] But AWS will likely perpetuate and intensify this trend, not least by opening up new possibilities for holding nuclear submarines carrying ballistic missiles at risk.[51] Thus, when nuclear weapons or strategic command and control systems are, or are perceived to be, at greater risk, conventional capabilities end up increasing instability at the strategic level.

Today's unmanned systems have already increased the risk that military force will be used in scenarios where manned systems would previously have presented decision-makers with bigger, caution-inducing hurdles – a connection recently confirmed in war-gaming exercises.[52] Of course, swarming AWS need not necessarily lead to escalation under all conditions. In asymmetric scenarios involving adversaries who lack AWS capabilities, the escalatory mechanisms developed above would not take effect. In symmetric settings, by contrast, they would certainly exacerbate the overall development toward an increased risk of crisis instability and escalation.

Preventive arms control for AWS?

Due to their detrimental impact on global peace and strategic stability, AWS have sparked a lively international debate among arms-control experts. Since 2013 this debate has included the United Nations. The main venue for UN deliberations on AWS is the Convention on Certain Conventional Weapons (CCW) in Geneva (where AWS used to be referred to as 'lethal autonomous robots' and are now called 'fully' or 'lethal' autonomous weapon systems – the latter designation spawning the clumsy yet widely used acronym LAWS).[53]

Unease with AWS is growing in Geneva. After three 'informal meetings of experts' (leading to continued and intensified deliberations on the issue through a 'Group of Governmental Experts' in 2017), 19 governments have called for a preventive prohibition – commonly referred to as a 'ban' – on AWS, which could be concluded via a sixth CCW protocol.[54] Interestingly, while the notion that autonomous weapon systems may offer certain military benefits is being upheld mainly by Israel and the US, neither they nor any other state party to the CCW has so far argued unambiguously in favour of the development and deployment of AWS.

It is worth clarifying that arms control in the form of a preventive AWS prohibition or ban would not mean prohibiting or controlling specific technologies as such. The wide dissemination and dual-use potential of AI and robotics, the two prime technologies driving AWS, suggest that this would not only be a futile endeavour, it would also be severely misguided in light of the various benefits that could potentially flow from the maturation of these technologies with regard to civilian applications, the self-driving car being just one prominent example.[55] In close connection to this, a number of examples suggest that the private sector would welcome a ban on AWS since companies do not want their products to be associated with 'killer robots'. In August 2017, 116 AI and robotics company leaders – including Tesla's Elon Musk and DeepMind's Demis Hassabis and Mustafa Suleyman – published an open letter, urging the United Nations to increase its arms-control efforts.[56] Google had stated that it was not interested in military robotics years before, eventually selling the robot-maker Boston Dynamics, which it had owned for a brief period and which was well known at the time for its close ties to the US military.[57] The Canadian robot-maker Clearpath Robotics even officially joined forces with the international Campaign to Stop Killer Robots, asking 'everyone to consider the many ways in which this technology would change the face of war for the worse' and calling for robotic products to be created solely 'for the betterment of humankind'.[58]

In short, preventive arms control for AWS would not mean the regulation or prohibition of specific technologies, nor even countable (stockpiles of) individual weapon systems.[59] Instead, it would mean regulating or prohibiting a defined military practice, particularly certain applications of specific technologies for military purposes. An example of such an approach can be found in the preventive prohibition on blinding laser weapons added to the CCW in 1995.[60] This prohibition protects soldiers' eyes on the battlefield without banning laser technology in all its other military and civilian uses.

When it comes to achieving a preventive prohibition on AWS, all governments are still – more or less – in the same boat. Some states may be in the lead in technological terms, but there is not yet a clear division between haves and have-nots. And while some may hope for AWS to yield specific benefits, no one is oblivious to the risks of developing such systems, at least judging from the current deliberations in Geneva.

Three alternatives to a ban, possibly in some combination, are conceivable. One is an internationally agreed moratorium on the development and deployment of AWS. This might buy time for further research and development, and additional consideration of the risks and benefits of AWS. This seems an unlikely and unwise next step, however, due to the dual-use nature of AWS technology and thus the immense ease with which such an agreement could be spoiled. A second alternative is a non-binding agreement on best practices or a 'code of conduct' with an emphasis on compliance with existing international humanitarian law and more rigorous unilateral weapons reviews in accordance with Article 36 of Additional Protocol I to the Geneva Conventions.[61] This approach attempts to address legal concerns but does nothing to counter the detrimental effects of AWS on strategic stability. Moreover, it would be incomplete, because only a few states conduct Article 36 weapons reviews – without any obligation to share the results, one might add. The third possibility is an agreement between the major powers and states leading in AWS technology that curbs strategic-escalation risks. This could entail limiting or even precluding AWS interactions, especially swarms, as well as excluding specific targets, such as nuclear weapons, from AWS attacks.[62] The resulting loss of military capabilities would be so great, however, that it seems unlikely that any AWS-capable state would agree to it. Nor does this solution address concerns related to international humanitarian law. It is also worth mentioning that none of these options would address the fundamental ethical problem posed by AWS – that killing people with an anonymous, unaccountable algorithm arguably amounts to a violation of human dignity. Verifying compliance would also be a problem. Non-binding agreements would by definition not be subject to verification, but even an international, legally binding moratorium, which *would* be subject to verification, would present difficulties – just as in the 'zero solution' case of a prohibition. However, a ban might promise enough advantages to prompt the international community to actually muster the resources required for addressing the verification problem.

> *Verification would be a problem*

In light of these considerations, the best solution would be to use the current window of opportunity to firmly establish and codify a bright red line against autonomous weapon systems that take life-and-death decisions out of human hands. This would not be easy, but the long list of concerns raised by AWS from the perspective of international law, ethics and, as argued here, global peace and strategic stability suggests that the international community would be well advised to collectively stop the race toward full autonomy in weapon systems. A legally binding, preventive, multilateral arms-control agreement comprehensively prohibiting the deployment and use of AWS would not only be the most logically consistent, morally desirable and politically prudent solution, it would also deal with all current concerns in one fell swoop.[63]

Could a ban on autonomy in weapon systems ever be verified? After all, autonomy is, as noted, essentially a question of software, potentially consisting of little more than a checkbox to be clicked on a graphical user interface. In other words, AWS and remotely controlled weapon systems may appear identical from the outside. Any existing, hardware-based verification method, let alone a quantitative approach based on counting systems or measuring specific system features, is useless in this case. Yet no state would be willing to allow the software that runs its weapon systems to be inspected. Even if it did, cheating would be all too easy since the software could be changed back within minutes after inspection.

An alternative would be to approach the problem from an *ex post* point of view. A treaty requiring meaningful human control over weapon systems, 'specifically in the "critical functions" of selecting and attacking targets', as the International Committee of the Red Cross suggests,[64] would oblige states parties to install digital 'glass boxes' in all relevant weapon systems to keep secure and reliable records of all sensor and control data exchanged between the system and human operators or supervisors.[65] In cases of suspected illegal use of autonomous systems, any state party to the treaty could be asked to produce (in encrypted form, and handed to an international monitoring organisation) the relevant records to ensure an orderly forensic inquiry into questions of compliance.

Arms control for autonomy in weapon systems, especially regarding verification and compliance, would not be easy to accomplish. Arms control almost never is. However, as weapons technology advances, so too do technologies that can be leveraged for the purposes of arms control. It could be, for example, that novel, inherently manipulation-resistant database solutions such as blockchain could play a role in improving the glass-box approach. Any number of working, creative solutions as yet unknown to the world could potentially be achieved by mustering political will and dedicating more resources to an inquiry into these issues.

Maintaining meaningful human control over the use of weapon systems and life-and-death decision-making in warfare is a worthy and sensible goal for legal, ethical and strategic reasons. A preventive prohibition of AWS would go a long way toward achieving it, and would come with the additional benefit of curbing the upward spiral towards operational speeds beyond human fail-safe capabilities. Speed is undoubtedly a tactical advantage on the battlefield, and humans are slower than machines. But strategic stability is essential for survival. When it comes under threat, some remainder of human slowness is a good thing.

Notes

1 Future of Life Institute, 'Autonomous Weapons: An Open Letter from AI & Robotics Researchers', http://futureoflife.org/open-letter-autonomous-weapons/.

2 US Department of Defense, 'Autonomy in Weapon Systems', Directive no. 3000.09, 21 November 2012, http://www.esd.whs.mil/Portals/54/Documents/DD/issuances/dodd/300009p.pdf.

3 See, for example, the Campaign to Stop Killer Robots website, http://stopkillerrobots.org/.

4 See Jürgen Altmann and Mark Gubrud, 'Anticipating Military Nanotechnology', *IEEE Technology and Society Magazine*, vol. 23, no. 4, 2004, pp. 33–40; Jürgen Altmann, *Military Nanotechnology: Potential Applications and Preventive Arms Control* (Abingdon: Routledge, 2006), Section 6.1.2; Armin Krishnan, *Killer Robots: Legality and Ethicality of Autonomous Weapons* (Farnham and Burlington, VT: Ashgate, 2009), Chapter 6; Jürgen Altmann, 'Preventive Arms Control for Uninhabited Military Vehicles', in Rafael Capurro and Michael Nagenborg (eds), *Ethics and Robotics* (Heidelberg: Akademische Verlagsgesellschaft, 2009); Jean-Marc Rickli, 'Strategic Stability, Non-State Actors and Future Prospects', Presentation at CCW Meeting of Experts on LAWS, Geneva, 16 April 2015, http://www.unog.ch/80256EDD006B8954/(httpAssets)/B6E6B974512402BEC1257E2E0036AAF1/$file/2015_LAWS_MX_Rickli_Corr.pdf; I. Lachow, 'The Upside and Downside of Swarming Drones', *Bulletin of the Atomic Scientists*, vol. 73, no. 2, 2017, pp. 96–101; and Wendell Wallach, 'Toward a Ban on Lethal Autonomous Weapons: Surmounting the Obstacles', *Communications of the ACM*, vol. 60, no. 5, 2017, p. 31.

5 Ronald C. Arkin, 'The Case for Ethical Autonomy in Unmanned Systems', *Journal of Military Ethics*, vol. 9, no. 4, 2010, pp. 332–41.

6 Noel Sharkey, 'Grounds for Discrimination: Autonomous Robot Weapons', *RUSI Defence Systems*, vol. 11, no. 2, 2008, pp. 86–9.

7 See Human Rights Watch, 'Mind the Gap: The Lack of Accountability for Killer Robots', 9 April 2015, https://www.hrw.org/report/2015/04/09/mind-gap/lack-accountability-killer-robots; and Robert Sparrow, 'Killer

Robots', *Journal of Applied Philosophy*, vol. 24, no. 1, 2007, pp. 62–77.

8 See Peter Asaro, 'On Banning Autonomous Weapon Systems: Human Rights, Automation, and the Dehumanization of Lethal Decision-making', *International Review of the Red Cross*, vol. 94, no. 886, 2012, pp. 687–709; Christof Heyns, 'Report of the Special Rapporteur on Extrajudicial, Summary or Arbitrary Executions', A/HRC/23/47, 9 April 2013, http://www.ohchr.org/Documents/HRBodies/HRCouncil/RegularSession/Session23/A-HRC-23-47_en.pdf; and Robert Hart, 'The Case for Banning Autonomous Weapons Rests on Morality, Not Practicality', *Bulletin of the Atomic Scientists*, 24 April 2017, http://thebulletin.org/case-banning-autonomous-weapons-rests-morality-not-practicality10707.

9 Charli Carpenter, 'Beware the Killer Robots: Inside the Debate over Autonomous Weapons', *Foreign Affairs*, 3 July 2013, http://www.foreignaffairs.com/articles/139554/charli-carpenter/beware-the-killer-robots#cid=soc-twitter-at-snapshot-beware_the_killer_robots.

10 Open RoboEthics Initiative, 'The Ethics and Governance of Lethal Autonomous Weapons Systems: An International Public Opinion Poll', 9 November 2015, http://www.openroboethics.org/wp-content/uploads/2015/11/ORi_LAWS2015.pdf.

11 Paul Scharre, 'Autonomous Weapons and Operational Risk', Center for New American Security, February 2016, available at https://www.cnas.org/publications/reports/autonomous-weapons-and-operational-risk.

12 See Scott D. Sagan, *The Limits of Safety: Organizations, Accidents and Nuclear Weapons* (Princeton, NJ: Princeton University Press, 1993).

13 Russia suspended its CFE participation in 2007 and halted it completely in 2015.

14 US Congress, Office of Technology Assessment, *Ballistic Missile Defense Technologies*, OTA-ISC-254 (Washington DC: US Government Printing Office, September 1985), pp. 119, 128. See also the literature in Appendix L of this report.

15 *Ibid.*, pp. 119, 120.

16 'Treaty on Conventional Armed Forces in Europe', 19 November 1990, available at http://www.osce.org/library/14087.

17 US Department of Defense, 'Unmanned Systems Roadmap 2007–2032', 2007, pp. 53, 54, http://www.dtic.mil/cgi-bin/GetTRDoc?Location=U2&doc=GetTRDoc.pdf&AD=ADA475002.

18 The most recent example is US Department of Defense, 'Unmanned Systems Integrated Roadmap: FY2013–2038', 2013, http:/www.defense.gov/Portals/1/Documents/pubs/DOD-USRM-2013.pdf.

19 Jon Cartwright, 'Rise of the Robots and the Future of War', *Guardian*, 21 November 2010, https://www.theguardian.com/technology/2010/nov/21/military-robots-autonomous-machines.

20 Article 36, 'Killer Robots: UK Government Policy on Fully Autonomous Weapons', 19 April 2013, http://www.article36.org/weapons-review/killer-robots-uk-government-policy-

on-fully-autonomous-weapons-2/.

21 US Department of Defense, 'Department of Defense Announces Successful Micro-Drone Demonstration', *CHIPS: The Department of the Navy's Information Technology Magazine*, 9 January 2017, http://www.doncio.navy.mil/%285udzc155ibdgke454epoce55%29/CHIPS/ArticleDetails.aspx?ID=8575.

22 David Smalley, 'LOCUST: Autonomous, Swarming UAVs Fly into the Future', Office of Naval Research, 14 April 2015, https://www.onr.navy.mil/Media-Center/Press-Releases/2015/LOCUST-low-cost-UAV-swarm-ONR.aspx.

23 US Department of Defense, 'Unmanned Systems Roadmap 2007–2032', p. 49.

24 Aaron Mehta, 'Work: Autonomy in Flight Likely Before Ground', DefenseNews, 30 March 2016, http://www.defensenews.com/story/defense/land/army/2016/03/30/bob-work-autonomy-flight-ground-systems-robot-ai/82427024/.

25 'David Ignatius and Pentagon's Robert Work Talk About New Technologies to Deter War', *Washington Post*, 30 March 2016, https://www.washingtonpost.com/video/postlive/david-ignatius-and-pentagons-robert-work-on-efforts-to-defeat-isis-latest-tools-in-defense/2016/03/30/0fd7679e-f68f-11e5-958d-d038dac6e718_video.html.

26 Philip E. Ross, 'Velodyne Announces a Solid-State Lidar', IEEE Spectrum, 19 April 2017, http://spectrum.ieee.org/cars-that-think/transportation/sensors/velodyne-announces-a-solidstate-lidar.

27 In the case of LIDAR this adaptation might, for example, include ensuring that it can operate under highly adverse conditions, or making efforts to achieve signature reduction.

28 See this data set on the developing role of artificial intelligence in weapon systems: Heather M. Roff and Richard Moyes, 'Project: Artificial Intelligence, Autonomous Weapons, and Meaningful Human Control', Arizona State University, Global Security Initiative, Autonomy, Robotics & Collective Systems, 2016, https://globalsecurity.asu.edu/robotics-autonomy. See also Heather M. Roff, 'Weapons Autonomy is Rocketing', *Foreign Policy*, 28 September 2016, http://foreignpolicy.com/2016/09/28/weapons-autonomy-is-rocketing/.

29 See Chuck Hagel, 'Reagan National Defense Forum Keynote', Simi Valley, CA, 15 November 2014, http://www.defense.gov/News/Speeches/Speech-View/Article/606635; and Dan Lamothe, 'Pentagon Chief Overhauls Silicon Valley Office, Will Open Similar Unit in Boston', *Washington Post*, 11 May 2016, https://www.washingtonpost.com/news/checkpoint/wp/2016/05/11/pentagon-chief-overhauls-silicon-valley-office-will-open-similar-unit-in-boston/.

30 We are thankful to an anonymous reviewer for pointing this out to us.

31 The ten countries possessing these weapons by 2016 were China, Iran, Iraq, Israel, Nigeria, Pakistan, Somalia, South Africa, the UK and the US. New America's 'World of Drones', the source of this list, today names some 28 countries as having armed drones. However, this updated number includes states that only have develop-

ment programmes and demonstrators. See New America, 'World of Drones', http://securitydata.newamerica.net/world-drones.html.

32 Tair Eshel, 'China Tested an Upgraded CH-4 "Rainbow" Weaponized Drone', *Defense Update*, 5 June 2016, http://defense-update.com/20160605_improved_ch-4_rainbow.html.

33 Modes of attack could, for instance, include crashing the system through a specific window, landing on a desk and exploding or stinging like an insect.

34 See Scharre, 'Autonomous Weapons and Operational Risk'.

35 See David Hambling, *Swarm Troopers: How Small Drones Will Conquer the World* (Venice, FL: Archangel Ink, 2015).

36 Jeremy Hsu, 'Any Ban on Killer Robots Faces a Tough Sell', *Discover Magazine*, 29 April 2017, http://blogs.discovermagazine.com/lovesick-cyborg/2017/04/29/any-ban-on-killer-robots-faces-a-tough-sell/#.

37 Paul Scharre, 'Counter-Swarm: A Guide to Defeating Robotic Swarms', *War on the Rocks*, 31 March 2015, http://warontherocks.com/2015/03/counter-swarm-a-guide-to-defeating-robotic-swarms/.

38 For more on the concept of 'normal accidents', see Charles Perrow, *Normal Accidents: Living with High-Risk Technologies* (New York: Basic Books, 1984).

39 Michael Eisen, 'Amazon's $23,698,655.93 Book About Flies', Michaeleisen.org, 22 April 2011, http://www.michaeleisen.org/blog/?p=358.

40 US Commodity Futures Trading Commission and US Securities & Exchange Commission, 'Findings Regarding the Market Events of May 6, 2010', 30 September 2010, https://www.sec.gov/news/studies/2010/marketevents-report.pdf.

41 Gary Shorter and Rena S. Miller, 'High-Frequency Trading: Background, Concerns, and Regulatory Developments', Congressional Research Service, 19 June 2014, http://fas.org/sgp/crs/misc/R43608.pdf.

42 See Sagan, *The Limits of Safety*; Bruce G. Blair, *The Logic of Accidental Nuclear War* (Washington DC: Brookings Institution Press, 1993); Ron Rosenbaum, *How the End Begins: The Road to Nuclear World War III* (London: Simon & Schuster, 2011); and Eric Schlosser, *Command and Control: Nuclear Weapons, the Damascus Accident, and the Illusion of Safety* (London: Penguin, 2013).

43 Frank Sauer and Niklas Schörnig, 'Killer Drones – The Silver Bullet of Democratic Warfare?', *Security Dialogue*, vol. 43, no. 4, 2012, pp. 363–80.

44 Christof Heyns, 'Report of the Special Rapporteur on Extrajudicial, Summary or Arbitrary Executions', A/68/382, 13 September 2013, http://justsecurity.org/wp-content/uploads/2013/10/UN-Special-Rapporteur-Extrajudicial-Christof-Heyns-Report-Drones.pdf.

45 Two examples of such miniature aircraft, which have already been deployed, are TiGER from MBDA and *Switchblade* from AV Inc., which have wingspans of only tens of centimetres, and can carry a small explosive charge within a radius of three and ten kilometres, respectively. They operate via remote control and a video feed. See David Crane, 'MBDA TiGER (Tactical Grenade Extended Range) Small UAS/UAV (SUAS/

SUAV)/Mini-Flying Bomb/"Kamikaze Drone"', *Defense Review*, 31 October 2011, http://www.defensereview.com/mbda-tiger-tactical-grenade-extended-range-mini-flying-bombkamikaze-drone-for-tactical-reconnaissance-and-precision-kill-missions-is-low-observable-seriously-lethal-kittys-got-a-temper/; and AV Inc., 'Switchblade', 2017, http://www.avinc.com/uas/view/switchblade. Future concepts foresee micro weapons that fly or crawl, and biohybrids using implants in small mammals or insects. Research on biohybrids has been funded for some time by the US Defense Advanced Research Projects Agency. See US Air Force Research Laboratory, 'US Air Force Flapping Wing Micro Air Vehicle', 16 July 2009, https://www.youtube.com/watch?v=_5YkQ9w3PJ4; Sanjiv K.Talwar et al., 'Behavioural Neuroscience: Rat Navigation Guided by Remote Control', *Nature*, vol. 417, no. 6884, 2002, pp. 37–8; and Alper Bozkurt, 'Research Paves Way for Cyborg Moth "Biobots"', *NC State News*, 20 August 2014, http://news.ncsu.edu/2014/08/bozkurt-moth-jove-2014/.

46 We are thankful to an anonymous reviewer for prompting us to further clarify this important point.

47 See Patrick Tucker, 'The Pentagon Is Nervous About Russian and Chinese Killer Robots', Defense One, 14 December 2015, http://www.defenseone.com/threats/2015/12/pentagon-nervous-about-russian-and-chinese-killer-robots/124465/; and Heather Roff, 'The New Mineshaft Gap: Killer Robots and the UN', Duck of Minerva, 20 April 2015, http://duckofminerva.com/2015/04/the-new-mineshaft-gap-killer-robots-and-the-un.html.

48 George N. Lewis and Theodore A. Postol, 'How US Strategic Antimissile Defense Could Be Made to Work', *Bulletin of the Atomic Scientists*, vol. 66, no. 6, 2010, pp. 8–24.

49 Eugene Miasnikov, 'Long-Range Precision-Guided Conventional Weapons: Implications for Strategic Balance, Arms Control and Non-Proliferation', paper commissioned by the International Commission on Nuclear Non-proliferation and Disarmament, June 2009, http://www.armscontrol.ru/pubs/en/em090918.pdf.

50 'Treaty Between the United States of America and the Russian Federation on Measures for the Further Reduction and Limitation of Strategic Offensive Arms', 8 April 2010, http://www.state.gov/documents/organization/140035.pdf.

51 Sebastian Brixey-Williams, 'Will the Atlantic Become Transparent?', Second Edition, British Pugwash, November 2016, http://www.basicint.org/sites/default/files/Pugwash_TransparentOceans_update_nov2016_v1%281%29.pdf. Regardless of whether the autonomous underwater vehicles are armed themselves, or serve simply to localise and track enemy submarines so that they can be attacked by other weapons, the destabilising effects on deterrence are the same.

52 Center for a New American Security, 'Game of Drones: Wargame Report', 29 June 2016, http://drones.cnas.org/reports/game-of-drones/.

53 See Frank Sauer, 'Stopping "Killer

Robots": Why Now Is the Time to Ban Autonomous Weapons Systems', *Arms Control Today*, vol. 46, no. 8, 2016, pp. 8–13; and Frank Sauer, 'Autonomous Weapons Systems. Humanising or Dehumanising Warfare?', *Global Governance Spotlight*, no. 4, 2014, http://www.sef-bonn.org/fileadmin/Die_SEF/Publikationen/GG-Spotlight/GGS_2014-04_en.pdf.

54 Details of the meetings can be found at United Nations Office at Geneva, '2014 Meeting of Experts on LAWS', http://www.unog.ch/80256EE600585943/%28httpPages%29/A038DEA1DA906F9DC1257DD90042E261?OpenDocument; United Nations Office at Geneva, '2015 Meeting of Experts on LAWS', http://www.unog.ch/80256EE600585943/%28httpPages%29/6CE049BE22EC75A2C1257C8D00513E26?OpenDocument; and United Nations Office at Geneva, '2016 Meeting of Experts on LAWS', http://www.unog.ch/80256EE600585943/%28httpPages%29/37D51189AC4FB6E1C1257F4D004CAFB2?OpenDocument. The 19 governments to have called for a ban include (as of April 2017) Algeria, Argentina, Bolivia, Chile, Costa Rica, Cuba, Ecuador, Egypt, Ghana, Guatemala, Holy See, Mexico, Nicaragua, Pakistan, Panama, Peru, State of Palestine, Venezuela and Zimbabwe. See Campaign to Stop Killer Robots, 'Report on Activities', Convention on Conventional Weapons, Fifth Review Conference, United Nations Geneva, 12–16 December 2016, http://www.stopkillerrobots.org/wp-content/uploads/2013/03/CCW_ReportRC_Feb2017.pdf.

55 Civilian applications of AI/robotics pose their own sets of problems, but these are beyond the scope of this article.

56 Future of Life Institute, 'An Open Letter to the United Nations Convention on Certain Conventional Weapons', https://futureoflife.org/autonomous-weapons-open-letter-2017.

57 Peter Kafka, 'Google Wants Out of the Creepy Military Robot Business', *Recode*, 17 March 2016, https://www.recode.net/2016/3/17/11587060/google-wants-out-of-the-creepy-military-robot-business.

58 Meghan Hennessey, 'Clearpath Robotics Takes Stance Against "Killer Robots"', Clearpath Robotics, 13 August 2014, https://www.clearpathrobotics.com/2014/08/clearpath-takes-stance-against-killer-robots/.

59 See Altmann, *Nanotechnology*, Chapter 5; and Jürgen Altmann, 'Nanotechnology and Preventive Arms Control', Forschung DSF, no. 3, 2005, sections 4.1, 4.2, http://www.bundesstiftung-friedensforschung.de/images/pdf/forschung/berichtaltmann.pdf.

60 United Nations Office at Geneva, 'The Convention on Certain Conventional Weapons', http://www.unog.ch/80256EE600585943/(httpPages)/4F0DEF093B4860B4C1257180004B1B30?OpenDocument.

61 This article states that in 'the study, development, acquisition or adoption of a new weapon, means or method of warfare, a High Contracting Party is under an obligation to determine whether its employment would, in some or all circumstances, be prohibited by this Protocol or by any other rule of international law applicable to the High Contracting Party'. See

'Protocol Additional to the Geneva Conventions of 12 August 1949, and Relating to the Protection of Victims of International Armed Conflict (Protocol I)', 8 June 1977, https://ihl-databases.icrc.org/applic/ihl/ihl.nsf/Article.xsp?action=openDocument&documentId=FEB84E9C01DDC926C12563CD0051DAF7.

62 We owe this suggestion to an anonymous reviewer.

63 Space constraints preclude us from discussing the scope of this prohibition in more depth; suffice it to say that there are valid arguments for extending it to development and testing, as well as to policing and other circumstances as well.

64 International Committee of the Red Cross, 'Autonomous Weapon Systems: Implications of Increasing Autonomy in the Critical Functions of Weapons', 1 September 2016, https://www.icrc.org/en/publication/4283-autonomous-weapons-systems.

65 More precisely, 'A time slice of the data stream immediately prior to and including the selection and engagement commands could be designated as the primary record of [every] engagement. This record would be held by the state party, but a cryptographic code called a "hash" of the record would be recorded by a "glass box" (not "black [box]" because its hardware and software would be known and open) together with a time stamp of the moment the engagement command was issued.' See Mark Gubrud and Jürgen Altmann, 'Compliance Measures for an Autonomous Weapons Convention', International Committee for Robot Arms Control (ICRAC), Working Paper Series #2, 2013, https://icrac.net/wp-content/uploads/2016/03/Gubrud-Altmann_Compliance-Measures-AWC_ICRAC-WP2-2.pdf. This proposal also contains details about what exactly might be prohibited and which exceptions with regard to systems in use for defence against incoming missiles might be accepted. It outlines a wide framework for compliance that begins with the philosophical and legal principle that violent force must always be under human control, and comprises transparency and confidence-building measures, inspections, technical safeguards and forensic investigation of suspicious incidents.

Nuclear Legacies of the First Gulf War

Rebecca Friedman Lissner

Although the ultimate political success of the Gulf War remains contested, the United States' military success was staggering.[1] US conventional war-fighting abilities – largely untested in combat since Vietnam – demonstrated the potential of the information revolution, as precision-guided munitions enabled pinpoint strikes against regime targets and global positioning system (GPS)-guided troops manoeuvred in the desert with unprecedented coordination.[2]

The experience of the Gulf War was formative for the United States' post-Cold War strategic thinking. Washington had overestimated the Iraqi threat – and, by extension, that of the Soviet Union and its client states – and underestimated the United States' own military dominance. It was especially formative for US thinking about nuclear weapons. The Gulf War highlighted the danger posed by nuclear proliferation to regional powers, and the United States' insufficient tools to counter it. Finally, the Gulf War reshaped how American policymakers and war planners conceived of nuclear weapons' role in the United States' national-security strategy.

These lessons explain the broad trajectory of US nuclear and non-proliferation policy after the Cold War, and continue to carry weight today. Yet the world has changed significantly since 1991, and, as Washington confronts pressing proliferation threats while also undertaking a massive nuclear-modernisation programme, it is worth re-evaluating these lessons in the light of two and a half decades of new evidence.

Rebecca Friedman Lissner is a Stanton Nuclear Security Fellow at the Council on Foreign Relations. She previously served as a Special Advisor to the Deputy Secretary at the US Department of Energy. This article draws on a longer study, 'Assessing the Nuclear Lessons of the First Gulf War', published by the CSIS Project on Nuclear Issues.

Survival | vol. 59 no. 5 | October–November 2017 | pp. 143–156 DOI 10.1080/00396338.2017.1375265

Proliferation risk

During *Desert Storm* and afterwards, inspectors found that the Iraqi nuclear programme was substantially more advanced than US intelligence had previously indicated. The underestimate came as a shock. The post-war Gulf War Air Power Survey, an after-action report prepared for the US Air Force, described it starkly:

> The Iraqi nuclear program was massive, for most practical purposes fiscally unconstrained, closer to fielding a nuclear weapon, and less vulnerable to destruction by precision bombing than Coalition air commanders and planners or U.S. intelligence specialists realized before Desert Storm.[3]

Indeed, prior to the war, war planners had identified only two nuclear targets; after the war, UN inspectors uncovered more than 20 sites, of which 16 were significant facilities. The miscalculation was all the more alarming to policymakers because of the specific method Iraq used to create fissile material: the Iraqi facilities employed electromagnetic isotope separation to enrich uranium, a process that used vast quantities of electricity.[4] Bush administration officials were confounded – and alarmed – that US intelligence had not picked up on such intensive energy consumption.[5]

After-action reports also revealed that the US-led bombing campaign had failed to substantially degrade the Iraqi nuclear programme, as well as Saddam Hussein's arsenal of *Scud* missiles. Even the much-lauded precision systems, famously capable of penetrating individual windows of Baghdad buildings, made few inroads on key targets related to Iraq's nuclear-weapons programme. Having inspected Iraqi facilities after the war's end, the UN drew a damning conclusion: the air campaign had no more than 'inconvenienced' the Iraqi nuclear programme.[6] Difficulties in destroying Iraqi *Scuds* and chemical-weapons caches further undermined policymakers' confidence that rogue states' nuclear-weapons programmes could be degraded militarily – even with new, high-end systems.[7]

As a result of these revelations, counter-proliferation rose to the top of the Bush administration's strategic objectives. According to American scholar Janne Nolan's account of this period: 'In the aftershock of Operation

Desert Storm, the redefinition of proliferation from a diplomatic priority to an urgent military priority became a central preoccupation of policymakers'.[8] Nuclear proliferation was the most extreme concern because nuclear weapons would provide aggressor states with the capability to counter superior US forces asymmetrically, threatening emergent US hegemony as well as myriad regional interests.[9]

Such conclusions extended beyond the Bush White House to influence Democrats who later staffed the Clinton administration at the highest levels. For example, Representative Les Aspin – who was then the chairman of the House Armed Services Committee and would subsequently serve as president Bill Clinton's first secretary of defense – offered Saddam Hussein's Iraq as the template for future 'threat driver[s]'.[10] Indeed, other pariah states with potential nuclear, chemical and biological programmes were measured against Iraq as a 'threat yardstick' to determine the extent of their aggressiveness, as well as the military resources necessary to counter them.[11] Iraq's use of ballistic missiles during the Gulf War heightened this concern.[12] By the mid-1990s, as Hans Kristensen and Joshua Handler put it, '"countering" the acquisition and use of weapons of mass destruction by regional proliferators … [became] a central focus of [US] nuclear strategy'.[13]

Lessons from Iraq also galvanised interest in bolstering the non-proliferation regime. Beginning in 1993, the International Atomic Energy Agency (IAEA), with US encouragement, initiated an effort to supplement the Nuclear Non-Proliferation Treaty (NPT) with extra safeguards against secret nuclear programmes.[14] Although Iraq had been a party to the NPT, it exploited a loophole in the treaty that effectively limited safeguards to the inspection and monitoring of declared (as opposed to clandestine) facilities. The Additional Protocol, formalised in 1997, sought to identify and deter construction of secret nuclear sites ('undeclared facilities') by giving the IAEA inspectors broader inspection authority.[15]

Proliferation response

Fearful of future Iraq-like regional contingencies in which an adversary would be nuclear-armed, US policymakers reconsidered the counter-proliferation capabilities required to meet post-Cold War threats.

Advanced conventional capabilities, the Gulf War made clear, would play a greater role in all aspects of national-security policy, including counter-proliferation. Indeed, the United States' conventional preponderance in the Gulf War convinced US strategists that high-tech conventional weapons could increasingly substitute for nuclear weapons in addressing the most likely post-Cold War contingencies. US military performance in the Gulf War substantiated the administration's view that, in the words of secretary of state James Baker, 'precision guidance enables the conventional weapons of today to destroy targets that in years past were assigned primarily to nuclear weapons'.[16]

But even with a greater role for conventional systems, nuclear weapons retained a role in counter-proliferation. The commander of Strategic Command (STRATCOM), General Lee Butler, advocated for a conception of nuclear deterrence that encompassed nuclear proliferation.[17] Butler's was not an isolated view: in 1992, then-secretary of defense Richard Cheney issued a nuclear-weapons employment policy which 'formalized procedures for nuclear operations against countries with the potential to develop weapons of mass destruction'.[18] In particular, nuclear weapons remained useful for deterrence against WMD-armed adversaries, as well as possible first use against hardened nuclear facilities as part of a preventive or pre-emptive attack.[19] The strategy of maintaining nuclear capabilities as a hedge against future proliferation contingencies endured through the Clinton administration's major nuclear-policy statements, specifically the 1993 bottom-up review,[20] the 1994 nuclear posture review (NPR) and Presidential Decision Directive 60 in 1997.[21] Similarly, the George W. Bush administration's 2002 NPR emphasised threats from 'terrorists or rogue states armed with weapons of mass destruction',[22] and the Obama administration's 2010 NPR made 'preventing nuclear proliferation and nuclear terrorism' its top objective.[23]

Adapting strategy

After the Gulf War, US nuclear posture and strategy adapted to and integrated with new conventional systems for maximal efficacy. The creation of STRATCOM cemented the convergence of nuclear and conventional missions.[24] As the nuclear mission refocused away from the Soviet Union and toward regional threats, STRATCOM assumed responsibility for rapid and flexible targeting – a major change from the single integrated operational plan (SIOP) that had characterised nuclear targeting during the Cold War.[25] An approach emphasising nuclear flexibility in response to regional contingencies persisted into the Clinton administration and beyond. The 2002 NPR, for example, introduced the concept of a 'new triad', one leg of which constituted 'offensive strike systems (both nuclear and nonnuclear)'.[26] The greater integration of nuclear and conventional war planning, combined with the fall of the Soviet Union, precipitated important changes to US nuclear posture. While the end of the Cold War likely had the greatest role in inspiring the Presidential Nuclear Initiatives – the reciprocal unilateral reductions in tactical nuclear weapons between the US and the Soviet Union (and then Russia)[27] – it is plausible that the Gulf War shaped the Bush administration's confidence in the determination that tactical nuclear weapons were no longer necessary to defend South Korea,[28] and the decision to cease 'normal' deployment of tactical nuclear weapons on surface ships, attack submarines and naval aircraft.[29]

The greater interchangeability of conventional and nuclear weapons had implications for conflict-escalation dynamics. The precise effect is difficult to measure, and because the United States has spent most of the past 25 years fighting unconventional wars against non-state actors, the necessity of climbing the escalatory ladder has remained blessedly remote. Nevertheless, primary and secondary sources suggest several ways in which the Gulf War may have shaped US strategists' and planners' thinking about wartime escalation.

Firstly, the fact that the Gulf War never escalated beyond conventional forces suggested that non-use norms would persist in the post-Cold War world.[30] President Bush explicitly rejected nuclear use in December 1990, prior to commencement of the air campaign against Iraq. The timing of this decision is significant because the president expected a tough fight against Saddam's million-man army, but nevertheless ruled out nuclear use. The military was apparently unaware of the president's decision; while war plans that included nuclear weapons were proposed, they were not seriously considered.[31]

Secondly, the demonstrated efficacy of conventional weapons may have pushed nuclear options farther up the escalatory ladder. For example, Bill Perry, who later became secretary of defense, wrote in 1992 that the conventional capabilities demonstrated in the Gulf raised the nuclear threshold for the first time since the 1950s; advanced-technology weapons might prove more effective deterrents, he argued, because unlike nuclear weapons these conventional systems were highly useable.[32] The result was that 'the United States would no longer need to extend its nuclear forces to deter nonnuclear attack' on allies – a conclusion that never became declaratory policy but nevertheless shows the important nuclear lessons drawn by influential elites from conventional warfare in the Gulf.

A third, contradictory lesson may also have emerged about the utility of nuclear weapons in certain contingencies. Advances in precision targeting created the possibility of smaller-scale nuclear strikes, possibly making nuclear weapons more useable. To some extent, this change reflects diminished fears of mutually assured destruction given that the most likely contingencies entailed regional powers with small or non-existent nuclear arsenals. Yet, coupled with advances in low-yield nuclear-weapons technology, the precision revolution augured by the Gulf War may have lowered the threshold for nuclear use over the long term by diminishing the anticipated destruction of a nuclear detonation. Indeed, Hans Kristensen and Joshua Handler contend that proliferation anxiety after the Gulf War inspired the US military to pursue new, low-yield miniature and 'exotic' nuclear options.[33]

A mixed record

If these are the lessons learned by US policymakers, have they proven correct over the past two and a half decades? In the realm of nuclear threats, covert nuclear proliferation by regional powers remains a primary national-security concern. Given the United States' global interests, as well as its continued conventional military superiority, nuclear weapons are an attractive asymmetric tool for states threatened by US power. Yet the nuclear-alarmist predictions of the 1990s have not been realised, and nuclear proliferation has posed less of a threat to American interests than many imagined. A proactive non-proliferation policy – characterised by vigorous diplomacy alongside military dominance – deserves much credit for this success, though North Korea stands out as a conspicuous failure.

In the case of Iraq, Gulf War-inspired alarmism resulted in a significant foreign-policy blunder. In contemplating the 2003 invasion, George W. Bush administration policymakers – many of whom had also served during the first Gulf War – extrapolated from previous experience and assumed that the Iraqi nuclear programme was farther along than intelligence indicated. Yet the 2003 Iraq War demonstrated that Saddam Hussein had an incentive to strategically misrepresent the progress of the Iraqi nuclear programme because of domestic political imperatives as well as regional power dynamics – even though this misrepresentation ultimately contributed to the coming of war with the United States.[34]

More broadly, the non-proliferation regime seems to have advanced US interests in countering the spread of WMD more effectively than US nuclear sabre rattling. At the same time as the military was developing new operational concepts for countering WMD, US diplomats led NPT signatory states in extending the treaty indefinitely at the 1995 review conference. In addition to its normative value in affirming the nuclear taboo – a taboo that would be undermined by American use of nuclear weapons to counter nuclear proliferation – the NPT provides a framework for deterring prospective proliferators through cost-imposing strategies such as sanctions.[35]

Although nuclear weapons remained a necessary component of the US defence posture, the Gulf War's demonstration of advanced conventional capabilities augured a new era of warfare in which the nuclear threshold could be substantially higher in comparison with the Cold War. With the precision revolution, targets could be hit with greater accuracy, permitting the substitution of smaller conventional payloads in place of nuclear weapons – a prospect illustrated by ongoing debates over 'conventional prompt global strike'.

As compared with these broadly useful conventional capabilities, the application of advances in precision strike to nuclear strategy received less attention. The low-yield nuclear options that some anticipated in the wake of the Gulf War have been slow to materialise. Between 1994 and 2004, Congress banned research and development on nuclear weapons of fewer than five kilotons in the Spratt–Furse precision low-yield weapon design (PLYWD) provision to the fiscal year (FY) 1994 National Defense Authorization Act. Though Congress repealed this provision in 2004, advocates of expanding low-yield options contend that the US military remains ill-equipped in that domain.[36] Despite its 2010 NPR commitment not to build new nuclear weapons, however, the Obama administration worked to enhance the flexibility of existing nuclear weapons. Modifications included in the B61-12 Life Extension Program seem to finally fulfil the post–Gulf War prediction that precision guidance would ultimately be married with lower-yield bombs. The B61-12 has an internal guidance system for targeting, as well as four yields – 0.3, 5, 10 and 50 kilotons – according to media reports.[37]

Perhaps more importantly, those who argued after the Gulf War that nuclear weapons would remain a necessary component of the US defence posture in the post-Cold War world were vindicated by the reaction of the United States' rivals. Initially, the shock and awe of the Gulf War seems to have convinced potential competitors that the United States' technological advantage was unbridgeable. The Russian military was reportedly impressed with the United States' skill in harnessing the 'revolution in military affairs', and the Gulf War convinced the Chinese that the United States was at least a generation ahead of its own military.[38] Yet, rather than deterring competition, this realisation instead made nuclear weapons more important in the eyes of conventionally weak states. India's chief of army staff famously summarised the lesson of the war for the rest of the world: 'Don't fight the Americans without nuclear weapons.'[39] The example of US-sponsored regime change in Iraq in 2003 made this imperative all the more acute. For those states that cannot afford a conventional hedge against US military power, nuclear weapons appear the best asymmetric option; and even states that can afford to compete conventionally, such as China and Russia, have pursued advanced conventional capabilities alongside (as opposed to instead of) nuclear modernisation.

The strategic challenge is now twofold: addressing 'vertical' proliferation by Russia and China as they pursue broad military-modernisation programmes, and countering 'horizontal' proliferation by new nuclear states such as North Korea. Competing with prospective great-power rivals such as China and Russia requires that the United States continue to maintain its conventional edge by pursuing further advances in the precision-strike regime as part of a broader push for defence-technology innovation. Additionally, sustaining nuclear deterrence will require modernisation of the United States' ageing arsenal, through the acquisition of updated delivery systems as well as weapons refurbishment.

Meanwhile, the advancement of North Korea's nuclear programme represents the greatest failure of the United States' post-Cold War non-proliferation policy. Despite more than two decades of effort, American policymakers have been unable to identify a combination of carrots and sticks sufficient to persuade the North Koreans to abandon their nuclear programme. The hyper-authoritarian North Korean regime, supported by Chinese patronage and equipped with significant conventional military capabilities, has proven remarkably resistant to normative and economic pressures. It would be overly fatalistic to assume, however, that North Korea was destined to acquire nuclear weapons and increasingly sophisticated delivery systems – rather, Pyongyang benefited from the United States' intense focus on the Middle East. North Korea and Iraq emerged in the early 1990s as the two most salient nuclear-proliferation threats in regions of critical interest to the United States. Precisely because of the legacy of the First Gulf War, American policymakers were highly attuned to the danger of proliferation in Iraq, and went to war over an exaggerated Iraqi threat while taking too long to appreciate the far greater risk of North Korean nuclear acquisition. The United States' distraction in the Middle East was not lost on the North Koreans, who conducted their first nuclear test in October 2006, at the height of America's Iraq entanglement.

North Korea represents the greatest failure of post-Cold War non-proliferation policy

As North Korea approaches the capability to miniaturise a nuclear weapon and deliver it on an intercontinental ballistic missile, the United States now faces a scenario that challenges all three of the Gulf War's nuclear lessons. If tensions remain below boiling point, the central strategic problem will be deterrence – not only of a North Korean attack on the United States and American allies in the region, but also of nuclear transfers to state or non-state actors. If tensions on the Korean Peninsula do boil over, the United States will be faced with the decision whether to launch a preventive or pre-emptive war with North Korea. Despite the persistent norm against the use of nuclear weapons, such an attack could require the first use of nuclear weapons to penetrate hardened targets associated with the nuclear programme. While both of these scenarios assume a crisis during which the United States decides when and if to cross the nuclear threshold, North Korea could also launch a nuclear first strike, compelling the United States to mount a robust response. In any contingency, advanced conventional capabilities alone might not be sufficient to achieve the United States' objectives, and the United States' nuclear posture must be tailored to respond to the evolving North Korean threat.

Taken together, vertical and horizontal proliferation confront the United States with an uncomfortable reality: the era of uncontested military dominance inaugurated by the Gulf War has come to an end. Having receded into the background in the 1990s, nuclear weapons are once again central to international politics, and the US national-security establishment must grapple with the prospect of re-entering a world in which wartime nuclear detonations are all too plausible.

Notes

1 See Stephen Biddle, 'Victory Misunderstood', *International Security*, vol. 21, no. 2, October 1996, p. 139; and Joshua Rovner, 'Delusion of Defeat: The United States and Iraq, 1990–1998', *Journal of Strategic Studies*, vol. 37, no. 4, 2014, pp. 482–507.

2 Michael Gordon and Bernard Trainor, *The Generals' War: The Inside Story of the Conflict in the Gulf* (Boston, MA: Little, Brown, 1995), p. xii.

3 Eliot A. Cohen, *Gulf War Air Power Survey*, vol. 1 (Washington DC: Office of the Secretary of the Air Force, 1993), p. 78.

4 Federation of American Scientists, 'Iraqi Nuclear Weapons', May 2012, http://fas.org/nuke/guide/iraq/nuke/program.htm.

5 Author interview with George H.W. Bush administration Department of Defense (DoD) official, April 2015.

6 Cohen, *Gulf War Air Power Survey*, p. 82.

7 *Ibid.*, pp. 81, 83, 89.

8 Janne E. Nolan, *An Elusive Consensus: Nuclear Weapons and American Security after the Cold War* (Washington DC: Brookings Institution Press, 2001), p. 68.

9 See, for example, *National Security Strategy of the United States: 1991* (Washington DC: White House, August 1991), p. 31.

10 Les Aspin, *An Approach to Sizing American Conventional Forces for the Post-Soviet Era: Four Illustrative Options* (Washington DC: Government Printing Office, 1992).

11 *Ibid.* See also Nolan, *An Elusive Consensus*, p. 68; and Robert Blackwill and Albert Carnesale (eds), *New Nuclear Nations: Consequences for U.S. Policy* (New York: Council on Foreign Relations Press, 1993).

12 Hans M. Kristensen and Joshua Handler, *Changing Targets: Nuclear Doctrine from the Cold War to the Third World* (Amsterdam: Greenpeace International, 1995), p. 4.

13 *Ibid.*, p. 3.

14 Arms Control Association, 'The 1997 IAEA Additional Protocol at a Glance', April 2015, https://www.armscontrol.org/factsheets/IAEAProtoco.

15 Arshad Mohammed, 'Iraq, North Korea Failures Shadow Nuclear Talks with Iran', Reuters, 1 July 2015, http://www.reuters.com/article/2015/07/01/us-iran-nuclear-verification-idUSKCN0PB5HY20150701.

16 'Transition in Washington: Excerpts from Baker's Testimony before Senate Committee', *New York Times*, 18 January 1989, http://www.nytimes.com/1989/01/18/us/transition-in-washington-excerpts-from-baker-s-testimony-before-senate-committee.html?src=pm&pagewanted=1.

17 Nolan, *An Elusive Consensus*, p. 67.

18 *Ibid.*, pp. 64–5.

19 For an unclassified discussion of what an offensive counter-proliferation operation of this kind might look like, see Philip Zelikow, 'Offensive Military Operations', in Blackwill and Carnesale (eds), *New Nuclear Nations*, pp. 162–95.

20 Kristensen and Handler, *Changing Targets*, pp. 6–7.

21 See Josiane Gabel, 'The Role of U.S. Nuclear Weapons after September 11', *Washington Quarterly*, vol. 28, no. 1, Winter 2004–05, p. 185; and William M. Arkin, 'Calculated Ambiguity: Nuclear Weapons and the Gulf War', *Washington Quarterly*, vol. 19, no. 4, 1996, p. 13.

22 'Nuclear Posture Review [Excerpts]', 8 January 2002, http://web.stanford.edu/class/polisci211z/2.6/NPR2001leaked.pdf.

23 US Department of Defense, *Nuclear Posture Review Report* (Washington DC: DoD, April 2010), http://www.washingtonpost.com/wp-srv/politics/documents/2010NuclearPostureReviewReport.pdf?sid=ST2010040601660.

24 Gregory Gilmour, 'From SAC to STRATCOM: The Origins of Unified Command over Nuclear Forces', Master's Thesis, Naval Postgraduate School, June 1993, pp. 58–9, http://www.dtic.mil/dtic/tr/fulltext/u2/a268609.pdf.

25 Nolan, *An Elusive Consensus*, p. 65. See also interview with Richard Cheney, Miller Center Oral History Project, 2000, http://millercenter.org/oralhistory/interview/richard-cheney.

26 'Nuclear Posture Review [Excerpts]'.

27 Susan Koch, *The Presidential Nuclear*

Initiatives of 1991–1992 (Washington DC: National Defense University Press, September 1992), http://ndupress.ndu.edu/Portals/68/Documents/casestudies/CSWMD_CaseStudy-5.pdf.

28 This shift on tactical nuclear weapons was reflected in the Bush administration's arms-control position. Paul Wolfowitz, 'Shaping the Future: Planning at the Pentagon, 1989–1993', in Melvyn P. Leffler and Jeffrey W. Legro (eds), *In Uncertain Times: American Foreign Policy after the Berlin Wall and 9/11* (Ithaca, NY: Cornell University Press, 2011), p. 55.

29 Interview with Clinton administration official, November 2014. On the Presidential Nuclear Initiatives' changes to nuclear force posture, see Hans Kristensen, 'The Neither Confirm Nor Deny Policy: Nuclear Diplomacy at Work', Nuclear Information Project, February 2006, http://www.nukestrat.com/pubs/NCND.pdf.

30 *Ibid.*, pp. 83–94.

31 Although secretary of state Jim Baker led the Iraqis to believe nuclear retaliation was possible if Saddam used chemical weapons, nuclear use by the US had been ruled out by president Bush in December. See James Baker and Thomas DeFrank, *The Politics of Diplomacy* (New York: Putnam, 1995), p. 197; Michael Gordon and Bernard Trainor, *The General's War* (London: Little, Brown and Company, 1995), p. 197; and Arkin, 'Calculated Ambiguity', p. 3.

32 Bobby Inman et al., 'U.S. Strategy after the Storm', in Joseph S. Nye and Roger K. Smith (eds), *After the Storm: Lessons from the Gulf War* (Lanham, MD: Madison Books, 1992), p. 241.

33 Kristensen and Handler quote George Miller, Lawrence Livermore associate director, drawing direct connections between the Gulf War's 'revelation' of Iraqi nuclear capability and its demonstration of precision delivery, which together suggest the possibility of low-yield nuclear weapons directed at counter-proliferation targets. Kristensen and Handler, *Changing Targets*, pp. 13–14.

34 David A. Lake, 'Two Cheers for Bargaining Theory: Assessing Rationalist Explanations of the Iraq War', *International Security*, vol. 35, no. 3, Winter 2010–11, pp. 29–30.

35 On the nuclear taboo, see Nina Tannenwald, 'Stigmatizing the Bomb: Origins of the Nuclear Taboo', *International Security*, vol. 29, no. 4, 2005, pp. 5–49. On the effectiveness of sanctions, see Nicholas L. Miller, 'The Secret Success of Nonproliferation Sanctions', *International Organization*, vol. 68, no. 4, 2014, pp. 913–44.

36 Keir A. Lieber and Daryl G. Press, 'The Nukes We Need', *Foreign Affairs*, November 2009, http://www.foreignaffairs.com/articles/65481/keir-a-lieber-and-daryl-g-press/the-nukes-we-need; Kier A. Lieber and Daryl G. Press, *Coercive Nuclear Campaigns in the 21st Century: Understanding Adversary Incentives and Options for Nuclear Escalation* (Monterey, CA: Naval Postgraduate School, March 2013), https://www.hsdl.org/?view&did=734062.

37 Mike Hoffman, 'Nuclear Bomb Upgrade Could Violate Key Treaty', *Defensetech*, 28 February 2014.

38 See, for example, Thierry Gongora and Harald Von Riekhoff, *Toward a Revolution in Military Affairs?: Defense and Security at the Dawn of the Twenty-First Century*, Contributions in Military Studies (Westport, CT: Greenwood Press, 2000), p. 97; and David L. Shambaugh, *Modernizing China's Military: Progress, Problems, and Prospects* (Berkeley, CA: University of California Press, 2002).

39 Christopher F. Chyba, 'Time for a Systematic Analysis: US Nuclear Weapons and Nuclear Proliferation', *Arms Control Today*, vol. 38, no. 10, 2008, pp. 24–9.

Review Essay

We Can't Go On Living Like This

Gordon Barrass

Gorbachev: His Life and Times
William Taubman. London and New York: Simon & Schuster and W.W. Norton, 2017. £25.00/$39.95. 880 pp.

Mikhail Gorbachev wanted to revitalise the moribund Soviet system by giving socialism a 'human face', thereby securing for his country an honourable place in the vanguard of world history. Even though this Tolstoyan undertaking ended in Shakespearean tragedy, horrendous slaughter was avoided and great things were achieved.

In an outstanding biography, William Taubman shows his mastery in bringing this narrative together and enlivening it with an extraordinary range of sources and poignant vignettes. Many of the brightest gems come from the diaries of Anatoly Chernyaev – Gorbachev's foreign-policy adviser and alter ego – which are full of penetrating insights into personalities and events, often related with his characteristically wry humour.[1]

Thanks to Taubman's literary skills, one feels one is eavesdropping on Gorbachev's life – his hopes and triumphs, his doubts and misjudgements and downright failures, both public and private. By going on to ask why Gorbachev and others acted as they did, Taubman illuminates not only the

Gordon Barrass is Visiting Professor at LSE IDEAS, where he focuses on strategy and assessments. He had much to do with Soviet affairs during his years in the United Kingdom's Diplomatic Service and as a member of the Joint Intelligence Committee (1988–93). His book on *The Great Cold War* (Stanford University Press, 2009) examined the perceptions that each side had of the other.

Survival | vol. 59 no. 5 | October–November 2017 | pp. 157–166 DOI 10.1080/00396338.2017.1375266

way the Soviet elite thought, but how the Soviet system functioned – or why it failed to do so.

Gorbachev's rise is a tale of talent blessed by good fortune. He spent most of his first 50 years nearly 1,600 kilometres by rail from Moscow in the province of Stavropol, north of the Caucasus Mountains and midway between the Black and Aral seas. His early years were not promising, as Gorbachev's family struggled to survive on a collective farm out on the grain-growing steppes of the province. Nevertheless, his father and maternal grandfather both remained optimistic, and encouraged the young Mikhail to better himself.

In his school's meagre library, Gorbachev found a book left over from Tsarist times that profoundly influenced him. It was a collection of essays by Vissarion Belinsky, who in the 1840s proclaimed that socialism could only be achieved if it respected the individual. Gorbachev went on to become devoted to the great works of Russian literature that likewise addressed the big issues of life (pp. 29–30).

Amazing good luck followed in 1948, when Gorbachev was awarded the Order of the Red Banner of Labour, signed by Josef Stalin himself, for helping his father bring in a bumper harvest. Without that coveted honour, he would never have made it into Moscow University, where there were teachers who opened up his mind and widened his horizons; nor would he have married his fellow student, the vivacious and highly intelligent Raisa Titorenko.

Over the next 15 years, Gorbachev rose from being head of the Komsomol in Stavropol city to being the party boss for the whole region. He showed such respect and love for Raisa that local women would encourage their husbands to follow his example (p. 103). From the outset, Mikhail and Raisa talked about everything, including what they found out about the harsh realities of everyday local life.

It was during these years that Gorbachev's contacts with the outside world began to challenge his conviction that the Soviet system could be made to work. The first such challenge came from Eastern Europe when, in

1967, Zdenek Mlynár, his old friend from university days, told him that he was now convinced that socialist societies could never flourish unless they became genuinely democratic – a goal Mlynár tried to achieve the following year as one of the leaders of the Prague Spring (pp. 116–17).

The second challenge came from the West. As a rising young member of the Central Committee, Gorbachev was sent on official trips to Italy, France, Germany and the Benelux countries, sometimes accompanied by Raisa. They were not only impressed by the prosperity and culture they found there, but (perhaps more importantly) they felt entirely comfortable in the West, an experience no Soviet leader had had before. In Italy, Raisa was thrilled to see a statue of Giuseppe Garibaldi that portrayed the unifier of Italy with his wife, which confirmed her view of the importance of leaders' wives (pp. 149–53).

Because of his position as party boss, Gorbachev became acquainted with Yuri Andropov, head of the KGB and arguably the smartest man in the Politburo, who holidayed in Stavropol province. The two men shared a liking for music and literature, and a dislike of alcohol. Some nights they would grill shashlik (skewered meat), while Andropov sang songs that were ideologically suspect (p. 138).

With Andropov's backing, Gorbachev returned to Moscow in 1978 to be the party secretary in charge of agriculture. He had made it this far by seeming to be an ideal, youthful product of the system, yet he was concealing his belief that communism needed a human face (p. 689).

On becoming a full member of the Politburo in 1980, Gorbachev invited the Andropovs, now their next-door neighbours in Moscow, to a picnic 'as in the good old days' near Stavropol. Andropov declined, saying that before the two of them reached Gorbachev's house, Leonid Brezhnev would know about it and many questions would be asked (p. 174).

During these years, Gorbachev began to realise that the Soviet Union was run as a 'hierarchy of vassals … a caste system based on mutual protection',[2] and that the roots of its problems ran deep. When apologising to a foreign visitor for being late because he had been busy trying to solve some urgent problem in the agricultural sector, his guest asked when this problem had arisen. 'In 1917', Gorbachev replied with a wry smile (p. 253).

Gorbachev's real breakthrough came when Andropov, who had succeeded Brezhnev as general secretary of the Communist Party's Central Committee in 1982, told him to begin preparing himself to lead the party. Two years later, Andropov was dead and had been succeeded by the already aged Konstantin Chernyenko. After the funeral, Chernyenko and his senior colleagues met with a number of Western leaders, none of whom surprised them more than British prime minister Margaret Thatcher. The 'Iron Lady' spoke in seductively breathy tones about the importance of 'peace'. In doing so, she was exploiting not only her charm, but also the fact that among the Western leaders, she knew the most about the growing Soviet paranoia, thanks to the reports she was receiving from Oleg Gordievsky, British intelligence's well-placed KGB source in London.[3]

At the end of 1984, Gorbachev visited Thatcher in London. Following their discussions, the prime minister told the world that Gorbachev was a man she 'could do business with', and privately urged US president Ronald Reagan to meet him. One factor that has generally been overlooked behind the success of Gorbachev's visit is the very constructive use that the British continued to make of Gordievsky's intelligence.[4]

Three months later, Chernyenko, too, was dead and Gorbachev had been appointed party leader. Just before he accepted that post, he told Raisa that he had to take on this mighty burden because 'We [the Soviet people] can't go on living like this' (p. 209).

Ending the Cold War

In making itself one of the world's two superpowers, the Soviet Union had come to the brink of bankruptcy. Its defence expenditure was roughly the same as that of the US, while its economy was merely one-third as large. To make matters worse, Gorbachev had to deal with Reagan, the first American president to believe that the US could force the 'evil empire' to end the Cold War. Even after five years in power, Reagan's steely determination to pile pressure on the Soviet Union was undiminished.

Within the Soviet leadership, there was already a growing awareness that their country could not continue the confrontation with the US and NATO.[5] On the nuclear front, the Americans already had *Pershing* II missiles that could strike Moscow with virtually no warning. Moreover, they were researching a space-based anti-ballistic-missile system that would block a retaliatory Soviet strike. On the conventional front, they were not only developing weapons that threatened the formidable Soviet tank armies with obsolescence, but they also had a lead in electronic warfare that the Russians could not match.[6]

As the stoic Soviet people were not themselves demanding change, Gorbachev was able to concentrate on what he saw as the key issue: freeing them from the siege mentality that constrained innovation. His first priority was 'scaling down the arms race'.[7] The big question was the terms on which the Cold War would be settled.

In addition to ending the arms race with the West, Gorbachev had three additional tasks on his agenda: getting Soviet troops out of Afghanistan, integrating the Soviet Union into Europe and settling regional disputes in Southern Africa and Central America. This approach obliged him to act like a Western politician, carefully choosing his words to keep the support of different groups on various issues in changing times.

Fortunately, Reagan, like Gorbachev, was in no doubt that personal chemistry could produce miracles (p. 276). The ice was broken when they first met at the Geneva Summit in 1985, and by the time Gorbachev paid his first visit to the US in 1987, he and Reagan were not only able to sign the Intermediate-Range Nuclear Forces (INF) Treaty, but also a 'framework' treaty for negotiations to make deep cuts in each side's strategic missile forces. Then, in December 1988, Gorbachev caused an even greater sensation when he declared at the UN General Assembly that, over the next two years, there would be massive cuts in Soviet conventional forces in Europe. Moscow, he assured listeners, was not going to use force anywhere (p. 442).

Despite this gesture, the administration that took office in January 1989 under George H.W. Bush judged the Cold War to be far from over, and doubted whether Gorbachev really wanted it to end. (Many key people in London shared that view – one that I had been challenging from the Cabinet Office since early 1988, with limited success.) While the US reassessed relations with Gorbachev, momentous changes were sweeping across Eastern Europe. Within a few months of the Berlin Wall coming down in November

1989, Gorbachev was the only communist leader left in Europe – and he now faced the dramatic prospect of a reunited Germany.

Nevertheless, when Bush and Gorbachev finally met in Malta in December 1989, they were able to make considerable headway in resolving outstanding issues. Bush felt the need to support Gorbachev's domestic reforms. For his part, Gorbachev reversed decades of Soviet efforts to evict the US from the continent by describing its presence as important for the future of Europe (p. 499).

Reforming the Soviet system

The Malta Summit made the world safe for implementing Gorbachev's reforms. Unfortunately, this had become a greater challenge since 1986, when the price of oil, the Soviet Union's main source of hard currency, plunged by two-thirds to a mere $10 a barrel, in large part as a result of Reagan having persuaded Saudi Arabia to boost production. Moscow's foreign debt, already over $30 billion, began surging upwards.

Gorbachev's strategy was to lead the transformation from the top, and to implement it through the party machine. He brought a stunning change in leadership style to this task, reflecting his youthful energy, optimism and willingness to talk with ordinary people (p. 228). Videos of his first address in Leningrad, for example, 'were soon selling for five hundred rubles on the black market, an outlet normally reserved for bearded bards singing dissident ballads' (p. 214).

Gorbachev began by mobilising support for 'restructuring' the economy (perestroika), a term more acceptable to the party than 'reform'. In doing so, Gorbachev showed himself to be a consummate politician and brilliant tactician. He even persuaded the Communist Party to give up its monopoly of power and take part in a new, democratically elected People's Congress, from which a new Soviet government would be constituted (p. 691).

Whereas Gorbachev's liberal supporters wanted him to lead a new democratic party, he was unwilling to let the Communist Party, 'this lousy, rabid dog', off the leash (p. 591). As a result, Boris Yeltsin, his arch rival, was able to demonstrate his superior grasp of the new populist game. One of Yeltsin's key moves was to get himself elected as president of the

Russian Republic, by far the biggest of the union's 15 so-called republics, by popular vote.

It was, however, Yeltsin's persistent goading of Gorbachev to pursue far-reaching political changes that turned tensions between the two men into deep, mutual hatred (p. 330). As Taubman graphically puts it, 'In a Shakespearean sequence of events Yeltsin not only became Gorbachev's gravedigger, but brought down the whole Soviet system' (p. 333).

Gorbachev's many opponents were horrified by this turn of events. His concessions to the Americans on arms control, the loss of Eastern Europe and the reunification of Germany had infuriated them. So, too, had his stripping the party of its monopoly of power, the worsening food shortages across the country, the increase in violence and the rise of nationalism in the other republics. As Vladimir Kriuchkov, then head of the KGB, put it, '[our] biggest mistake was to misunderstand Gorbachev' (p. 227).

Meanwhile, in Washington, the CIA had concluded that 'The Gorbachev era is effectively over'. The Bush administration now focused on 'locking in' the gains Gorbachev had already allowed the US to make, rather than anticipating a post-Gorbachev era (p. 588).

In summer 1991, Gorbachev ignored an explicit American warning that his opponents were preparing to oust him. He did so believing he could persuade Yeltsin to agree to the republics having more power within the Soviet Union and thus satisfy his opponents (p. 585). While Gorbachev was on holiday in Crimea, the plotters made a farcical bid for power.

Once again, Yeltsin seized the initiative, rallying over 50,000 people to defend the Russian parliament building in Moscow. Four days later, the coup collapsed and Gorbachev returned safely to Moscow. Nonetheless, Yeltsin triumphed over him by delivering a humiliating denunciation of his failures. The following day, Gorbachev resigned as head of the party, which ceased to exist only a few days later.

Given all he had done on arms control, German unification and Iraq, Gorbachev was embittered that Western leaders (with the exception of German chancellor Helmut Kohl) had failed to give him a massive aid package that could have enabled him to bribe the republics into accepting some new form of federation. Western leaders, however, were cautious, believing that, without serious reforms in place, and given that Soviet hard-currency debt was already approaching $80bn, any financial support would be money down the drain (pp. 589–97).

As levels of violence rose and the spectre of the union disintegrating loomed larger, Gorbachev concluded that any attempt to use the army to restore order would risk civil war.[8] With Gorbachev unable to demonstrate his authority, Yeltsin and the leaders of Ukraine and Belarus were quick to sign a pact replacing the Soviet Union with a Commonwealth of Independent States. To add insult to injury, they first telephoned Bush to tell him what they had done, only informing Gorbachev afterward.

Although this 'soft landing' was acceptable to the West, it was not what Gorbachev had intended for his country.[9] On 25 December 1991, the Soviet Union came to an end. That evening, the 'nuclear button' was passed into the hands of Boris Yeltsin, president of Russia, the borders of which had shrunk to where they had been in 1653.

An ending and a new beginning

Could it have ended differently? Of course, but in all probability the Soviet Union would have eventually found itself once again in a Time of Troubles. Taubman concludes that Gorbachev's 'over-confidence in himself and his cause gave him the courage to reach so high that he over-reached – and then warped his judgment when what he was trying to build started to shatter' (p. 692). As Gorbachev himself later lamented, one of the key difficulties was that 'Our Russian mentality required that the new life be served up on a silver platter immediately … without reforming society' (p. 3).

Yet, as Taubman points out, Gorbachev's achievements were many: he destroyed what was left of totalitarianism in the Soviet Union; and he brought freedom of speech, assembly and conscience to people who had never known it. By introducing free elections and creating parliamentary institutions, he laid the groundwork for democracy (p. 688). 'Despite his flaws and his failures to achieve his noble aims', Taubman concludes, Gorbachev 'was a tragic hero who deserves our understanding and admiration' (p. 693).

The day after Gorbachev stepped down as president of the Soviet Union, he told Italian journalists that democracy and human rights were important everywhere, but added,

> We have our own reality, inspired by tradition, history, a unified country that has formed by a natural process. Yes, like many of my compatriots, I have spiritual ties to Europe, but I am no less bound to the East ... Russia must recognize that it is a bridge between the two cultures ... and, simultaneously, part of human civilization.[10]

Russia's national identity and links with Europe were on Tsar Alexander I's mind as he marched into Paris in 1814 – and have yet to be settled more than 200 years later.

Notes

1 Chernyaev's diaries are available on the website of the George Washington University National Security Archive at http://nsarchive.gwu.edu/rus/Chernyaev.html.

2 Zdenek Mlynar and Mikhail Gorbachev, *Conversations with Gorbachev* (New York: Columbia University Press, 2002), p. 4.

3 Gordon S. Barrass, *The Great Cold War* (Stanford, CA: Stanford University Press, 2009), p. 304.

4 Oleg Gordievsky, *Next Stop Execution* (London: Macmillan, 1995), pp. 310–11.

5 S. Akhromeyev and G. Kornienko, *Glazami Marshala I Diplomata* [Through the Eyes of a Marshal and a Diplomat] (Moscow: Mezhdunarodnye otnosheniia, 1992), pp. 315–16.

6 Christian Nuenlist (ed.), *Records of the Committee of Ministers of Defence, 1969–1990* (Washington DC: Parallel History Project, 2001), p. 13.

7 Anatoly Chernyaev quoted in William C. Wohlforth (ed.), *Witnesses to the End of the Cold War* (Baltimore, MD: Johns Hopkins University Press, 1996), p. 15.

8 Mark Kramer, 'The Collapse of the Soviet Union (Part 2)', *Journal of Cold War Studies*, vol. 5, no. 4, Fall 2003, p. 9.

9 Barrass, *The Great Cold War*, p. 369.

10 Andrei Gratchev, *Final Days: The Inside Story of the Collapse of the Soviet Union* (Boulder, CO: Westview Press, 1995), p. 190.

Review Essay

Hillbilly Insurgency

John A. Gans, Jr

Hillbilly Elegy: A Memoir of a Family and Culture in Crisis
J.D. Vance. New York: Harper, 2016. $27.99. 272 pp.

There was a time when America's heartland was seen as critical to the nation's strength. Its food, factories and coal powered the nation; its men and women fought its wars; and its white-picket-fenced small towns evoked the American dreams of foreigners. During the Cold War, none other than Soviet premier Nikita Khrushchev visited one such town – Ames, Iowa – because he was 'curious to have a look' at America while in the country for meetings in 1959.[1]

US president Dwight D. Eisenhower used that curiosity to his advantage by strategically scheduling his summit with Khrushchev at the end of the Soviet leader's grand tour. By using Camp David as a carrot, Eisenhower hoped to keep the fiery premier on his best behaviour. But the president also wanted Khrushchev to visit an American factory town that was 'universally and exclusively inhabited' by its workers, to see 'decent, fine, comfortable homes', and to meet a 'happy … free people, doing exactly as they choose'.[2]

Khrushchev did not visit Middletown, Ohio – a town that would have fit Eisenhower's description six decades ago – but readers can do so today in J.D. Vance's bestselling memoir *Hillbilly Elegy*. Although Vance describes his life story as 'superficially boring' (p. 204), the memoir is a searing look

John A. Gans, Jr, is a professorial lecturer at the Johns Hopkins School of Advanced International Studies and a Resident Fellow at the German Marshall Fund. These views are his own.

 DOI 10.1080/00396338.2017.1375268

into a part of the United States that is 'hemorrhaging jobs and hope' (p. 1), and a startling introduction to the friends and family he affectionately calls 'hillbillies' – who, the book makes clear, are not the happy people of Eisenhower's America but instead increasingly 'isolated, angry [and] distrustful' (p. 148).

'Hillbilly' is an American term, but the fears and frustration Vance sees in Middletown and communities like it across the country are not unique to the US. The same 'stress, sadness, fear, anxiety' that many working-class Americans feel about a world that they believe no longer serves their needs can also be seen in Europe, Asia, the Middle East and elsewhere (p. 224). American hillbillies and others like them around the globe, as well as the populists some tend to support, have something else in common: they are now taking steps – such as voting for US President Donald Trump – to upset the global order and the globalists they blame for their struggles.

Hillbilly heartland

The Vance family number among the millions of white, working-class Americans, typically of Scots-Irish descent, found predominantly in and around the Appalachian Mountain region of the United States. They are hill people, or hillbillies. Vance finds his roots in Kentucky coal country, in a town named after Andrew Jackson, the populist hero, seventh US president, and inspiration for the tone of Trump's inaugural address. Content for generations to mine for coal and live in Kentucky, members of the Vance family, like others, could not resist the lure of the industrialising north, which, according to Vance's book, needed two things from the mountains, 'coal and hill people' (p. 28).

Two separate migrations after the first and second world wars brought hillbillies to Ohio, Michigan, Illinois, Indiana, Pennsylvania and elsewhere. They also spread 'hillbilly values', a heritage that has remained largely unchanged for generations (p. 21). Vance notes that the hillbilly diaspora inherited many good traits, among them an 'intense sense of loyalty', a 'fierce dedication to family and country' and what he refers to at one point as a devotion to 'Christian duty' (pp. 3, 86). He even-handedly admits, however, that some 'bad' traits have also been passed down, including a dislike for 'outsiders or people who are different' (p. 3).

This hillbilly heritage may have toughened members of the Vance family for the transition to their new home, but it also held some of them back as times changed. Vance's grandparents relocated to Middletown, Ohio, recruited by the American Rolling Mill Company (Armco Steel), which promised them a better life outside of the mines. Though they found financial success, achieving a middle-class lifestyle for themselves and their growing family, this success could not dispel, but only masked, the 'cultural unease' they carried with them (p. 36).

According to Vance, the combination of hillbilly culture's 'robust sense of honor, devotion to family, and bizarre sexism' all too frequently produced 'explosive' results (p. 41). Growing up in a self-described 'clan of lunatics' (p. 17) with tendencies toward violence and substance abuse (alcohol in his grandparents' time and prescription drugs in his mother's), Vance's formative years were filled with 'never-ending conflict' (p. 74). Though his 'old fashioned, quietly faithful, self-reliant, hardworking' grandparents displayed a 'measured optimism', his mother – and, says Vance, his 'whole neighborhood' – was angry, distrustful and hopeless (p. 148).

The generational change corresponds with the nation's economic evolution and the Midwest's stagnation. Japan's Kawasaki Steel Corporation bought the struggling Armco, which at the time was the fifth-largest US steelmaker, in 1989.[3] In an increasingly global, corporate and automated era, AK Steel, as it became, could not remain the same generous employer and city partner it once was. In turn, employees and their families could no longer sustain the middle-class lives of their parents, reducing Middletown to 'little more than a relic' of Eisenhower-era 'American industrial glory' (p. 50). According to Vance, many in the city, like those across the nation's 'hollowed out' manufacturing heartland, lost 'economic security and the stable home and family life that comes with it' (p. 5).

But Vance is rightly unwilling to blame this outcome only on economic difficulties. He also cites a cultural tendency to react to 'bad circumstances in the worst way possible', and to act in ways that encourage 'social decay instead of counteracting it' (p. 7) – a tendency he finds anecdotal evidence for within his own family. His mother's drug use and inability to hold a job, for example, created an uncertain and anxious home for the young Vance. His community's despair nearly became his own: when his mother demanded a sample of his clean urine so she could pass a drug test at work, Vance relented, but writes that 'something inside me broke' that day (p. 132).

Hillbilly meets world

Fortunately, Vance's grandmother, or 'Mamaw', stepped in to save him. Under Mamaw's roof, Vance began to thrive. Her rules, boundaries and insistence he focus on school and early jobs gave Vance a taste of a different approach to life, an experience he describes time and again in *Elegy*. When exposed to the unfamiliar, whether at his grandmother's home, during a visit to an uncle in California or in a court room where he had come to testify after another violent fight with his mother – and where he spent a few hours observing the professionals – Vance came to see there were 'people who … were different from us' (p. 79). Each of these experiences helped to prepare him for the two big leaps that would ultimately make his life – and this book – a happier one: the first into the US Marine Corps and the second to Yale Law School. Vance's challenge was to ensure that hillbilly culture and pathology did not undermine him as he attempted to make these transitions.

Though love of country runs deep in the Vance clan, military service did not. Mamaw opposed his enlistment, warning him that with 'everything that's going on in the world, you'll get your head blown off' (p. 157). Vance, however, believed he 'had no other choice' (p. 157). Unprepared for college and unwilling to settle for nothing, Vance saw the Marine Corps more as an opportunity for a better life than an opportunity to serve. The Marines did their part, teaching him how to 'live like an adult', in his words, and showing him more of the world, including war (p. 174).

Vance's memoir is far from a war story, however. The author admirably refrains from exaggerating his experiences as a public-affairs officer, a choice that gives weight to the one anecdote he does share. Rather than complain about the damage done by the American intervention in Iraq or fetishise its local culture, Vance recalls how a visit to an impoverished Iraqi school, at which a young boy was overjoyed by a small gift, gave him a newfound appreciation for how 'lucky' he was to be American and loved by a family, even if it was full of lunatics (p. 173).

Vance arguably experienced greater culture shock in New Haven, Connecticut, where, after excelling at university, he found the classes at the top-ranked Yale Law School far easier to master than the class differences. As a hillbilly, a veteran and the product of a public college, he encountered frequent reminders of his outsider status. When interviewing for a prestigious law firm at a high-end restaurant off campus, for example, Vance found himself overwhelmed by everything from the quality of the crystal to the conversation at the table. When offered a choice of water, still or sparkling, he hesitated, guessed, and then, shocked by the carbonation, sent it back, believing something was 'wrong with that water' (p. 212).

The episode demonstrates why the class divide can be so difficult for some hillbillies to bridge, but also why, despite occasionally spitting out his water or wearing the wrong shoes to interviews, Vance was able, with a little help from non-hillbilly friends and faculty, to not only keep up, but to get ahead. By the end of his time at Yale, he had secured a spot on the law review, lined up a prestigious clerkship and prepared himself for success on the other side of the divide. He was now an Ivy-league-branded, over-paid, white-collar professional.

Vance describes the change not just in terms of his professional achievements but his entire worldview. He had, in his own words, 'harbored resentment' for his 'entire life' (p. 173). Yet his experiences in Iraq, at Yale, during his upward ascent and among new friends introduced him to an optimism he had never known. This changed his view both of his own life and of hillbilly life more generally. He writes that his 'increasing optimism … contrasted starkly with the pessimism of so many of [his] neighbors' (p. 188). Having come to feel like an 'alien' in the hillbilly heartland (p. 195), he began to see its problems anew, and grew frustrated with those who he believed were misdiagnosing the ills of his community.[4]

Hillbilly struggle

Few scholars or policy experts, in Vance's eyes, have identified the real problem hillbillies face: the pessimism that stalks them from birth (p. 8). Using polling, he argues that no group in America is 'more pessimistic than working class whites', less than half of whom expect 'their children will fare better economically than they have' (p. 194). In the years following the Great Recession, Vance sees 'something almost spiritual about the cynicism of the community, something that went much deeper than a short-term' downturn (p. 188).

The hillbillies Vance knows in Middletown and elsewhere are more 'socially isolated than ever' (p. 4). Many have 'dropped out of the labor force or have chosen not to relocate for better opportunities', and feel betrayed by 'an economy that failed to deliver the most basic promise of the American dream' (pp. 4, 189). Hillbilly men, in Vance's opinion, 'suffer from a peculiar crisis of masculinity in which some of the very traits that our culture inculcates make it difficult to succeed in a changing world' (p. 5).

It is clear from trends in the United States and other industrialised nations that this toxic brew of resentment poses political, social, economic and spiritual challenges. The politics of *Elegy* may be dated – Donald Trump is not mentioned – but Vance's lengthy discussion of Barack Obama still serves to illuminate the attitudes that continue to shape American politics. The now former president, in Vance's telling, struck 'at the heart of our deepest insecurities' (p. 191). Hillbillies 'believe that the modern American meritocracy was not built for them', but rather for people like Obama, another Ivy-league-branded, over-paid, white-collar professional – and bestselling author to boot (p. 191).

It is frustrating, however, that Vance has chosen mostly to ignore race in his treatment of Obama and the hillbilly problem. If Obama and post-Yale Vance are 'alien' to hillbillies, what to make of their embrace of a thrice-married, 'billionaire', Queens-accented television star who lived in a gilded penthouse in New York before moving to the White House? Especially after President Trump's comments sympathising with the white supremacists who gathered in Charlottesville, Virginia, in August 2017, Vance seems too dismissive of the possibility that Trump's race had something to do with his appeal, and with the contempt that many felt for the president he replaced.

Hillbilly insurgency

Toward the end of the book, Vance writes that his life is in many ways an 'anomaly' (p. 204). Surviving a disadvantaged childhood, earning a world-class education and developing a prestigious career are the stuff of American legends and, it turns out, Hollywood movies.[5] Vance knows how lucky he was. He praises the individuals, many imperfect, who propelled him upward even if they remained on spoiled ground themselves, and concedes that, had any of them been removed 'from the equation', he would have been 'screwed' (p. 239).

'Screwed' is how too many in America's working-class communities feel about their lives and futures. But that feeling extends far beyond the United States to homes and communities around the world. Vance's is a story about the white working class in America, but there are people like his family members everywhere. They may not aspire to the American dream, but they share the growing fear that an anxiety-free night's rest, let alone dreams of any kind, is becoming a luxury afforded only to the rich, connected and worldly. With the election of Trump, the Brexit vote, the strong performance of Marine le Pen in the French presidential race, and the rise of other protest and populist movements across the world, it appears that large numbers of people have decided that they're just not going to take it anymore.

The world has thankfully moved on from the state-driven ideological struggle that once pitted Khrushchev against Eisenhower. But the divide between those who espouse a globalist system for organising the world and those who back a more populist approach seems to be growing wider by the day. Globalists may still be more powerful, standing at the helm of businesses, markets, governments, international organisations and printing presses, but some hillbillies and others like them around the world, along with the populists who have stoked their fears, are mounting an insurgency, working to slow and upset the plans and policies of globalists they no longer trust with their well-being.

Although they cannot take down the globalised order in one shot, they can with their tweets, votes and small acts of resistance make it less efficient, effective and attractive while trying to woo others to their cause. Whether by spreading conspiracy theories about the alliances and agreements that anchor the US-led international order, mounting aggressive campaigns to contract or crater the single market in Europe and free trade in North America, or supporting candidates bent on starving or stymieing international organisations, they are steadily escalating the asymmetric fight against globalisation that has simmered since the 1990s.

Vance's book makes clear why this globalist–populist fight will continue, and why the hillbilly insurgency could persist and even triumph in what will be, as Eisenhower said of the Cold War, 'a prolonged and complex struggle'.[6] Though he criticises the dark side of their culture, Vance, knowingly and rightly, describes hillbillies as some of the 'toughest goddamned people on this earth', willing – perhaps too much so – to fight for their kin, their community and their country (p. 255). Anyone tempted to underestimate them would be wise to remember that. The world should also recall how successful insurgencies can be, and that effective counter-insurgency requires a better understanding of the opposition. With his *Elegy*, Vance makes an introduction, demonstrating through his own life story all that hillbillies can overcome.

Notes

1 Chalmers M. Roberts, 'Our Least Diplomatic Visitor', *Washington Post*, 4 February 1979.

2 Dwight D. Eisenhower, 'The President's News Conference at Gettysburg, Pennsylvania', 12 August 1959, available at http://www.presidency.ucsb.edu/ws/?pid=11466.

3 Jonathan P. Hicks, 'Talking Deals; Armco's Accord With Kawasaki', *New York Times*, 6 April 1989.

4 Vance provides a veritable literature review of the latest findings from the fields of sociology, economics and more as to the worth and wisdom of food stamps, school vouchers, drug rehab and more. See, for example, pp. 116, 126–7 and 195.

5 It was announced in April 2017 that *Hillbilly Elegy* had been optioned by a Hollywood movie studio. Mike Fleming, Jr, 'Imagine Lands J.D. Vance's Rust Belt Memoir "Hillbilly Elegy"; Ron Howard to Direct Film', Deadline.com, 10 April 2017, http://deadline.com/2017/04/j-d-vance-hillbilly-elegy-ron-howard-directing-rust-belt-memoir-1202067052/.

6 Dwight D. Eisenhower, 'Farewell Radio and Television Address to the American People', 17 January 1961, available at http://www.presidency.ucsb.edu/ws/?pid=12086.

Book Reviews

South Asia

Teresita C. Schaffer

Choices: Inside the Making of India's Foreign Policy
Shivshankar Menon. Washington DC: Brookings Institution Press, 2016. $26.00. 159 pp.

Shivshankar Menon is one of the most gifted people to lead the Indian Foreign Service, both in terms of his intellectual grasp of strategy and foreign policy, and in his diplomatic skills. In this slim volume, he uses five complex decisions in which he participated as examples of the way Indian policy deals with the inevitable competition among its foreign-policy goals. The 1993 Border Peace and Tranquility Agreement with China drew on his background as one of India's 'China cadre'; the others – the US–India nuclear agreement, India's response to the bloody attacks on Mumbai in 2008, the end of the Sri Lankan civil war in 2009 and India's decision to adopt a no-first-use policy for nuclear weapons – occupied the later parts of his career, including his time as foreign secretary and as India's national security adviser.

Menon's basic argument is that India is on its way to becoming a great power, and that, at this stage, its policy combines bold goals and cautious tactics. As a practitioner, he recognises that serious policymaking is rarely black and white, and usually involves trade-offs among important national goals. His title, *Choices*, reflects this.

Those who have dealt with India from the outside often observe that choices do not come easily to India's diplomatic establishment, especially when, as often happens, they pit some of India's idealistic goals against its more hard-nosed geostrategic interests. In that case, as this book illustrates, realism usually has the edge, though policy continues to be articulated in the

 DOI 10.1080/00396338.2017.1375271

idealistic language that India gave the world in the 1950s and has modulated gradually ever since.

As India's power expands and its international profile becomes more prominent, India's preferred policy stance – non-alignment or, as one hears more frequently nowadays, strategic autonomy – and its geostrategic requirements are likely to be in tension with increasing frequency. Relations with China in particular are likely to generate more than their share of competing objectives, with the strategic challenge from China pulling India in one direction and the increasingly important India–China economic relationship in another. I would have welcomed a bit more discussion of this prospect. Menon's book is an excellent and authoritative guide to how some of the stars in India's foreign-policy leadership think about the inevitable trade-offs they deal with.

Pakistan's Inter-Services Intelligence Directorate: Covert Action and Internal Operations
Owen L. Sirrs. Abingdon: Routledge, 2016. £110.00/$155.00. 317 pp.

Owen Sirrs is a professor at the University of Montana, and his CV lists stints with the US Defense Intelligence Agency and the US military in Afghanistan. His book on *Pakistan's Inter-Services Intelligence Directorate* has pulled together material previously discussed in an enormous number of books and articles by participants in Pakistan's intelligence adventures, both from Pakistan and from other countries, as well as by observers of them. Sirrs paints a picture of an agency that has from its inception been an important player in Pakistan's troubled security policy – but also in 'black operations' in its domestic politics. Known as ISI, the agency famously reports both to the army chief and to the prime minister or president of Pakistan. Thus, when the national leadership is civilian and weak, it becomes an instrument of military domination.

The book has some interesting material, but also curious gaps and mistakes. The maps are practically unusable, for example. While his bibliography is long, it omits some surprising sources; some of his juiciest stories are unsourced; and there is no mention of interviews even though a number of the dramatis personae would surely have been willing to be interviewed. All told, he paints a picture of an agency that operates within the army's orders but largely outside the legal and judicial framework. He argues that ISI's poor understanding of the dynamics of East Pakistan contributed importantly to Pakistan's ultimate loss of Bangladesh, and that the agency similarly misunderstood the Kashmiris, leading to the debacle of Pakistan's attempted conquest of Kashmir in 1965. He credits ISI with a better understanding of Afghanistan – and with relentless pursuit of the army's, and former president Muhammad Zia-ul-Haq's, goal of a subservient government in Kabul, while running roughshod over the 'strategic partnership' with the United States. He correctly acknowledges that the United States and Pakistan had significantly different strategic objectives in Afghanistan. This is still true.

One well-connected Pakistani friend commented to me that 'there is a great deal we simply don't know about ISI'. This book doesn't change that – indeed, it illustrates the problem. By pulling together the main features of the story, this book represents a useful resource for scholars. But it will inevitably leave them with a great many unanswered questions.

Half Lion: How P.V. Narasimha Rao Transformed India
Vinay Sitapati. Guragon: Penguin Random House India, 2016.
₹699.00. 391 pp.

Vinay Sitapati begins his account of the complex and contradictory political career of P.V. Narasimha Rao, India's ninth prime minister (1991–96), by citing a story from the *Bhagvata Purana*, one of the ancient writings that have shaped India's cultural traditions. Narasimha, half-man and half-lion, is able to slay a mighty demon because of the ambiguities and contradictions he embodies. Sitapati's book is an admiring account of how this ancient hero's namesake was able to be, by turns, fox, lion and mouse, and in the process to transform India's economy, politics and military power.

It is widely believed that Manmohan Singh, a PhD economist and skilled technocrat who would himself become prime minister in 2004, was the architect of India's transformation. Sitapati sets out to challenge this conventional wisdom. The author rightly credits Singh with developing the intellectual framework within which India's economic transformation took place. But he makes a good case that only the prime minister could supply the political cover Singh needed to put in place a major deregulation, and that Rao, however improbable his selection as prime minister may have been, did the job with a level of Machiavellian guile, cunning and sometimes concealed decisiveness that few believed him capable of.

Rao himself was not a natural choice to introduce and sustain such dramatic changes in India's state-centric economic management. He had been an enthusiastic participant in the earlier system. Nothing in his previous career suggested that he would have much interest in upending the 'license permit raj' that was so central to India's economic management and political deal-making. And yet, once convinced that this was necessary, Rao was able to take decisive – and sometimes devious – action, resulting in the greatest growth spurt independent India had known. Sitapati goes on to describe how Rao introduced elements of a welfare state and used these to strengthen the political consensus behind deregulation. He credits Rao with preserving the option to test a nuclear device, which his successor, Atal Bihari Vajpayee, actually implemented. His major failure, in Sitapati's eyes, was the destruction of the Babri Mosque in 1992, carried out by operatives of the Bharatiya Janata Party who essentially betrayed a bargain Rao believed their leaders had struck with him.

At the time of these events, Rao did not come across as a heroic figure. I remember, as a US diplomat, calling on him when he was out of office, and finding him worn down with cares and rather taciturn. A few months later, in the wake of Rajiv Gandhi's assassination, he had manoeuvred his way into the prime ministership – and power had put a new spring in his step. He had admirers among Indian political analysts and historians, but he was not widely liked. His cautious style generally served him well, but did not make him popular. The poignant story of how his erstwhile colleagues in the Indian National Congress shunned him when he died illustrates how lonely he had become. They forced the family to move the funeral out of Delhi, to his original hometown of Hyderabad; newly minted prime minister Dr Manmohan Singh promised to have a memorial built in Delhi, but nothing came of it; and most conspicuously, the funeral cortège leaving Delhi stopped outside the locked gate of the Congress party headquarters, but contrary to other former leaders, the body was not brought inside.

Nonetheless, Rao certainly deserves to be remembered as one of those who created today's India. Sitapati's lively and readable account will help to make this happen.

When Crime Pays: Money and Muscle in Indian Politics
Milan Vaishnav. New Haven, CT: Yale University Press, 2017.
£25.00/$40.00. 410 pp.

Milan Vaishnav tackles the tantalising issue of corruption in Indian politics on three levels: as a storyteller, a political scientist and a policy thinker.

The most compelling, in my view, is the story he tells through the eyes, careers and fans of such colourful politicians as Pappu Yadav, Ateeq Ahmed, Mohammed Shahabuddin and Arvind Kejriwal. He starts by highlighting the stunning number of Indian politicians who have been charged with crimes. By 2014, 34% of India's national parliamentarians had pending criminal cases against them, and for 21%, these involved serious offenses (p. 10). The trend in recent years has been relentlessly upward, in both categories. The core of Vaishnav's argument is that this does not represent an information gap on the part of India's voters. Rather, it reflects the voters' judgement that their politicians' criminal pedigrees put them in a position to provide better services to constituents and, in places marked by ethnic or caste rivalry, to help their confrères beat out their ethnic or caste competitors. The main characters are unforgettable. The logic of the 'market' for criminally tainted politicians is distressingly strong, and very persistent.

The most ambitious level of this book is Vaishnav's political-science analysis. He works over the numbers with great care, demonstrating with multiple approaches to statistics what his anecdotes illustrate.

His policy recommendations are the most depressing feature of the book. Vaishnav has put together an impressive and quite creative list of policy measures that might eventually change voters' calculus about whether criminal muscle really is a prerequisite for providing constituent services. But these reforms – even those that draw on institutions already in use in India – promise to be difficult. He argues, for example, for putting in place 'smarter regulations', and for starting from scratch to reinvent and modernise a panoply of laws dating from the mid-nineteenth century and drafted by the British imperial authorities. He makes an excellent case for both recommendations. But reading these proposals as the US Congress struggles to tackle the future of healthcare, tax reform or even the ordinary annual budget, one wonders how many of these extraordinarily difficult tasks the Indian legislature would be able to tackle during any given five-year electoral cycle. The goals make one want to stand up and cheer; the complexity of actually achieving them is daunting.

This is an important book. Milan Vaishnav has gotten deeply into the weeds of Indian politics, and presents in granular detail a remarkable picture of how India's political machinery works. His depiction of the people involved alone makes it a must-read for anyone who cares about the political future of the world's largest democracy. Vaishnav closes with some observations on other countries in which the same problems might recur. Political junkies interested in other countries as well should read and ponder this book.

Rivers Divided: Indus Basin Waters in the Making of India and Pakistan
Daniel Haines. London: C. Hurst & Co., 2017. £35.00/$45.00. 264 pp.

As a US diplomat specialising in South Asia, I came to this book as an admirer of the Indus Waters Treaty, signed in 1960 between the governments of India, then headed by Jawaharlal Nehru, and Pakistan, under Field Marshal Ayub Khan – the most enduring agreement ever signed by those two hostile neighbours.

Only once had I been exposed to the contrary point of view. Toward the end of a conference on Kashmir, I found myself sitting at dinner next to Roger Fisher, whose slim volume *Getting to Yes* has introduced generations of Americans to the art of negotiation. Fisher had assisted the World Bank president with the Indus treaty negotiations early in his legal career. I asked him if anything about the negotiations had surprised him.

His response surprised *me*. Fisher was disappointed that the agreement had not adopted the optimum usage of all the Indus Basin water. The Indus Waters Treaty provided for a 'divorce', with Pakistan taking all the water in the three western rivers and India having predominant rights to the three eastern ones. To me, that was brilliant. The two hostile riparians would not have to interact on contentious issues on a daily basis. In my view, this contributed to the treaty's survival through three wars. Fisher, who had hoped for a 'joint custody arrangement', found the treaty a waste of water resources.

Daniel Haines takes us behind the curtain. He not only provides a lucid account of the ingredients that went into the treaty, including the ecology and economy of the river basin and the negotiating history both within and between the two countries involved; he also deals at length with the philosophical difference I discovered in talking to Roger Fisher. The American lawyer David Lilienfeld had pushed – successfully at first – for a 'whole basin' approach, hoping that the experience of cooperating in an agreement where the scientific data drove everything else would yield not just economic but also political benefits.

Haines's account makes clear that this model was too difficult for either country to pull off. India and Pakistan started with incompatible positions on how rivers figured in national sovereignty, views that were intensified by their mutual hostility and need to defend their nascent independence. Moreover, the earlier history of dealing with Indus Basin-related issues when the British ruled the subcontinent had yielded ample disagreements between central and local authorities, which played out in some degree in the treaty negotiations.

Haines goes one step further and argues that the treaty was an expression of Cold War politics. I don't altogether accept this. Certainly, US interest in peacemaking between India and Pakistan, and in promoting economic development in the Third World, was partly motivated by a desire for strengthening US influence. But this general goal would not necessarily have required a deep US involvement in treaty negotiations.

Haines is fascinated by Lilienfeld and his influence on the early stages of the process. I was fascinated by his account – but unpersuaded that Lilienfeld had the right answer. Pursuing the hydrologically ideal solution would, in my view, have been a classic case of the best being the enemy of the good. Haines does not explicitly say so in the book, but I believe he would agree.

The Indus Waters Treaty has been back in the news for the last decade or so, with active disputes over Indian proposals to construct waterworks along the upper reaches of the rivers the treaty allotted to Pakistan. Anyone who wants to understand the possibilities and limitations of dealing with these disputes should read Haines's book. I suspect, however, that they will come away feeling, like me, that a good riverine divorce is better than a bad joint river-custody arrangement.

Middle East

Ray Takeyh

The Six Day War: The Breaking of the Middle East
Guy Laron. New Haven, CT: Yale University Press, 2017.
£20.00/$28.00. 368 pp.

The 50th anniversary of the 1967 Arab–Israeli war has brought forth a slew of new books. The Six-Day War was certainly one of the most lopsided conflicts in the annals of the modern Middle East, with Israel managing to triumph over the collective militaries of Egypt, Syria and Jordan. The results of the war may be clear-cut, but its origins are murky. It was a war that no one wanted, and yet a series of actions and reactions caused the region to once more descend into violence. Guy Laron's *Six Day War: The Breaking of the Middle East* is a detailed and impressive account that does much to illuminate the origins of this elusive conflict. Michael Oren's *Six Days of War* has long set the bar for the field, standing alone over a mass of largely mediocre accounts. Laron offers a thoughtful diplomatic counterpoint to Oren's military history.

In 1967, Egypt's aged and exhausted revolutionary leader, Colonel Gamal Abdel Nasser, was being assailed by younger militants in Syria and taunted by conservative monarchies. The radical Syrian republic wanted Nasser to redeem his Arab-nationalist pledge to wage a decisive battle against the Jewish state. The Ba'athist leaders in Damascus, who had little or no direct experience with Israeli armour, seemed to believe their own rhetoric and did much to inflame the region by facilitating Palestinian infiltrations of Israel. Nasser knew better. He wanted to lead the radical camp without following through on its promise to push Israel into the sea. In the meantime, the conservative monarchies – under attack by Nasser's propaganda machine for insufficient resolve – were asking why the lion of Arabism was shielding himself behind UN peacekeepers. Ironically, one of Nasser's mockers, King Hussein of Jordan, would eventually ally with him and thus lose substantial portions of his kingdom.

Laron's study draws on a multiplicity of archives, making good use of Soviet and Eastern European depositories. He highlights a neglected dimension of the war: tensions in civil–military relations. It appears that in all the nations involved, the generals wanted war more than the civilians did. This was especially the case in Israel, where prime minister Levi Eshkol had to constantly beat back demands from his army chiefs for war. But such pressures were not limited to Israel. Nasser also faced rivals in the armed forces who seemed to relish the chance to punish Israel. The Israeli generals' desire for war may be understandable given their decisive military edge, but it is hard to see why the commanders of the sluggish Egyptian army thought they could hold their own.

The role of the United States in this conflict seems curious by its absence. By 1967, Lyndon Johnson was drowning in the morass of Vietnam. America preferred not to have another crisis on its hands, but seemed incapable of mustering the necessary diplomatic muscle to stop it. Eshkol hoped that Johnson would somehow come to his aid and help him fend off his generals, but to no avail. The war that followed continues to cast a long shadow over the region.

Nasser's Peace: Egypt's Response to the 1967 War with Israel
Michael Sharnoff. Abingdon: Routledge, 2017. £85.00/$100.00. 233 pp.

The unresolved Palestinian question is often seen as the legacy of the 1967 war. Suddenly, Israel was in possession of both the West Bank and Gaza, bringing it into direct rule over a large Palestinian population. The other side of the story is that the war, ostensibly launched by the Arab states to achieve Palestinian self-determination, did much to undermine that cause.

In his commendable new book, Michael Sharnoff examines Nasser's last years in power, offering a critical portrait of the champion of Arabism, whose tenure was marked by disastrous wars, domestic mismanagement and incompetent tyranny. Nasser was not without his gifts, of course, mesmerising crowds with his soaring rhetoric and manipulating Westerners with private assurances of pragmatism. The fact that his public face often contradicted his private pledges comes across vividly in these pages.

In a sense, Nasser was a tragic figure, imprisoned by forces that he himself had unleashed. It was Nasser's strident pan-Arabism that was used against him by Syrian radicals, who taunted him into a war with Israel that he did not want. That same Arabism also prevented him from forging a peace with Israel that he knew was necessary. Yet even though the war shattered his economy and destroyed his military, he was still not prepared to relinquish the mantle of Arab leadership.

Sharnoff chronicles Nasser's confused moves in the aftermath of the war. On the one hand, the most important priority for Nasser was no longer to liberate Palestine but to reclaim the territories that he had lost to Israel. This necessitated limiting his horizons, settling with conservative Arab monarchies and dealing with the United States. He achieved some of these objectives in part. The reconciliation with Saudi Arabia came easily, as Riyadh was prepared to offer Nasser a way back so long as he left the country alone – the price for Saudi petro-dollars was Nasser's acquiescence to the reactionary forces he had always mocked. The Egyptian colonel may have been effective at manipulating Dwight Eisenhower during the Suez Crisis, but Lyndon Johnson, distracted by the war in Vietnam, needed assurances that Nasser would make peace with Israel before getting involved in the talks. This would become the land-for-peace formula that has guided the talks between Israel and its Arab nemesis ever since.

Nasser was ultimately unable to entirely abandon his ideological identity, eventually adopting an Egypt-first posture. The implementation of this policy would be left to his more enterprising successor, Anwar Sadat, who waged a more successful war than Nasser had and regained the territory that he had lost. Unlike Nasser, Sadat was prepared to pay the price of being ousted from the ranks of Arab radicals. To be sure, Nasser's guile was still on display, as he made promises to both American and Soviet emissaries that his spokesmen decried in public. But this was not the 1950s, and there was no one to take the place of the Bandung generation of neutralists who had successfully manipulated Cold War rivalries. The Americans were too wise, the Soviets too cynical and the Israelis too powerful for such ploys to work. Nasser had to sue for peace, something he refused to do. He died with his revolution exhausted, his army shattered, his land occupied and his successor ready to abandon his legacy.

The Future of Leadership in the Shiite Community
Mehdi Khalaji. Washington DC: Washington Institute for Near East Policy, 2017. 124 pp. Available at http://www.washingtoninstitute.org/policy-analysis/view/the-future-of-leadership-in-the-shiite-community.

The political wrangling to determine who will succeed Iran's Supreme Leader Ali Khamenei has begun in earnest, yet the backroom dealings and subtle signals coming from Tehran are lost on most Western analysts. Mehdi Khalaji is an exception: a one-time seminarian, he knows his way around Iran's clerical estate. *The Future of Leadership in the Shiite Community* reflects his experience, erudition and unparalleled knowledge of one of the Islamic world's more opaque institutions. The monograph's endnotes should put paid to the claim that a paucity of sources makes research in this area difficult to carry out – Khalaji has dug up memoirs, religious texts and press interviews to buttress his arguments.

As for the question of who will succeed Khamenei, Khalaji seems to identify a leading candidate, Mahmoud Shahroudi, the former head of the judiciary. As the monograph attests, he is a problematic choice. Shahroudi was born in Iraq, still a sore point for Persian nationalists who do not share their clerical elders' transnationalism. In the past, he expressed scepticism of the *Wilayat al-Faqih*, the notion that a single religious jurist should assume political power. (Despite Iran's experiment with clerical rule, the idea of a single ayatollah wielding temporal powers was at once a contentious idea in the seminaries.) He is also known for his corruption, having indulged in his share of financial misconduct. And yet, among the coterie of clerics that Khamenei has cultivated, Shahroudi does have a measure of theological learning. He also has experience with the bureaucracy, and his background in supporting anti-Saddam guerrillas demonstrates his dexterity in dealing with paramilitary forces. He is reliably anti-Western and has little use for the democratic trappings of Iran's constitution. Still, if the best the Islamic Republic can offer as a successor to Khamenei is a corrupt cleric imported from Iraq, the regime seems headed for rough times.

Khalaji concedes that the succession process may yet yield some surprises. But his impressive monograph leaves little room for doubt that the 1979 revolution has done real damage to the Shia clerical order. The intermingling of faith and politics has sullied the reputation of the men of God, hollowed out the seminaries, and created a measure of public apathy toward Shi'ism and hostility toward its clerical guardians. This is surely not how the founder of the revolution, Ayatollah Ruhollah Khomeini, expected the system to evolve, but the experience of the past three decades illustrates that even the best-laid plans can still go awry.

Democracy and the Nature of American Influence in Iran, 1941–1979

David R. Collier. Syracuse, NY: Syracuse University Press, 2017. $44.95. 448 pp.

As documentary evidence has become available, scholars have begun to re-examine the Pahlavi dynasty in Iran and its tumultuous tenure. A number of outstanding biographies and books on the 1953 coup that restored Shah Mohammad Reza Pahlavi to power have provoked a lively debate. David

Collier's comprehensive but uneven book is the latest addition to the genre. The author gets some of the big themes right: the shah's relentless quest for absolute power did prove his undoing; Iran did have nascent democratic movements, often led by wise aristocrats who might have skilfully guided the ship of state; and the United States did at times subordinate its values to the need for Cold War stability.

The author's account is weakest where he assesses the first two decades of the shah's rule. Collier has an evident fondness for the word 'control'. According to him, America controlled Iranian politicians, sought to control Iran's oil and did much to control its destiny. For a book that insists on assigning agency to the Iranians, the locals frequently fade from the scene, functioning mostly as the pawns of malevolent forces beyond their influence. This is a shame, especially given that a series of colourful Iranian prime ministers did much to save their country in the 1940s and 1950s. It was Ahmad Qavam who coaxed Josef Stalin out of Azerbaijan in 1946, and Mohammad Mossadeq who reclaimed Iran's oil from Britain in 1951. Thus, two great powers that had historically abused and exploited Iran were gently ushered out by its politicians. The shah should have trusted this establishment instead of eviscerating it.

Collier's assessment of the oil-nationalisation crisis seems regrettably conventional. The Truman administration's many efforts to resolve the crisis through diplomacy are largely ignored, and Dwight Eisenhower is superficially presented as a dullard easily manipulated by the devious Dulles brothers (secretary of state John Foster Dulles and CIA director Allen Dulles) into supporting the coup that overthrew Mossadeq. All this to take over Iran's oil, with anti-communist rhetoric serving to conceal mercantile motives. Such polemics fail to address the complex origins of the events and their lasting consequences.

Collier is at his best when assessing the 1960s, a remarkable decade usually overlooked in favour of the coup and the revolution. John Kennedy emerges as one of the outstanding personalities of this period: he and his enterprising aides, Walt Rostow and Robert Komer, seemed to have appreciated the necessity of reform in Iran. The shah responded with the White Revolution that made land reform its central ambition. Although these reforms suffered from poor planning and were haunted by the spectre of the authoritarianism that was gradually descending on Iran, they still led to the empowerment of numerous peasants and workers.

The final decade of the shah's tenure is given surprisingly short shrift in this account. The archives of the Nixon and Carter administrations seem not to have been explored, with the book's final chapters relying mostly on secondary sources. The Iranian revolution, which must stand as one of the great revolts of the twentieth century, is given little attention. Those who wish to learn why Iran had a revolution, and why the revolutionaries succeeded, must look elsewhere.

In the end, Collier's account is an important reminder that the Pahlavi dynasty offers historians much scope for exploring the many tensions and contradictions that eventually provoked the demise of one of the Middle East's seemingly formidable monarchies.

From Independence to Revolution: Egypt's Islamists and the Contest for Power
Gillian Kennedy. London: C. Hurst & Co., 2017. £25.00. 262 pp.

With its intact borders, important cultural and educational institutions, and even a vibrant press, Egypt, the most populous Arab country, was once considered the epicentre of Arab politics. The notion that religion should inform politics is not unique to Egypt, but the Muslim Brotherhood – which has proved to be one of the most consequential Islamist organisations in history – originated there. Since then, the organisation's branches have popped up throughout the Middle East, with its proxies and emulators seeking to replicate the Egyptian experiment. Gillan Kennedy's compact and judicious study of Islamism in Egypt during the reign of the Free Officers is an important addition to the evolving literature on this subject.

The author begins her study with the familiar terrain of Gamal Abdul Nasser's revolution, which pragmatically reached out to the Brotherhood to begin with, only to relegate it to the margins of society later on. This was the age of Arab nationalism, with its presumptions of modernity that left little room for religious activism. Nasser's ambitions were not limited to displacing his erstwhile Islamist allies, but stretched to dominating Egypt's politics as a means of establishing its hegemony in the Middle East. As with most Third World leaders, Nasser saw in socialism a way of not just controlling the means of production but establishing a personalised dictatorship. The state nationalised industry and agricultural lands, took over the banking system and promised employment for all college graduates in the burgeoning bureaucracy. The result was economic stagnation and a heavily bureaucratised state that provided poor services and low wages for its servants. Islamists were not the only ones repressed, but unlike some they managed to maintain a measure of activism in Nasser's enveloping dictatorship.

In an ironic twist of history, it was Israel that came to the rescue of Egypt's beleaguered Islamists. The Six-Day War devastated Nasser's military, discredited the shibboleths of Arab nationalism and led to cries for authentic solutions to Arab problems. No group had railed against imported ideologies more than the Islamists, who now experienced a revival of their fortunes. Their message seemingly validated and their rivals all but discredited, the men promising salvation stepped forth to claim their moment.

The Islamists were granted an additional advantage when Anwar Sadat rose to the presidency determined to displace his leftist rivals by making common cause with the forces of tradition. As Kennedy deftly demonstrates, Sadat's pragmatism empowered the Islamists while further radicalising the movement. The Muslim Brotherhood responded positively to Sadat, approving of his privatisation measures and his more successful war against Israel. In the process, however, the organisation's complicity with power paved the way for even more radical Islamists to emerge, proffering their own critiques of the state and its Muslim enablers.

The question that lingers through much of this account is whether the experience of wielding power moderates the Islamists. Before the advent of the Arab Spring, academics assured themselves that Islamist radicalism was caused by the exclusion of its adherents from power. Once vested with the responsibilities of state, they would yield to the mandates of governance and eschew ideological experiments. Having since had the opportunity to observe the rule of ideologues who claim to know the mind of God, the proponents of such notions would be well advised to discard them.

Economy
Erik Jones

Public Debt, Inequality, and Power: The Making of a Modern Debt State
Sandy Brian Hager. Oakland, CA: University of California Press, 2016. £27.95/$34.95. 157 pp.

Public debt has increased dramatically in recent decades, and particularly in the aftermath of the economic and financial crisis. Income inequality has increased as well. These two developments have overlapped insofar as the top income earners have come to hold an ever-greater concentration of the public debt. In turn, this concentration represents a twofold challenge: control over the public debt gives high-income households (and large corporations) potential influence over public policy, as well as substantial claims on current tax revenues. In a worst-case scenario, the rich will push governments to structure their fiscal accounts in ways that transfer resources from society at large into the pockets of those who are well off.

According to Sandy Brian Hager, the worst-case scenario may already be upon us. Pulling together disparate data series to reveal who holds outstanding US government bonds, he shows that debt holdings have become more concentrated in the hands of wealthy households and corporations. He demonstrates how this concentration is correlated with the growth in income inequality and the decline in effective marginal tax rates. He suggests that foreign holders of US government-backed instruments give big domestic bondholders even more leverage over politics and policy. And he uses textual analysis of the annual 'Economic Report of the President' to argue that bondholder interests have become increasingly predominant in public-policy discourse.

There is much to like about this volume. It is clear and concise. It points to policy measures that have done much to resolve the recent crisis – such as quantitative easing – and that would do much to improve public finances – such as a more progressive effective marginal tax-rate structure. Most importantly, it seeks to translate the arcana of public finances into the more familiar language of policy discourse that any interested reader should be able to decode.

Nevertheless, the argument has problems. The 'bondholder class' is presented as a kind of singular entity that knowingly manipulates government policy for its own gain. The fact that rich people have many of the same political inclinations does not give them awareness or coherence as a 'class' (in the Marxist sense). Moreover, their intervention is not required to make the story hold together. The government can either tax the rich or borrow from the people who have savings (also known as 'the rich'). The US government does both. And while the effective marginal tax rate has declined for high-income earners, the overall tax taken from that group has increased both in absolute terms and as a share of total revenue. This is the admittedly tarnished silver lining of rising income inequality.

Moreover, the government is not giving the rich much in terms of interest rates (or yields) on the money it has borrowed. On the contrary, the more the government borrowed during the recent crisis, the higher the price it charged for its bonds. This was not in the interests of bondholders, who were not in the market for short-term gains, but the alternatives were worse – witness the growing pressure in the US to raise taxes and the brinkmanship in Congress over the debt ceiling. There is no conspiracy here, just interdependence. The rich only gained their wealth because of the relatively smooth functioning of the financial economy; they will only benefit from that wealth if the financial economy does not collapse. Meanwhile, the American people show little appetite for entitlement reform. There seems ample reason to expect further debate on the possible reintroduction of more progressive effective marginal tax rates.

The Power of a Single Number: A Political History of GDP
Philipp Lepenies. Jeremy Gaines, trans. New York: Columbia University Press, 2016. $30.00. 186 pp.

In order to determine how much tax can be extracted from a group of people, some understanding is needed of how much money they have and how much they make. To increase wartime production, it is necessary to ascertain how productive resources are being used and identify the potential implications of any redeployment. To escape from an economic crisis, it is important to know how that crisis began in the first place. And to promote economic development, some way of measuring progress must be established. As Philipp Lepenies explains, the calculation of what is today called the 'gross domestic product' (GDP) lies at the intersection of all these ambitions. That 'single number' serves as a tool for the state to determine how much money it can raise, how big a military it can field, what to do when things go wrong and how to make the world a better place.

The almost cult-like status of GDP in modern politics is understandable given the usefulness of having a reliable measure of national income, output and expenditure. Far more surprising is the fact that, less than a century ago, standardised national accounting did not really exist – a point made to great effect by Lepenies. And while there were political economists who recognised the need for some reliable measure of economic performance dating back to the emergence of the modern state in the early seventeenth century, the intellectual effort needed to justify, create and agree upon an accounting standard was immense. Moreover, most of the great innovators either died before their preferred measures were adopted, lost important battles over how the data would be collected or disappeared into relative obscurity despite their success.

This story is important because it explains many of the deficiencies of the 'single number' in use today. As Lepenies describes it, the gross domestic product is an instrument of state that gives pride of place to manufacturing output and market prices, because these are better proxies for what can be taxed. It treats military expenditure on a par with consumption and investment because such equal treatment (rather than regarding military expenditure as a deadweight loss) is necessary to plan a war effort. It relies on three different techniques for calculation (output, income, expenditure) because so much of what should be measured is not recorded directly and thus needs to be estimated and cross-checked. It ignores a large number of cultural and social factors that would only complicate the task of making comparisons across countries or providing recognisable benchmarks for achievement. And it focuses more attention on aggregate performance than on the distribution of wealth or income. GDP is not neutral, it is functional. At its core, it relies on a political arithmetic.

The implication, Lepenies concludes, is that the needs of the present may extend far beyond the capabilities that the gross domestic product represents. The number will continue to attract cultish devotion, and yet its usefulness will diminish. Indeed, that may already have happened. We should not expect, however, to see another magic number rise up to take its place. The gross domestic product was centuries in the making. It rests on a complex nest of compromises that are both substantive and methodological. And its emergence was historically contingent on a peculiarly Anglo-American synthesis of economic traditions and political imperatives. It is as difficult to imagine replacing it as living without it.

The End of Theory: Financial Crises, the Failure of Economics, and the Sweep of Human Interaction
Richard Bookstaber. Princeton, NJ: Princeton University Press, 2017. $29.95. 226 pp.

Imagine two worlds. In one of them, people with the best of intentions nevertheless interact with one another in ways that no one likes; try to learn from their mistakes, but accept that they cannot predict the future; and realise that sometimes there are no short cuts to getting things right. In the other, people never interact in ways that conceal their underlying motivations; do not learn from their mistakes because they never make 'mistakes' (in the conventional sense of the word); trust that they can make the future predictable by working to make people's motives more transparent, including by revealing any institutional incentives; and believe that such predictions can be achieved through mathematical shortcuts, with no need to rely on lived experience. The first world is the one we live in. The second is the one economists imagine. That is why, as Richard Bookstaber argues, economists systematically fail to anticipate and understand meltdowns and crises.

The solution, Bookstaber insists, is to embrace the world as it is rather than imagining something that is more tractable for mathematical modelling. The goal is not to submit ourselves to the tyranny of lived experience, but rather to embrace a modelling strategy that takes advantage of, rather than ignoring, the basic elements of the human condition. The models would start with real-world agents, describing how they navigate the world in terms of their relationships and the simple decision rules they deploy in the face of changing circumstances. It would assess the many different iterations of their interaction to suggest a universe of possibilities – both intended and unintended. By analysing these scenarios as unfolding narratives, it should be possible to isolate the crucial elements that place our real-world agents in jeopardy. The institutional environment can then be tweaked in ways that help fend off calamity.

There is much promise in this line of argument. Economic theory does rest on unrealistic assumptions, and it did fail to anticipate the most recent economic crisis – not to mention crises past. Meanwhile, evolutionary biologists have made great strides in showing how simple, rule-based models that focus on individual agents as they interact with one another can reveal patterns that mirror what we see in the world around us, and yet would be hard to identify using an alternative set of modelling conventions. If we could find a way to use this kind of agent-based modelling to illustrate dynamics that would otherwise remain hidden from view until we experienced them, it would be well worth the effort of re-engineering the way we study finance and economics to reflect this approach.

Contrary to its title, however, *The End of Theory* does not replace mainstream economics. Sure, economists have their failings, but they also have their successes. Any reasonable replacement theory should be able to acknowledge and replicate those insights. Yet Bookstaber's analysis does not do so, and the agent-based modelling he uses in his illustrations cannot do so. As for the ability of these models to predict the next crisis, I remain dubious. We do not need a multi-agent adaptive model to spot the problem of portfolio contagion, whereby crises spread from one market to another because portfolio managers need to meet ever increasing liquidity requirements. Bookstaber offered a more compelling account of that phenomenon in his previous book, which antedated the recent crisis. Much of the emphasis he places on liquidity management can be justified using lived experience as well. The recent crisis was expensive in terms of jobs lost and capital destroyed. If Bookstaber is arguing that we need some sophisticated model to convince policymakers to learn from this painful episode, I might have to reconsider my assessment of the world we live in.

Adaptive Markets: Financial Evolution at the Speed of Thought

Andrew W. Lo. Princeton, NJ: Princeton University Press, 2017.
$37.50. 483 pp.

Andrew Lo's adaptive-markets hypothesis demonstrates the promise of evolutionary biology and multi-agent adaptive modelling more fully than does Bookstaber's *The End of Theory*. Like Bookstaber, Lo begins with a critique of economists' fascination with mathematical modelling and the strong professional consensus surrounding the belief that financial markets are efficient. The difference is that Lo is more willing to admit that the efficient-markets hypothesis works. Financial-market participants can absorb huge amounts of information in vanishingly short periods of time; their pricing decisions can communicate that information in a streamlined format; and the results can be verified independently through comparisons with other information-harvesting techniques, such as in-depth surveys (for consumer products) or public-opinion polling (for voting intentions and hence election outcomes).

Just because the efficient-markets hypothesis works, however, does not mean it is 'right' – any more than Newtonian physics is a true depiction of the material world. Human behaviour departs from the assumptions underpinning the financial-markets hypothesis in a number of ways. Many of these deviations – for example, the phenomenon of loss aversion – have been catalogued by behavioural economists. The problem is that observed behaviour does not constitute a predictive theory. We can see bias, but determining how that bias contributes both to the 'normal' functioning of the economy between crises (as anticipated by the efficient-markets hypothesis) and to the sudden onset of a crisis (when predictions based on the efficient-markets hypothesis break down) is more difficult. As Lo insists, 'it takes a theory to beat a theory' (p. 75). A new theory should be able to capture all that its predecessors have to offer while adding new features.

Lo's adaptive-markets hypothesis is just such a replacement. The essence of the theory is the same as that outlined by Bookstaber: human beings make decisions based on shortcuts; those shortcuts evolve to fit a particular context; and when people use those shortcuts out of context, bad things happen. Lo uses this simple framework to reveal the conditions under which the efficient-markets hypothesis would appear to hold, thus validating the contributions of mainstream economics as a special case. He then shows how the same framework can be used to explain the evolution of the various quirks identified by behavioural economists in terms of loss aversion, risk aversion, framing effects and the like. Critically, Lo shows that such quirks are not 'irrational', but they may be 'maladaptive', depending upon the environment (p. 189). Finally, Lo shows how the context of such assessments varies depending on whether all market participants experience the same shocks or whether the experience of some participants is idiosyncratic.

The notion of idiosyncrasy is important because it allows Lo to draw on the experience of hedge funds as a kind of natural experiment. According to the efficient-markets hypothesis, hedge-fund managers should not be able to beat the market. Experience shows, however, that some fund managers are successful for extended periods. Lo uses his adaptive-markets hypothesis to explain why market pricing does not follow a random walk. He reveals how hedge funds have emerged to exploit systematic deviations using various strategies and techniques. And he shows how the success of those funds invites both imitation and competition until the original deviation no longer exists. The process is not always a smooth one; sometimes whole groups of hedge funds collapse. The important thing is to understand the underlying pathology as the key not only to fixing finance, but also to harnessing financial markets to tackle the world's most significant problems. This book is essential reading.

Warnings: Finding Cassandras to Stop Catastrophes
Richard A. Clarke and R.P. Eddy. New York: Ecco, 2017. $29.99.
416 pp.

For any given crisis there is always someone who saw it coming, who may not have known the precise date on which it would arrive, but who had a sense of the mechanism at work and the magnitude of the coming impact. Such people do not rely on guesswork – they are typically experts using hard data and proven models to illustrate cause and effect. Their predictions are usually made publicly and repeatedly, but all too often, no one sees fit to listen or, if the message is received, to take steps to avoid the catastrophe or mitigate its effects. In many cases, serious crises might have played out differently if only the people responsible for protecting the public interest had paid attention to the warnings and reacted accordingly.

Richard Clarke and R.P. Eddy present two sets of case studies to demonstrate that Cassandra, the prophetess of Greek myth who can see the future and yet is condemned to be ignored, is always with us. One set focuses on past crises, including the Fukushima nuclear disaster, the subprime-mortgage debacle, the collapse of Bernie Madoff's fraudulent investment scheme, Hurricane Katrina and the emergence of ISIS. The other set focuses on crises that have not yet come to pass but involve foreseeable threats such as meteor strikes, global warming, artificial intelligence, nuclear winter and genetic engineering. All of these cases feature an individual who uses publicly available information combined with extensive training and experience to identify a problem as it is emerging. These individuals commit themselves to the cause of avoiding catastrophe, but find themselves confronting a mixture of opposition and indifference. This narrative structure makes for engaging reading. Each chapter unfolds like a blockbuster movie – many of which have already been made.

The book's individual stories are less interesting, however, than its overall message as a collection. The effect of the ensemble is to reveal that the world is an unbelievably dangerous place, with problems unfolding both in plain view and out of sight, over a range of time horizons, and requiring not just immediate but sustained attention. Moreover, each hazard poses its own complications, even if the impact is almost always the same in terms of loss of life, social disruption and economic hardship. It is easy to sympathise with those policymakers who, like the authors in their previous role as public servants, are responsible for setting priorities and allocating resources. It is also possible to understand, although much harder to sympathise with, those policymakers who find themselves wishing the world were a simpler place, and that some of its more intractable problems would just go away.

Clarke and Eddy stress the dangers of ignoring the warnings of experts, no matter how inconvenient or out of step with the prevailing consensus. Their solution is not to chase every possible problem but to make sure that each is at least acknowledged – both at the highest levels of government and by the many departments and stakeholders, including the public, that would be implicated in forging a response. Such acknowledgement is the first step in creating accountability. Politicians and policymakers can and must set priorities; they should also be held responsible when the threats they ignore manifest. In Clarke and Eddy's telling, Cassandras only exist after the fact. Governments need to develop their capacity to listen more carefully before crises break out.

Cyber Security and Emerging Technologies

Thomas Rid

The Hacked World Order: How Nations Fight, Trade, Maneuver, and Manipulate in the Digital Age
Adam Segal. New York: PublicAffairs, 2016. $26.99. 306 pp.

For a quarter century now, cyber security has been creeping up the list of national-security priorities. In 2016, the issue even broke into US presidential politics in unprecedented and unforeseen ways. Russian interference in that year's election involved no high-tech cyber war, but a relatively simple hack-and-leak operation adapted from the Cold War's active-measures playbook. The cyber-security debate is only just beginning to take stock of this momentous event.

Adam Segal's *The Hacked World Order*, published a few months before the leaks started, serves as a useful snapshot of where things stood around the time the computers of the Democratic Party's National Committee were being breached. Segal provides useful historical and conceptual background to a reinvigorated discussion. Although it contains a certain amount of unhinged hyperbole – Segal approvingly quotes Henry Kissinger to the effect that 'cyberspace challenges all historical experience' (p. 10) – this ambitious book has much to offer.

'Year zero', for Segal, runs from June 2012 to June 2013. That year, nation-states 'visibly reasserted' their control over data in search of power, wealth and influence, 'laying to rest the already battered myth of cyberspace as a digital utopia' (p. 1). During those 12 months, the US admitted to developing Stuxnet; Iran mounted a counter-attack against US financial institutions; tens of thousands of hard drives owned by Aramco, Saudi Arabia's oil giant, were destroyed; and unprecedented volumes of classified documents that had been exfiltrated from US National Security Agency (NSA) networks were leaked by Edward Snowden. In Segal's post-2013 hacked world order, new strategic cultures of 'cyber power' are emerging. This power can be seen in four areas: in a country's infrastructure prowess, which allows it to contribute to the running of the internet itself; in a government's ability to leverage its private sector; in its possession of tech-savvy intelligence agencies and armed services; and finally, as Segal boldly argues, in the state's control over 'an attractive narrative of cyberspace' (p. 38). The author is one of the foremost authorities on China's technology policy, and he is particularly convincing on this subject.

Occasionally, the analysis would benefit from better attention to detail. Quantum computing would not, even in theory, 'enable the decryption of any information' (p. 228). The NSA announced in 2015 that it is preparing for the 'upcoming quantum resistant algorithm transition', and there are even public-key algorithms that are currently invulnerable to quantum computing. Disappointingly, *The Hacked World Order* also trades in too many clichés ('physical space matters much less in the cyber age', p. 10). This problem is to some degree unavoidable in a short introductory text with such a vast scope. Still, intelligence agencies cannot, as Segal claims, 'go to Google [and] Facebook' to 'gather huge amounts' of private data 'with little effort' (p. 119). The NSA and Britain's Government Communications Headquarters (GCHQ) did not do so before 2013, and attempting to do so has become even harder since then. For most users, personal-communication apps are more secure than ever. This is, ironically, at least partly the result of the Snowden leaks and Silicon Valley's reaction to the often exaggerated press coverage of the NSA revelations. The Snowden files were keenly studied not only by journalists, pundits and privacy activists – adversarial intelligence agencies also took careful note. The most aggressive ones will surely have realised how easy it would be to hack the world order — and open societies with a free press in particular — through leaked dumps of controversial documents.

Der Desinformant: Erinnerungen eines DDR-Geheimdienstlers
Horst Kopp. Berlin: Das Neue Berlin, 2016. €16.99. 254 pp.

In late 2016, just as active measures were making a comeback, a remarkable book appeared in Germany: *Der Desinformant* (The Disinformant), by Horst Kopp. The 83-year-old author served as an officer in Abteilung X, the infamous active-measures department of East Germany's Ministry of State Security (Stasi). For more than 20 years, Kopp helped deceive and influence West German politicians and journalists. The goal of the Stasi's 'active measures', according to a ministerial memo from 2 January 1963 quoted by Kopp, was 'to hit [the adversary] at the base and in the hinterland, to expose him, to disturb his power, to fracture and to paralyze' (p. 93). Perhaps no intelligence agency was more masterful at disinformation than the Stasi. Certainly, Kopp and his colleagues benefited from their geographic, cultural and linguistic closeness to their target.

Kopp ran 27 agents during his time at Department X, most of them journalists, and almost all of them under false flag, meaning these individuals did not know they actually served the Stasi. His career-defining accomplishment – tipping the first-ever vote of no confidence in the West German Bundestag in late April 1972 – was one of the most brazen and successful disinformation operations of the Cold War. The Christian Democrats (CDU), then in opposition, should have been able to oust Chancellor Willy Brandt, a Social Democrat, with some promised help from the Liberals. But Kopp and his colleagues deceived and bribed two CDU MPs into defecting from their own party. Thus, the Stasi secretly shaped the outcome of a historical Bundestag vote, keeping Brandt in power and humiliating the CDU. Kopp ran one of the defectors, Leo Wagner, through an intermediary, and meticulously prepared contacts, arguments and the transfer of funds.

Kopp himself was never a defector. His organisation simply ceased to exist. The Hauptverwaltung Aufklärung (HVA), the Stasi's foreign-intelligence arm, saw itself as relatively uncorrupted by the excesses of domestic surveillance. Nor does the author write as if admitting some mistake, or condemning the HVA's disinformation operations as morally wrong. Kopp confidently documented his work. So how does he justify the lying and deception? When I asked him this in person during an interview in Kyritz in May 2017, he passed me a handwritten note stating 'A.–M. Examples, FAZ, 20/2/2004, page 11'. 'Look it up', he said. 'The other side did it too.' Kopp's oblique note, it turned out, referred to a tame story of West Germany trying to lure Eastern defectors.

The Disinformant is the second book to emerge from the Stasi's Department X. The first – *Auftrag: Irreführung* (Mission: Deception) by Günter Bohnsack and Herbert Brehmer, published in 1992 when memories were still fresh – has become something of a classic among the small group of historians working on active measures. The book confirmed, for example, the German intelligence community's attribution and analysis of major Stasi active measures from 1985. Sergey Kondrashev, who led the KGB's active-measures efforts, praised it as one of the two best books ever written on influence operations. Remarkably, it has never been translated into English.

Such operator accounts of disinformation campaigns are invaluable at a time when disinformation is making a comeback. The Stasi books illustrate the depth of experience in Eastern bloc intelligence organisations, and demonstrate how long it can take for the most sophisticated operations to see the light of day. They also sound a note of warning, echoed by the historical debate surrounding Stasi operations in Germany: not even the testimonies of the perpetrators can resolve the finer points of attribution, vulnerable as they are to self-interest, fading memory and, alas, disinformation.

Drone: Remote Control Warfare
Hugh Gusterson. Cambridge, MA: The MIT Press, 2016.
£19.95/$24.95. 199 pp.

The irony is bitter: the administration of Barack Obama, a thoughtful law professor and reluctant warrior, forged and fine-tuned a terrifying assassination machine, only to pass it on to Donald Trump. But even under Trump's more democratically minded predecessor, America's extraordinary drone programme was kept as secret as possible. Today, the data and the future of 'remote control warfare' are more obscure than ever.

Hugh Gusterson is an anthropologist at George Washington University who focuses on nuclear weapons. In the past, he has been fiercely critical of the US military's use of anthropologists in counter-insurgency. With *Drone*, he applies his anthropological toolset to an analysis of the changing nature of warfare itself. Hackneyed notions of American 'empire' and drones as a 'colonial' technology notwithstanding, this book is an inspiration.

According to Lieutenant-General David Deptula, a US Air Force pioneer of remotely piloted aircraft, 'the real advantage of unmanned aerial systems is that they allow you to project power without projecting vulnerability' (p. 22). President Obama found these weaponised platforms attractive for precisely that reason — they promised to help keep the US out of quagmires. If a drone crashed in Helmand, its pilot could still pick up some groceries on his way home from work in Nevada. Drones meant more precision strikes in theatre, at lower risk for American operators.

But the effects of drones on warfare have been profound. Drone technology, Gusterson argues, has 'remixed' war (p. 29). Before the technology was invented, war consisted of what Gusterson describes as a tightly packed and spatially concentrated ensemble comprising weapon, weaponeer and target. He cites Carl von Clausewitz's notion of war as a 'duel' or 'competition' as the best expression of this classic view of armed conflict (p. 45). Remote-control warfare 'disarticulated' this assembly – spatially, temporally and conceptually. With logistics and command-and-control chains spanning literally the entire planet, and multiple agencies in different bases taking advantage of unmanned 'platforms' circling remote skies, drones expand the space of war for the weaponeer, even as they compress space for their targets, who cannot escape the machines' humming omnipresence. Drones also expand time for the weaponeer, requiring never-ending hours of observation and reconnaissance, and causing operators to report experiencing hits 'in slow motion' (p. 46). For their targets, meanwhile, *Hellfire* missiles strike like a flash from the blue.

Finally, remote-control warfare, according to Gusterson, 'remixes' the concept of war itself. If war, as classically understood, involves the mutual exchange of death blows, are drones even weapons of war? 'With the help of the drone', Gusterson concludes, 'war is fragmenting into something else for which we do not yet have a good name' (p. 44). In his view, a duel without the opportunity for 'reciprocal injury' is no longer a contest, and thus no longer war.

For a slim book, *Drone* has remarkable range: Gusterson provokes on a conceptual level, yet displays good attention to detail throughout, contrasting, for example, the experience of landing piloted aircraft with that of landing an aircraft remotely, without the subtle physical and visual feedback that airborne pilots receive from the machine and its environment. It may be that a certain ethnographic empathy helped him to make some surprisingly nuanced and helpful observations on the controversial issues of valour and post-traumatic stress disorder as well.

The Red Web: The Struggle Between Russia's Digital Dictators and the New Online Revolutionaries

Andrei Soldatov and Irina Borogan. New York: PublicAffairs, 2015. $17.99. 370 pp.

Andrei Soldatov and Irina Borogan are two of Russia's best-known investigative journalists. Their previous book, *The New Nobility*, chronicled the evolution of Russia's intelligence and security establishment in the years following the Cold War. *The Red Web* tells the story of the struggle for the Russian internet, with the state's powerful forces pitched against a group of online activists.

On 17 August 2009, the Sayano–Shushenskaya hydroelectric power station on the Yenisei River in Siberia suffered a catastrophic accident that killed more than 70 workers. Keith Alexander, while still director of the NSA, once cited the incident as an example of what a 'cyber attack' could achieve, even though a material failure, and not a cyber attack, caused the accident. Soldatov and Borogan discuss the Sayano–Shushenskaya dam incident for a more hard-hitting and less hypothetical reason: in the incident's aftermath, Russian authorities, for the first time, expelled an Interfax agency journalist for being too critical – and brought in an independent blogger to cover the relief operation in a more sympathetic way. Two months later, the LiveJournal blogger was invited to join the Kremlin press pool.

Soldatov and Borogan are storytellers as well as, occasionally, protagonists. This set-up works well, making *The Red Web* even more engaging. The chapter on Edward Snowden's association with Russia is particularly intriguing. 'Snowden may not have known or realised it', the authors write, 'but his disclosures emboldened those in Russia who wanted more control over the Internet' (p. 209). His arrival in Moscow from Hong Kong in 2013 coincided with a 'large-scale offensive' against internet freedom led by the Kremlin. Vladimir Putin was quick to see that the NSA defector was a political godsend, not just internationally but also domestically. Moscow's security agencies soon acquired more investigatory powers over internet communications under the pretext of protecting the personal data of Russian citizens against the excesses of American snooping that Snowden had allegedly exposed. 'Snowden could have done good things globally,' the authors quote one of Russia's most prominent internet activists as saying, 'but for Russia he was a disaster' (p. 220).

The authors' discussion of Russian internet ideals in the late 1990s and early 2000s is a welcome antidote to the vision being espoused by Silicon Valley in those high-minded times, and which lingers to this day. Russian activists simply wanted a free press and freedom from corruption, whereas utopians in the United States were looking to transcend the laws of physics in a 'virtual reality' and to homestead the new frontier of 'cyberspace'. At first glance, Russia's version of internet utopianism may appear mundane. At second glance, it may have been ahead of its time.

The Red Web elegantly blends technology, history and politics. If this indispensable book admits to any flaw, its lack of depth on the late 1990s in Russia, especially the fateful year of 1999, might qualify. It was during this crucial and fascinating period that age-old active measures and *kompromat* operations were brought online for the first time. The goal was to bring down some of the Kremlin's domestic opponents by creating dedicated websites to serve up a time-tested brew of part-fact, part-forgery.

Closing Argument

Charlottesville

Dana H. Allin

I

On the second of May 2008, Mildred Loving, a 68-year-old black woman, died of pneumonia in Central Point, Virginia.[1] In the same town 50 years earlier, Loving had been asleep in bed with her new husband, a white man, when sheriff's deputies broke into their house and arrested them both. The Lovings had been legally married in adjacent Washington DC, but this did not spare them several nights in jail and a plea-bargained felony conviction for violating Virginia's 'Racial Integrity Act' that included suspended one-year jail sentences and a 25-year banishment from the state. The sentencing judge, Leon Bazile, explained that the Virginia law, enacted in 1662, was in service of God's purpose when He placed the races on separate continents to prevent their mixing. The Lovings paid court fees and left the state to set up house in Washington. But they grew homesick for family, friends and the easy rolling hills of rural Virginia, and in 1963, with the civil-rights movement stirring new expectations, Mildred Loving wrote a letter about her plight to US attorney general Robert F. Kennedy. Kennedy encouraged her to contact the American Civil Liberties Union. ACLU lawyers took the Lovings' case through Virginia courts and up to the US Supreme Court, which, in 1967, reversed their conviction and effectively overturned the United States' remaining laws against 'miscegenation'.

Dana H. Allin is Editor of *Survival*, and IISS Senior Fellow for US Foreign Policy and Transatlantic Affairs.

Survival | vol. 59 no. 5 | October–November 2017 | pp. 201–212 DOI 10.1080/00396338.2017.1375273

The *Washington Post* and *New York Times* published obituaries for Mildred Loving a few days after her death, on Tuesday 6 May. Neither paper remarked on the overlapping significance of that Tuesday: to do so might not have been appropriate to an obituary; in any event, as the papers went to press, no one knew that the day would end with the decisive victory of Barack Obama in his long and drawn-out contest for the Democratic Party's nomination to be president of the United States. His big win over senator Hillary Clinton in that Tuesday's North Carolina primary, and her own meagre win in Indiana, extinguished any residual chance that Clinton might overcome Obama's lead in delegates to the Democratic nominating convention.

Like Mildred Loving's children, Barack Obama was the fruit of miscegenation – in his case, between a black Kenyan father and a white Kansan mother. He was born in 1961 in Hawaii, a newly admitted American state which, by nature of its location and heterogeneous population, was relatively tolerant on racial matters, and did not, in any event, have a law intended to prevent his very existence. But growing up a black boy in America in the 1960s meant becoming politically conscious in an era of civil-rights struggle. The struggle was glorious and inspiring and, in many respects, triumphant, but it could not in a decade erase the humiliations and oppression still inflicted daily on the descendants of slaves. For most of that decade, the Lovings were still banned as a couple from crossing south over any of the Potomac River bridges that a president Obama could reach in a 20-minute walk from the White House. If, in the months and years following the Supreme Court ruling, young Barack himself had been driven through Virginia or any southern state in a car with his white mother, he almost certainly would have encountered hostility and abuse. (This is something that the current author, a white man, knows personally, having been driven by his mother in 1970 from North Carolina to his home in Maryland with an eight-year-old African-American in the back seat next to him.)

Three years after Mildred Loving's death, and a little more than two years after Obama's inauguration as America's 44th president, reality-TV star Donald Trump sat down on the guest couch of a daytime talk show, *The View*. He was known to be contemplating – rather implausibly, it seemed at the time – a bid for the 2012 Republican presidential nomination. Co-hosts Barbara Walters and Joy Behar started by asking how Trump, as a twice-divorced 'social liberal', could expect to win over the Republican base. After a few more minutes of conversation, Trump showed them how. Behar had quoted him saying of Obama – 'He grew up and nobody knew him. Nobody knows who he is until later in his life. The whole thing is very strange' – and then she asked, 'What are you driving at there? Are you a "birther", Donald?' Trump's reply, spanning ten minutes of the hosts' interjections and his own gesticulations, is a document for history:

> Why doesn't he show his birth certificate? … If you go back to first grade, people remember me. Nobody … If you are going to be president of the United States, it says very profoundly you have to be born in this country. There's something about that birth certificate he doesn't like … I'm not a fan of George Bush, but George Bush was born in this country … I grew up in New York. I have seen scandal and I have seen fraud … The point is, I can't rely on some newspaper. I want him to show his birth certificate. There is something on that birth certificate that he doesn't like.

Trump decided not to run for president that year. But he did run away with the birth certificate question, becoming, over the next six weeks, America's high priest of birtherism. He thus established himself unambiguously and indisputably as a political racist – that is, a politician who, whatever his personal relationship with people of other races, openly and directly exploited racial fear and hatred. When, next time around, he did launch a presidential campaign, it was with a speech featuring the problem of Mexican 'rapists' who would finally be excluded by his 'great wall'. There followed an astonishing campaign of fabrication and falsehood: New Jersey Muslims cheered the fiery deaths of 9/11; 80% of white murder victims are killed by blacks; millions of illegal immigrants voted fraudulently for Hillary Clinton. (For the record: they didn't; 15%; and they didn't.) Trump called for a 'total and complete shutdown on Muslims entering the United States' and asserted casually that an Indiana-born judge with a Spanish surname could not impartially preside over a fraud case against him. All of this in a fever dream of mass rallies of Trump supporters thrilling to their candidate's incitements to violence. And the shock at the end: Donald Trump became the first political racist since, arguably, Woodrow Wilson to win the White House.

The Trump administration's beginning in birtherism – a conspiracy mania nurtured in the emotional conviction that America's first black president could not be legitimate – is important. To begin with, it announced that racism would dominate the campaign and, it seemed likely, the presidency. It also sharply established the 45th president in his historical role as Obama's antithesis. The two men stand as chronological and moral bookends. Trump was born in 1946, the beginning of the post-Second World War 'baby boom'. Obama was born in 1961, at what most demographers consider the end of that distinct generation. Morally, the two men face one another from distant shores. Trump was raised into the real-estate business of a father, Frederick Trump, who was arrested at a 1927 Ku Klux Klan rally in Queens – a 'near riot', according to the next day's *New York Times*. Fred Trump would be investigated by a Senate Committee for war profiteering. And he was the racist villain of verse found in the notebooks of Woodie Guthrie, who rented one of his Brooklyn apartments after returning from the war:

> I suppose
> Old Man Trump Knows
> Just how much
> Racial Hate
> he stirred up
> In the bloodpot of human hearts
> When he drawed
> That color line
> Here at his
> Eighteen hundred family project[2]

In 1973, both father Fred and son Donald, by this time president of the family company, were named as defendants in a US Justice Department suit against Trump Management for discriminating against blacks. Donald Trump angrily denied the charges, claiming, as the *New York Times* later reported, that 'the government was trying to force him to rent to "welfare recipients"', and he counter-sued for defamation. He ultimately settled in a consent decree which, he claimed, did not admit any guilt. But a *New York Times* investigation in 2016 made clear that the discrimination was real.[3] Thirteen years later, in 1989, Trump purchased full-page ads in all four New York daily newspapers, calling for the execution of the 'Central Park 5', young black and brown teenagers arrested for the savage 'wilding' gang rape of a white jogger in Central Park. The boys were not executed, but they did spend years in prison, until DNA evidence and another convict's confession conclusively exonerated them. Trump continued to insist that they were guilty.

This was 1980s, *Bonfire of the Vanities* New York, a place of surging new wealth and seething racial tension, not to mention exploding sexuality – and it was all Trump's element, including the sex. Obama was there too, from 1981 to 1985, but his was a different New York experience. He transferred for his third year of university from Occidental College, in California, to Columbia University in Harlem. He had grown into adolescence and manhood during a decade in which the desolation of riot-torn cities, the growing drug scourge, fears of urban crime and the unsettled nature of race relations – all in the context of economic and foreign-policy crisis – helped to feed a conservative political backlash among whites. Meanwhile, Obama was moving into the social circles of black college students who felt the anger, the disappointed expectations and the confusion of an African-American middle class that was trying to find its place in the racially polarised, crisis-torn and palpably violent America.

In his first book, *Dreams from My Father,* Obama set down his struggles with selfhood and racial identity in these years. He seems to have worked hard to embrace his black identity for the purpose of transcending it. In his electrifying speech to the 2004 Democratic convention in Boston, which nominated John Kerry for president, Obama spoke eloquently of the falsity of imagining that America was so utterly divided between conservatives and liberals, whites and blacks, or the religious and the secular. He continued to articulate a distinctive and upbeat brand of American nationalism. He thought of himself as a liberal version of Ronald Reagan, insofar as Reagan reached beyond traditional conservatives to assemble a game-changing coalition that famously included so-called 'Reagan Democrats'. Obama's supporters had hoped that he similarly could defy the categories of recent American polarisation. He did leave office with approval ratings higher than Reagan's. The polarisation, however, was somehow getting worse.

II

Trump's presidency has been a shambles in so many ways that it strains credibility to call his remarks, after August's events in Charlottesville, Virginia, the low point. Yet his several days of equivocation about whether to condemn Ku Klux Klansmen and neo-Nazis, one of whom killed a counter-protester in an ISIS-style car attack, touched a special nerve. Race is the distinctive problem of American history. It caused a great and savage civil war. And that civil war's unhealed wound was salted in Charlottesville, where armed, torch-bearing white supremacists marched to protect the monument to Robert E. Lee, the Confederate general who led the fight against America for the cause of preserving slavery.

Though some are now coming down, Confederate monuments are ubiquitous in southern and border, and even some northern, states of America, just as the treasonous Confederate flag, displayed as a banner of pride, was utterly commonplace in the America where Donald Trump and Barack Obama were raised. (Readers unfamiliar with the 1980s television series *The Dukes of Hazzard* should consult YouTube.) Both the flags and the monuments were explicit cultural signifiers. They were emblems of white supremacy, waved and built most energetically at specific historical junctures: the imposition of Jim Crow segregation in the late nineteenth and early twentieth centuries, and the reaction against civil-rights progress in the 1960s and 1970s. Yet, what caused special revulsion from Charlottesville was the Nazi dimension, including men marching past a synagogue chanting 'Jews will not replace us!'.

A parsing of the moral distinction between chattel slavery and Nazi genocide might be attempted, but is unlikely to edify. In the American context, however, the difference is that one was a legacy we had to acknowledge, while the other was an evil we could say that we fought. The Second World War and its meaning were part of the inheritance of the children of peace, Donald Trump's and Barack Obama's generation. And it was, in fact, an inheritance that made it difficult to remain indifferent to the other inheritance, the legacy of slavery. Even though they were cynical, jaded and often traumatised by the experience, the Americans who fought in or wrote about or directed the Second World War carried some of the moral dimension of the struggle into their post-war imagination. Part of this was propaganda, of course, or an *ex post facto* rationalisation, but it was present already in the 'Four Freedoms' charter of Roosevelt and Churchill, and it was spurred by the dawning enormity of the Holocaust, understood as a specifically racist crime. Thus, mostly in retrospect, and notwithstanding the reality that the Pacific war was charged with racial fear and hatred of Japanese, the Second World War became a war for racial decency.

This was clear enough in the immediate aftermath of Japan's surrender – as Minneapolis Mayor Hubert Humphrey demanded at the 1948 Democratic convention that his party 'get out of the shadow of states' rights and walk forthrightly into the bright sunshine of human rights'. It is not too much to say that the battle lines between Hillary Clinton and Donald Trump were set at that moment: North Carolina senator Strom Thurmond led his 'Dixiecrats' out of the Democratic Party; president Harry Truman embraced Humphrey's forthright liberalism. Two weeks later, Truman signed Executive Order 9981, desegregating the US armed forces – an act that remains one of the most significant human-rights advances in American history.

The armed forces were important not least because the war wasn't really over – it was morphing into the armed and dangerous truce of the Cold War. And that Cold War, giving rise to America's new global mission, was another reason it became impossible to abide the continuing subjugation of African-Americans. John F. Kennedy, for example, was somewhat irritated by the timing and impatience of the civil-rights movement, but he could see well enough that Bull Connor's brutality against peaceful protesters was a propaganda disaster in the American global contest with Moscow. In any event, while not passionately committed to civil rights, segregation offended his liberal intellect. It took his dark and complicated successor – another war veteran who was venal, profane and southern – to embrace civil rights as a burning cause, and it was appropriate that the words 'We shall overcome' were intoned in a Texas drawl as Lyndon Johnson stood before Congress to demand a voting-rights act after the outrages of Selma.

III

Joe Arpaio is the Bull Connor of our new century. The sheriff of Maricopa County, Arizona, until voted out of office in 2016, was an early Trump supporter, proudly embraced by the candidate. In July 2017, he was convicted and awaiting sentencing for criminal contempt, having refused to stop arresting people solely on suspicion that they were undocumented immigrants. Margaret Talbot in the *New Yorker* captured his special style:

> Arpaio, throughout his tenure, specialized in meting out theatrical punishments both petty and cruel. He required that detainees wear old-fashioned, black-and-white striped uniforms and pink underwear, presumably for the dollop of extra humiliation such costuming offered. He brought back chain gangs, including for women and juveniles. He housed detainees outdoors, under Army-surplus tents, in Phoenix temperatures that regularly soar well above a hundred degrees. 'I put them up next to the dump, the dog pound, the waste-disposal plant', Arpaio [said] … The sheriff called detainees 'criminals' when they had not been convicted and once referred to his jail as 'a concentration camp'.

A US Justice Department investigation found, in 2011, that Arpaio's department was 'profiling' to stop Latino drivers four to nine times more often than non-Latinos; that inmates who couldn't understand English commands were punished with solitary confinement and soiled sheets and clothing; and that his officers called Latinos 'wetbacks' and 'Mexican bitches'. Families of two separate men who died in 'restraint chairs' received settlements of more than six and eight million dollars when it was revealed that the men had been variously beaten, shocked with stun guns and suffocated.[4]

In August, after his week of blowback regarding Charlottesville, President Trump travelled to Phoenix, Arizona, for another campaign-style rally. White House aides were clearly dreading the event. In fact, his performance seemed more disjointed than usual, and too weird even for some of his die-hard supporters, who grew restless (to be fair, it was also very hot). Trump attacked Arizona's two senators, both Republicans who have criticised him, and one of whom, John McCain, is fighting brain cancer. And Trump hinted strongly that he would pardon Joe Arpaio. Three days later, he did so.

On its face, the president's power of pardon appears absolute. Yet this pardon crossed a line. Using pardoning power to immunise systemic police abuses against judicial review would pave the first piece of the road to a police state. There is some small comfort in thinking that Trump, inclinations notwithstanding, lacks the ambition and the competence to complete such a road – and that opponents would raise too many obstacles. Even if the damage to rule of law can be contained, however, American society is already significantly torn. This latest election cycle has unmistakably established the astonishing polarisation of American politics, and the fact that it is deeply racial. Throughout a presidential campaign in which it was widely assumed that Trump could not win the presidency, there was never any doubt that he would win a significant majority of the white vote.

The Republican presidential candidate, to be sure, generally wins a majority of whites. And subtracting *southern* whites from the polling numbers would yield a different result. Yet, it is precisely at this level of disaggregation that America's historical moment looks so puzzling, and worrying. In 1963, when Bull Connor, public-safety commissioner for Birmingham, Alabama, set fire hoses and police dogs on children, many southern whites supported him, but whites in the rest of the country were horrified. Partly as a consequence, president Johnson won a majority of

Republican senators and house members for the Civil Rights Act of 1964 and the Voting Rights Act of 1965.

It is very difficult to imagine that American whites would be more racist today than in 1963. Yet the great misunderstanding on the eve of the 2016 election was in assuming that traditional political models still functioned, and that by making overtly racist appeals to the most disaffected, Trump inevitably would lose the votes of more moderate Republicans.[5] This did not happen. Clearly, and despite his broad popularity on leaving office, Obama failed in his aspiration, professed in that 2004 speech, of transcending the polarisation. Short of changing the colour of his skin, Obama himself could not have taken greater care to avoid appearing as the tribune of an exclusive racial identity. Still, after Hillary Clinton's defeat, some liberal thinkers voiced their worry that the Democrats have become the party of identity politics, inspiring a countering white-identity movement that imperils the functioning of fundamental political consensus.[6] Such white identity, they argue, is based not so much on bigotry as on a diffuse anxiety about a country slipping away – their children's prospects fading at the same time as American demography shifts, inexorably, in a non-white direction. And while there is no logical link between those fading prospects and the shifting demography, the electoral consequences for a regionally disaggregated country are significant. Thus, although the Democrats have won the popular vote in six of the past seven presidential elections, they have been defeated twice more in the electoral college, and virtually routed in state legislatures and governors' mansions. And they have been beaten, less spectacularly but still decisively, in the US Congress. Democrats must, therefore, find a political strategy that better appeals to whites, and what these liberal critics propose is a reforging of the post-Second World War liberal vision of inclusive economic justice.

The case is arguable, and will be debated. It should not, however, obscure an understanding of the proximate cause of the Trump presidency. Russian intervention, and FBI director James Comey's public handling of the investigation into Hillary Clinton's email protocols, were significant factors. What made it close in the first place, however, was the fact that the overwhelming majority of Republican voters were going to vote for Trump, almost regardless of his behaviour. They were able to do so because this choice was validated by Republican leaders. Some of those leaders appear to have regrets. They made a Faustian pact, and it is starting to look – even in comparison to most such pacts – like a bad deal.

Notes

1 Portions of the following section are drawn from Dana H. Allin, 'The United States: An Extraordinary Election Campaign', in *IISS Strategic Survey 2008* (Abingdon: Routledge for the IISS, 2008), pp. 73–4.

2 Another verse in the same notebook refashions his Dust Bowl ballad, 'I Ain't Got No Home', into: 'Beach Haven ain't my home!/I just cain't pay this rent!/My money's down the drain!/And my soul is badly bent!/ Beach Haven looks like heaven/ Where no black ones come to roam!/ No, no, no! Old Man Trump!/Old Beach Haven ain't my home!'. See Will Kaufman, 'Woody Guthrie, "Old Man Trump" and a Real Estate Empire's Racist Foundations', *Conversation*, 21 January 2016, https://theconversation.com/woody-guthrie-old-man-trump-and-a-real-estate-empires-racist-foundations-53026.

3 Jonathan Mahler and Steve Eder, '"No Vacancies" for Blacks: How Donald Trump Got His Start, and Was First Accused of Bias', 27 August 2016, *New York Times*, https://www.nytimes.com/2016/08/28/us/politics/donald-trump-housing-race.html.

4 Margaret Talbot, 'Why Donald Trump Pardoned Joe Arpaio', *New Yorker*, 25 August 2017, http://www.newyorker.com/news/daily-comment/why-does-donald-trump-like-sheriff-joe.

5 Josh Marshall, 'A Theory of the Case', *Talking Points Memo*, 8 July 2017, http://talkingpointsmemo.com/edblog/a-theory-of-the-case.

6 See, for example, David Remnick's interview of Mark Lilla, 'A Conversation with Mark Lilla on His Critique of Identity Politics', *New Yorker*, 25 August 2017, https://www.newyorker.com/news/news-desk/a-conversation-with-mark-lilla-on-his-critique-of-identity-politics.